Set-Theoretic Multi-Method Rese

A state-of-the-art comprehensive exposition of combining qualitative comparative analysis (QCA) and case studies, this book facilitates the efficient use and independent learning of this form of set-theoretic multi-method research (SMMR) with the best available software. It will reduce the time and effort required when performing both QCA and case studies within the same research project. This is achieved by spelling out the conceptual principles and practices in SMMR, and by introducing a tailor-made R software package. With an applied and practical focus, this is an intuitive resource for implementing the most complete protocol of SMMR. Features include Learning Goals, Core Points, and Empirical Examples, as well as boxed examples of R codes and the R output it produces. There is also a glossary for key SMMR terms. Additional online material is available, comprising machine-readable datasets and R scripts for replication and independent learning.

Carsten Q. Schneider is Pro-Rector for External Relations and Professor of Political Science at Central European University (CEU), Vienna. He teaches set-theoretic methods worldwide and his research in comparative politics and social science methodology has appeared in leading international journals and publishing houses.

Methods for Social Inquiry

Editors
Colin Elman, Syracuse University
Diana Kapiszewski, Georgetown University
James Mahoney, Northwestern University

The *Methods for Social Inquiry* series comprises compact texts offering practical instructions for qualitative and multi-method research. Each book is accompanied by pedagogical data and exercises.

The books in the series offer clear, straightforward, and concrete guidance for teaching and using methods. While grounded in their relevant prescriptive logics, the books focus on the "how-to" of the methods they discuss – the practical tasks that must be undertaken to effectively employ them. The books should be useful for instruction at both the advanced undergraduate and graduate levels.

The books are tightly integrated with digital content and online enhancements through the Qualitative Data Repository (QDR). QDR is a new NSF-funded repository housing digital data used in qualitative and multi-method social inquiry. The pedagogical data (and related documentation) that accompany the books in the series will be housed in QDR.

Books in the series

1. Schneider, Carsten Q., *Set-Theoretic Multi-Method Research: A Guide to Combining QCA and Case Studies*
2. Kreuzer, Markus, *The Grammar of Time: A Toolbox for Comparative Historical Analysis*
3. Oana, Ioana-Elena, Schneider, Carsten Q. and Thomann, Eva, *Qualitative Comparative Analysis Using R: A Beginner's Guide*
4. Cyr, Jennifer, *Focus Groups for the Social Science Researcher*

Set-Theoretic Multi-Method Research
A Guide to Combining QCA and Case Studies

Carsten Q. Schneider
Central European University

Shaftesbury Road, Cambridge CB2 8EA, United Kingdom

One Liberty Plaza, 20th Floor, New York, NY 10006, USA

477 Williamstown Road, Port Melbourne, VIC 3207, Australia

314–321, 3rd Floor, Plot 3, Splendor Forum, Jasola District Centre, New Delhi - 110025, India

103 Penang Road, #05–06/07, Visioncrest Commercial, Singapore 238467

Cambridge University Press is part of Cambridge University Press & Assessment, a department of the University of Cambridge.

We share the University's mission to contribute to society through the pursuit of education, learning and research at the highest international levels of excellence.

www.cambridge.org
Information on this title: www.cambridge.org/9781009307147

DOI: 10.1017/9781009307154

© Carsten Q. Schneider 2024

This publication is in copyright. Subject to statutory exception and to the provisions of relevant collective licensing agreements, no reproduction of any part may take place without the written permission of Cambridge University Press & Assessment.

First published 2024

A catalogue record for this publication is available from the British Library

Library of Congress Cataloging-in-Publication Data
Names: Schneider, Carsten Q., 1972- author.
Title: Set-theoretic multi-method research : a guide to combining QCA and case studies / Carsten Q. Schneider.
Description: First edition. | Cambridge ; New York, NY : Cambridge University Press, [2023] | Series: Methods for social inquiry 1 | Includes bibliographical references and index.
Identifiers: LCCN 2023024831 (print) | LCCN 2023024832 (ebook) | ISBN 9781009307147 (hardback) | ISBN 9781009307192 (paperback) | ISBN 9781009307154 (epub)
Subjects: LCSH: Social sciences–Comparative method. | Social sciences–Mathematical models. | Qualitative research–Methodology. | Mixed methods research. | Set theory.
Classification: LCC H61 .S377 2023 (print) | LCC H61 (ebook) | DDC 300.72–dc23/eng/20230801
LC record available at https://lccn.loc.gov/2023024831
LC ebook record available at https://lccn.loc.gov/2023024832

ISBN 978-1-009-30714-7 Hardback
ISBN 978-1-009-30719-2 Paperback

Additional resources for this publication at https://doi.org/10.7910/DVN/URMOVC

Cambridge University Press & Assessment has no responsibility for the persistence or accuracy of URLs for external or third-party internet websites referred to in this publication and does not guarantee that any content on such websites is, or will remain, accurate or appropriate.

Contents

List of Figures		*page* ix
List of Tables		xi
Preface		xiii

1 Introduction: SMMR in a Nutshell 1
  1.1 Multi-Method Research 1
  1.2 Set-Theoretic Multi-Method Research 3
  1.3 Empirical Example 5
  1.4 The Elements of SMMR 7
    1.4.1 Cross-Case and Within-Case Levels 8
    1.4.2 Analytic Goals 11
    1.4.3 Types of Cases 11
    1.4.4 Single and Comparative Within-Case Designs 12
    1.4.5 Types of Sets 12
    1.4.6 Types of QCA Solution Formulas and Regularity Theory of Causation 13
    1.4.7 SMMR in a Nutshell 14
  1.5 Structure of the Book 15
  1.6 SMMR and Related Case-Oriented Approaches 17
  1.7 How to Use This Book 25
    1.7.1 Prerequisites 25
    1.7.2 Data and Resources 27
    1.7.3 Some Terminology 28

2 Basics of SMMR
  $A \Rightarrow Y$ 30
  2.1 Empirical Example 30
  2.2 Types of Cases in SMMR 33
    2.2.1 Crisp Sets 33

v

	2.2.2	Fuzzy Sets	35
2.3	Single-Case SMMR		39
	2.3.1	Descriptive Inference SMMR	39
	2.3.2	Causal Inference SMMR	41
2.4	Excursus: Forms of Broken Sufficiency Corridors		46
2.5	Comparative SMMR		48
	2.5.1	Descriptive Inference SMMR	49
	2.5.2	Causal Inference SMMR	54
2.6	Applying SMMR		58
	2.6.1	The smmr() Function	58
	2.6.2	Single-Case SMMR	60
	2.6.3	Comparative SMMR	62
2.7	Conclusion		66

3 Disjunctions
$A + B \Rightarrow Y$ 68

3.1	Empirical Example		69
3.2	The Challenge		72
3.3	The Solutions		73
	3.3.1	Climbing the Ladder of Generality	73
	3.3.2	Additional Sub-Types of Cases	74
	3.3.3	Additional Principles	75
3.4	Applying SMMR		79
	3.4.1	Descriptive Inference SMMR	80
	3.4.2	Causal Inference SMMR	86
3.5	Conclusion		90

4 Conjunctions
$A * B \Rightarrow Y$ 91

4.1	Empirical Example		91
4.2	The Challenge		95
4.3	The Solutions		96
	4.3.1	Climbing the Ladder of Generality	97
	4.3.2	Additional Principles	98
	4.3.3	Additional Formulas	110
4.4	Excursus: Necessary INUS Conditions		111
4.5	Applying SMMR		118
	4.5.1	Descriptive Inference SMMR	119
	4.5.2	Causal Inference SMMR	126
4.6	Conclusion		140

5	**INUS Conditions**		
	$A * B + C * D \Rightarrow Y$		141
	5.1	Empirical Example	142
	5.2	Descriptive Inference SMMR	145
	5.3	Causal Inference SMMR	150
	5.4	Conclusion	159
	5.5	Excursus: QCA Solution Types and Causal Inference SMMR Designs	161
6	**Necessary Conditions**		165
	6.1	Basics, $A \Leftarrow Y$	166
		6.1.1 Empirical Example	166
		6.1.2 Single-Case SMMR	168
		6.1.3 Excursus: Forms of Broken Necessity Corridors	174
		6.1.4 Comparative SMMR	178
		6.1.5 Applying SMMR	186
	6.2	Disjunctions, $A + B \Leftarrow Y$	193
		6.2.1 Empirical Example	194
		6.2.2 The Challenge	194
		6.2.3 The Solutions	196
		6.2.4 Applying SMMR	198
	6.3	Conjunctions, $A * B \Leftarrow Y$	208
		6.3.1 Empirical Example	209
		6.3.2 The Challenge	210
		6.3.3 The Solutions	210
		6.3.4 Applying SMMR	215
	6.4	Conclusion and Reflections on Necessary and Sufficient Conditions, $A * B + C * D \Leftrightarrow Y$	220
7	**Conclusions – SMMR in Practice**		222
	7.1	SMMR Principles and Established Case Selection Rules	223
	7.2	SMMR in Research Practice	225
		7.2.1 SMMR and the Different Uses of QCA	225
		7.2.2 Ideal-Typical vs. Applied SMMR	226
		7.2.3 Nonmodel-Related SMMR Goals	227
		7.2.4 Sequencing and Selecting SMMR Designs	228
		7.2.5 Selective Focus on Some Disjuncts or Conjuncts	229
		7.2.6 SMMR and Different Types of Sets	230
	7.3	Outlook – Where Could and Should We Go from Here?	234
		7.3.1 SMMR and Theory Evaluation	235
		7.3.2 SMMR and the QCA Robustness Test Protocol	236

	7.3.3 SMMR and Cluster Diagnostics	238
	7.3.4 SMMR and Time-Infused QCA Solutions	240
Appendix	**SMMR Principles**	243
	Glossary	245
	References	251
	Index	258

Additional resources for this publication at https://doi.org/10.7910/DVN/URMOVC

Figures

1.1	Causal mechanism linking supportive welfare regimes and low participatory inequality	6
1.2	XY plot: supportive welfare regime and low participatory inequality	6
1.3	Cross-case and within-case levels in SMMR	9
1.4	Flow chart of SMMR designs	15
2.1	XY plot: sufficient term for outcome "unpopular reforms" U	31
2.2	Cross-case condition and within-case level mechanism for outcome "unpopular reforms"	33
2.3	2×2 table: sufficient term for outcome U	34
2.4	Types of cases, crisp-set SMMR	34
2.5	Types of cases, fuzzy-set SMMR	37
2.6	Visualizations of a test corridor	44
2.7	Forms of broken sufficiency corridors	47
2.8	Comparative SMMR designs	50
3.1	XY plot: sufficient term LD, outcome HC	70
3.2	XY plot: sufficient term LH, outcome HC	70
3.3	XY plot: solution formula $LD + LH$, outcome HC	71
3.4	Cross-case and within-case levels for outcome "high perceived corruption"	72
4.1	XY plot: sufficient term $PD*RO$, outcome PC	94
4.2	Cross-case and within-case levels for outcome "no political contestation"	94
4.3	iir case: unique FC nonmember and attribution principle – XY plots	104
4.4	Typical cases: attribution principle – XY plots	105
4.5	Rank order of typical and iir case pairs for focal conjuncts in sufficient conjunctions	109
4.6	Rank order of typical and iir case pairs for necessary conjunct in sufficient conjunction	114

4.7	Necessary focal conjunct *FC* and forms of broken corridors *M*	116
5.1	XY plot: solution formula, outcome "low participatory inequality" *LPI*	144
5.2	XY plot: term *LM* ∗ *WC*, focal conjunct *WC*, and membership in mechanisms of typical and iir cases, outcome "low participatory inequality" *LPI*	153
5.3	XY plot: term *LM* ∗ *WC*, focal conjunct *LM*, and membership in mechanisms, outcome "low participatory inequality" *LPI*	154
5.4	XY plot: term *LM* ∗ *EP*, focal conjunct *EP*, and membership in mechanisms, outcome "low participatory inequality" *LPI*	159
5.5	XY plot: term *LM* ∗ *EP*, focal conjunct *LM*, and membership in mechanisms, outcome "low participatory inequality" *LPI*	159
6.1	XY plot: necessary condition ∼*DEP* for outcome "nonconflict" ∼*BDT*	168
6.2	Types of cases, crisp-set SMMR on necessity	169
6.3	Types of cases, fuzzy-set SMMR on necessity	170
6.4	Visualizations of test corridor, necessity	172
6.5	Forms of broken necessity corridors	174
6.6	Forms of feasible comparisons, necessity	179
6.7	XY plot: necessary disjunction *POV* + *COR*, outcome *BDT*	195
6.8	Cross-case and within-case levels for disjunctive necessity claim, outcome "conflict"	196
6.9	XY plot: necessary conjunction ∼*ECOD* + ∼*EDU*, outcome *BDT*	210
6.10	Rank order of typical and iir case pairs for focal conjuncts in necessary conjunctions	213
7.1	SMMR and the QCA robustness test protocol	237

Tables

2.1	Most parsimonious solution for outcome "unpopular reforms" *U*	31
2.2	Types of cases and analytic goals of within-case analysis ($S \Rightarrow U$)	38
2.3	Comparative SMMR designs and their goals	50
2.4	Matching of typical and deviant consistency cases	51
2.5	Matching of deviant coverage and iir cases	53
2.6	Matching of a typical case and an iir case	55
2.7	Matching of two typical cases	56
2.8	Function `smmr()`, argument `case` for SMMR on sufficiency	59
3.1	Most parsimonious solution, outcome "high perceived corruption" *HC*	69
3.2	Uniquely covered, jointly covered, and globally uncovered cases	74
3.3	Scenarios for comparison of typical and iir cases	79
4.1	Most parsimonious solution, outcome "no political contestation" *∼PC*	93
4.2	iir FC unique nonmember principle	100
4.3	iir FC unique nonmember principle, example	101
4.4	iir Case: Unique FC nonmember and attribution principles	103
4.5	Rank order of possible membership constellations between the focal conjunct and complementary conjuncts in a single typical case	106
4.6	Rank order of possible membership constellations between the focal conjunct and complementary conjuncts in a comparison of two typical cases	107
4.7	Rank order of possible membership constellations between the focal and complementary conjuncts in a comparison of typical and iir cases in a sufficient conjunction	108
4.8	Sufficient conditions, outcome "high-tech export success" EXPORT	112
5.1	Sufficient welfare regime conditions, outcome "low participatory inequality" *LPI*, most parsimonious solution	142

5.2	Truth table, outcome "low participatory inequality" *LPI*	144
5.3	Causal status of QCA solution types in light of within-case evidence	163
6.1	Necessary condition, outcome "nonconflict" $\sim BDT$	168
6.2	Types of cases and analytic goals of within-case analysis ($X \Leftarrow Y$)	170
6.3	Forms of comparisons and their goals in SMMR, necessity	179
6.4	Matching of typical and deviant consistency cases, necessity	181
6.5	Matching of typical and deviant relevance cases, necessity	182
6.6	Matching of a typical case and an iir case, necessity	184
6.7	Matching of two typical cases, necessity	184
6.8	Function `smmr()`, argument `case` for SMMR on necessity	186
6.9	SUIN conditions, outcome "conflict" *BDT*	194
6.10	Uniquely covered, jointly covered, and globally uncovered cases, necessity	197
7.1	Categorizing SMMR principles	224
A.1	List of SMMR principles	244

Preface

This book has been in the making, consciously and subconsciously, for quite a while. The conception of the idea of set-theoretic multi-method research (SMMR) as envisaged in this book can be traced back pretty clearly to one afternoon in the summer of 2012 in Ljubljana, Slovenia. I was teaching a course on qualitative comparative analysis (QCA) at the European Consortium For Political Research (ECPR) Summer School in Research Methods and Techniques and Ingo Rohlfing was teaching a course on case studies. We decided to hold one session together because in both our courses discussions kept coming up on how to best combine these two methods, which, clearly, do have an elected affinity. Our goal for this joint session was to present our first ideas and to discuss them with our students. The session went way over time and we left the room with the firm idea of condensing all that needs to be said about the combination of QCA and within-case analysis in one journal article. Well, here we are today, more than a decade later, after countless discussions, several conference presentations, a dedicated R function, and a handful of journal articles. This book is meant to consolidate, update, adjust, further refine, and comprehensively present in one place the insights gained over the past decade. In so doing, the goal of this book is to facilitate the understanding and practical use of SMMR.

As with any intellectual journey, one does not travel alone and I wish to thank my fellow travelers. First to mention here is Ingo Rohlfing with whom the project started. Throughout the years, we have jointly developed the SMMR framework on which this book is based. The adjustments and refinements to this framework that I offer in this book come in small, but sometimes crucial doses. For discussions on many of those new developments I am grateful to Nena Oana. Those exchanges of ideas often took place in relation to implementing SMMR into the R package `SetMethods` that Nena and I jointly develop. Nena's skills in making SMMR work in R have been invaluable. My thanks also go to the many participants in courses on QCA that I have been teaching over the past years, both at my home institution, Central European University (CEU), and at methods schools organized by ECPR, Global School in Empirical Research Methods (GSERM), Institute for Qualitative and Multi-Method Research (IQMR), International Political Science Association (IPSA), MethodsNET, and many other institutions that kindly invited me to share my ideas. Along that way, I have been fortunate to work with brilliant co-instructors – next to Nena, these were at different times Patrick Emmenegger, Airo Hino, Patrick Mello, Charles Ragin, Benoît Rihoux, Eva Thomann, and Claudius Wagemann – and teaching assistants who critically commented on various aspects of the SMMR framwork as it evolved over the years: Priscilla Álamos Concha, Dominik Brenner, Marcos Campos, Adrian Dusa, Nidia Murrieta Roque, Ekataryna Paustyan, Alrik Thiem, and Barbora Valikova. Manuel Bosancianu helped me prepare data on the within-case level mechanism used in Chapter 5.

For feedback on my work on SMMR and for their pathbreaking (and sometimes breathtaking) contributions to set-theoretic methods in recent years, which represent the ground on which SMMR is built, I owe gratitude to Gary Goertz and Jim Mahoney. Making sure that room for discussion was provided, even in the difficult pandemic period during which most of this book has been written, is a huge achievement of the team organizing the annual QCA event in Zurich: Manuel Fischer, Julia Leib, Johannes Meuer, Sofia Pagliarin, Ryan Rumble, and Christian Rupietta.

My deepest thanks go to my family – Sheila, Leo, and Giulia – for all their loving support when writing large chunks of this book in the middle of a pandemic that our family experienced in our new home city Vienna. I'd also thank our dog Laica, but she refuses to read English.

1
Introduction: SMMR in a Nutshell

This book is written for researchers who are interested in strengthening their descriptive or causal inference by combining two methods in a meaningful manner. More specifically, this book is for researchers who want to go beyond their findings generated by qualitative comparative analysis (QCA) by performing follow-up within-case analyses. Likewise, this book is also for case study researchers who usually perform within-case analyses and now seek to ascertain the empirical scope of their findings by inserting their case studies into a QCA design. This book is, thus, written for social researchers who feel that the use of just one method is not enough. Beyond that, the book is also for those who hold that the focus on only one level of analysis – either the cross-case or the within-case level – is inferior to the integrated analysis of both levels with the goal to enhance descriptive and causal inference.

1.1 Multi-Method Research

Multi-method research has become an almost universally accepted approach to enhancing social science research. As its name suggests, more than one method is applied for drawing either descriptive or causal inference on the conditions that drive a phenomenon of interest. As there are many methods, there are also plenty of shapes and flavors of multi-method designs. Of particular interest in the context of this book are those that combine methods for drawing inferences on the cross-case level, on the one hand, and the within-case level, on the other – probably the most common form of combining methods. What this book proposes is to adopt a set-theoretic perspective at both levels of analysis and to combine QCA with the within-case analyses of purposefully selected cases. For this, I use the label set-theoretic multi-method research (SMMR).

SMMR's stance that causal analysis requires both a cross-case effect and a within-case mechanism is fully in line with the writings of many methodologists and philosophers. Under the label of evidential pluralism, Russo and Williamson (2007) (see also Shan and Williamson, 2023) postulate that causal analysis requires evidence on difference making and on a mechanism. While initially designed for medical research, this position has been widely embraced by social science researchers, in particular those working on proper designs for multi-method research involving qualitative methods, such as Crasnow et al. (in press), Goertz and Haggard (in press), Mahoney (2021), or Rohlfing (2012). Runhardt (2022) outlines some challenges to implementing evidential pluralism via multi-method research designs. As this book will show, SMMR, with its "unifying framework" (Rohlfing and Schneider, 2018) of set theory both at the cross-case and the within-case levels, is able to master many of these challenges better than other multi-method approaches, in particular those that combine quantitative methods with qualitative case study approaches.

So far, the main multi-method focus in most of the social sciences has been on combining quantitative techniques at the cross-case level with qualitative techniques at the within-case level. Emblematic for this literature is Lieberman's nested analysis approach (Lieberman, 2005). The basic idea is to use a regression analysis to identify patterns at the cross-case level as a guide for selecting cases for process tracing at the within-case level, with the goal to either improve or test the cross-case regression model. Lieberman's proposal has been both criticized (e.g. Rohlfing, 2008) and refined (e.g. Weller and Barnes, 2016). Both Seawright (2016) and Goertz (2017) present a more comprehensive discussion on "combining qualitative and quantitative" tools. They lay out the role of qualitative case studies when combined not only with regression analysis, but also with (natural) experiments, matching techniques, or game theory.

One of the Achilles heels of multi-method approaches is that, more often than not, the assumptions that go into different methods are irreconcilable (Beach and Kaas, 2020; Bennett and Elman, 2006; Chatterjee, 2013). For instance, when combining regression analysis with case studies à la Lieberman's nested analysis, the ontological assumption at the cross-case analysis is that of average net effects and at the within-case analysis that of causally complex configurations or processes. In addition, more sophisticated quantitative case selection strategies, such as the pathway case by Gerring (2017) or the list of techniques outlined by Seawright and Gerring (2008), do not overcome this vexing problem. In Seawright (2016), the proposal for solving this Gordian knot of incongruity is to subordinate the qualitative part to the quantitative part. The latter does the heavy lifting of causal inference, whereas the former takes on the role of probing those assumptions that need to hold so that the plausibility of the causal inferences drawn with quantitative methods is increased. Humphreys and Jacobs (2015), in turn, propose a Bayesian approach as the framework in which qualitative and quantitative techniques can be integrated into one multi-method approach without contradicting one another.

In this book, I argue that SMMR overcomes the incompatibility problem of many multi-method approaches. SMMR achieves this by applying set-theoretic tools and notions at both the cross-case and the within-case levels of analysis and by guiding the analyses at both levels based on a series of case selection principles.

1.2 Set-Theoretic Multi-Method Research

In this book, I propose SMMR for combining cross-case and within-case analyses in an integrative framework. At both levels of analysis (cross-case and within-case), approaches are rooted in set theory and the analysis of set relations. This provides a unifying framework for descriptive and causal analysis in SMMR without ontological clashes (Rohlfing and Schneider, 2018). Integrated theories are defined as theories that cover both the cross-case level and the within-case level (Dessler, 1991; Goertz, 2017; Mahoney, 2021; Rohlfing, 2012). SMMR is geared toward developing or testing such theories. More specifically, at the cross-case level, the set-theoretic method of QCA is used to discern necessary and sufficient conditions for the outcome of interest. These findings are then used for identifying the appropriate cases for the within-case level analysis with the goal of analyzing the mechanism(s) that connect the necessary or sufficient conditions to the outcome at the cross-case level. SMMR with its combination of QCA and follow-up case studies gives empirical researchers exciting opportunities to build, test, and refine descriptive and causal explanations rooted in a set-relational framework.

Set-theoretic multi-method research (SMMR) is defined as the purposeful combination of QCA results obtained at the cross-case level for the study of mechanisms at the within-case level to formulate integrated, set-relational descriptive or causal inferences about a phenomenon of interest.

Qualitative comparative analysis can be combined with many different methods, including statistical methods (see e.g. Meuer and Rupietta, 2017a,b). At the core of this book and of SMMR is the combination of QCA and within-case analysis. This combination can occur in two possible sequences: we can run the truth table analysis first ("cross-case analysis first design") or start with the within-case part ("within-case analysis first"; Beach and Rohlfing, 2018). In a design performing the within-case analysis first, the within-case analysis either tests a hypothesis on a mechanism, or develops or modifies such a hypothesis in an exploratory fashion. The truth table analysis then builds on the within-case insights and probes set-relational patterns at the cross-case level. Within-case analysis first designs are valuable. They do not raise any particular research design issues, though. It even seems fair to say that any applied QCA that follows standards of good practice (Koivu et al., 2019; Schneider and Wagemann, 2010; Wagemann and Schneider, 2015) contains elements of within-case analysis first designs, simply because of the case-oriented nature of QCA as an approach (Berg-Schlosser et al., 2009).

Cross-case first designs raise methodological challenges.[1] This is why this book focuses on this type of SMMR. A cross-case analysis identifies patterns, based on which different types of cases are established. This information is then used for selecting cases for within-case analysis. In SMMR, it begins with the truth table analysis. The result of this cross-case analysis – the QCA solution formula – is then used for systematic case selection for within-case analysis with the goal to improve the QCA model or to probe the causal status of that model. In a sense, the cross-case part of SMMR can be perceived of as a procedure to sort cases into boxes. Cases from each box are adequate choices for different analytic goals during the second part of SMMR, the within-case analyses.

At the cross-case level, SMMR rests on the use of QCA. Over the past few decades, this technique has made inroads into various disciplines. Originally invented and developed in the fields of Political Science and Sociology (Ragin, 1987, 2000, 2008; Schneider and Wagemann, 2012), it is now also increasingly used in many other fields, such as business and management, environmental science, or public administration (Oana et al., 2021, chap. 1.3). This fact makes this book relevant for readers from all these and many other disciplines. The use of QCA – and its combination with within-case analysis – is not restricted to any field or discipline.

During the within-case analysis, many different, or in fact any, data analysis techniques can be applied – from quantitative analyses to archival research, interviews, participant observations, and so on. Whichever data and data analysis technique are most appropriate for uncovering information on the mechanism(s) can and should be chosen. This means that the within-case

---

[1] Among cross-case first SMMR designs, one could further distinguish between those that are more condition-centered and those that are more mechanism-centered (Beach and Rohlfing, 2018). This distinction rests on which of the two levels of analysis takes more room and attention. Any SMMR design must include both levels and cannot neglect any of the two.

analytic part of SMMR is not confined to process tracing, the method perhaps most associated with within-case analysis. The only thing that matters for SMMR is that, ultimately, the within-case evidence is translated into set membership scores and the logic of the within-case analysis is that of discerning set relations.

Also important to note is that the within-case analysis is useful for more than improving the cross-case model and probing its causal status. For instance, within-case evidence can contribute to probing the validity of data, reshaping the scope conditions, or reformulating the concepts under investigation (Rohlfing and Schneider, 2018). All of these are important benefits of within-case analysis and all of them are fostered by the SMMR designs introduced in this book. Yet the core focus of SMMR is model-related, that is, investigating the causal status of a QCA solution and enhancing, if needed, its descriptive accuracy by detecting conditions that are missing from the model.

1.3 Empirical Example

Throughout the book, I rely on examples of published research to explain and illustrate the principles and practices of SMMR. Often I will alter the original data or analytic setup to better focus on the methodological points I intend to make.

For illustrative purposes, take the study by Schneider and Makszin (2014). Their goal is to explain why in some countries social inequality does not lead to participatory inequality, defined as unequal turnout in elections across different social groups. At the cross-case level, they use QCA to analyze attributes of the welfare regime. They find several combinations of welfare state attributes that are sufficient for, or lead to, low levels of participatory inequality. Schneider and Makszin (2014) subsume these combinations under the concept of supportive welfare regime. At the within-case level, they find individual-level survey data evidence that cognitive and material resources and social engagement operate as the causal mechanisms linking the supportive welfare regime types to low participatory inequality.[2]

The argument by Schneider and Makszin (2014) can be graphically represented as shown in Figure 1.1. At the cross-case level – the QCA solution formula – we see that in countries with supportive welfare regimes, participatory inequality across different social groups is low. The hypothesized mechanism through which welfare regimes exert their effect on participatory equality

---

[2] In Chapter 5, I discuss the study of Schneider and Makszin (2014) in more detail.

Figure 1.1 Causal mechanism linking supportive welfare regimes and low participatory inequality

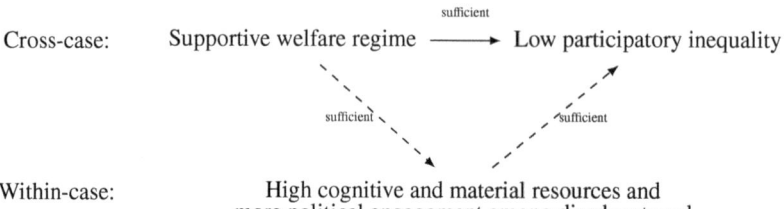

Figure 1.2 XY plot: supportive welfare regime and low participatory inequality

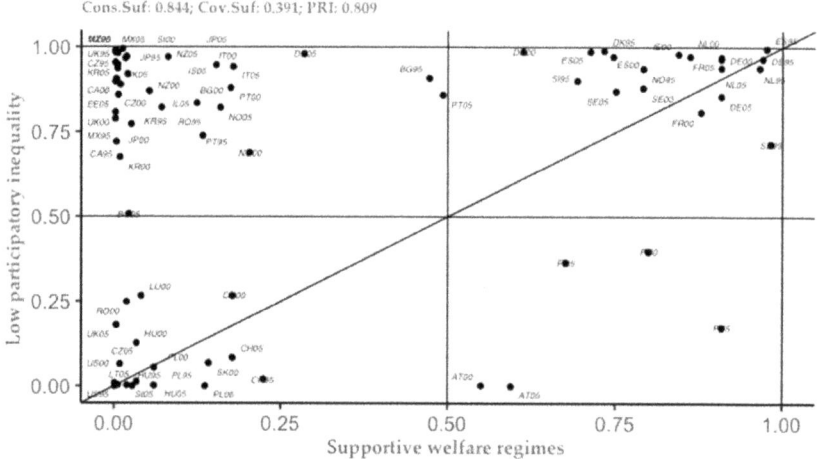

is that such regimes provide citizens from challenging social backgrounds with higher cognitive and material resources and social engagement than comparable citizens not living in such welfare regimes. Endowed with such resources and engagement, those citizens are more likely to participate in politics, which, in turn, produces low participatory inequality.

Figure 1.2 provides a graphical representation of each case's fuzzy set membership score in the supportive welfare regime plotted against their membership in the outcome low participatory inequality. This is an enhanced XY plot (Schneider and Rohlfing, 2013). It is very useful for understanding SMMR and I explain its features in detail below. For now, it suffices to understand that cases in the upper-right triangle, such as France in 1995 (FR95) or Spain in 2005 (ES05), are typical cases for the statement that having a supportive welfare regime is sufficient for low participatory inequality. In those cases, we expect to find the within-case causal mechanism "resources and engagement" to operate. In contrast, in cases in the lower-left quadrant, such as Czechia in 2005 or Hungary in 2000, neither of which are members of the set of countries with a supportive welfare regime nor of the set of cases with low participatory inequality, we expect to find that they are not members of any of the mechanisms. If both expectations are confirmed by empirical evidence, we have support for the causal mechanism claim depicted in Figure 1.1. Furthermore, cases in the lower-right quadrant, such as France in 1995, 2000, and 2005, are puzzling because they contradict the statement of sufficiency: they do have a supportive welfare regime but nevertheless do not show low participatory inequality. In contrast, cases in the upper-left quadrant, such as Portugal in 2005, do not contradict the sufficiency claim but are nevertheless puzzling, too. They do show the outcome low participatory inequality but do not have a supportive welfare regime.

Which cases should be selected for within-case analysis to achieve which analytic goal? The purpose of SMMR – and of this book – is to answer this question. In a nutshell, deviant cases (upper-left and lower-right quadrants in Figure 1.2) are needed for enhancing the descriptive inference. Typical cases and individually irrelevant (iir) cases (lower-left quadrant), in turn, are needed for causal inference.

1.4 The Elements of SMMR

This book takes as its basis previous work on SMMR, jointly authored with Ingo Rohlfing (Schneider and Rohlfing, 2013, 2016, 2019; Rohlfing and Schneider, 2013, 2018). It refines and, where necessary, rectifies the framework laid out in previous work: it formulates additional principles that guide case selection for within-case analysis, introduces more sub-types of cases, and spells out the principles and practices of SMMR on the analysis of necessity claims. In Section 1.6 and throughout the book, I also situate SMMR in relation to similar approaches to combining QCA with other, case-based methods.

One consequence of SMMR being a comprehensive answer to the typical challenges in applied social science research is that it requires the use of a dedicated software package. Only with the help of the smmr() function from the R (R Core Team, 2018) package SetMethods (Oana and Schneider, 2018) is it possible to properly implement SMMR. This is why in this book I not only explain in detail the logic of SMMR, but also the use of the smmr() function based on plenty of examples of applied SMMR, a glossary of key terms, and an index for better navigation.

In this section, I introduce the key elements of SMMR. These are the distinction between the cross-case and the within-case levels; descriptive and causal inferential goals; types of cases; single-case and comparative SMMR designs; and crisp and fuzzy set approaches. I also briefly address the topic of QCA solution types and causal inference, an issue I return to in greater detail in Section 5.4.

1.4.1 Cross-Case and Within-Case Levels

The distinction between the *cross-case* and the *within-case levels* is key to SMMR. It shares this feature with many well-known designs in the qualitative literature, such as the most different system design and the most similar system design (Mahoney, 2000; Przeworski and Teune, 1970). It is also in line with how many other (qualitative) multi-method researchers and methodologists approach the topic of causal analysis (e.g. Goertz and Haggard, in press; Mahoney, 2021; Rohlfing, 2012; Runhardt, 2022; Russo and Williamson, 2007). Figure 1.3 shows a graphical representation of the basic notion of different levels. At the cross-case level, we see the QCA solution S connected to outcome Y. This expression can be a statement of necessity or of sufficiency, or both. In this book, I mostly focus on studies whose goal is the detection of sufficient conditions. Compared to the others, this is by far the most dominant approach within applied QCA.[3]

At the cross-case level, the *solution formula* S can stand for a single set $(A \Rightarrow Y)$, a disjunction $(A + B \Rightarrow Y)$, a conjunction $(A * B \Rightarrow Y)$, or a disjunction of conjunctions $(A * B + C * D \Rightarrow Y)$, the highest form of complexity, and the one routinely encountered in applied QCA. The implications for SMMR are manifold. The more complex the QCA solution formula, the more sub-types of cases exist, and the more SMMR principles need to be taken into account when choosing cases for within-case analysis. This is why this book is structured along these elements of causal complexity. I begin with the simplest (and also least frequently encountered) scenario of a single sufficient condition and end with the most complex (and also most commonly encountered) form of a causally complex QCA solution formula, consisting of INUS conditions.[4] In QCA, three solution types are distinguished: conservative, intermediate,

---

[3] I discuss the implications for SMMR when encountering necessary conditions in Section 4.4 and in Chapter 6.

[4] INUS stands for an insufficient but necessary conjunct of unnecessary but sufficient conjunction (Mackie, 1965).

1.4 The Elements of SMMR

and most parsimonious (Ragin, 2008). All three solution types can be used in SMMR, a point I return to at the end of this chapter and in Section 5.4.

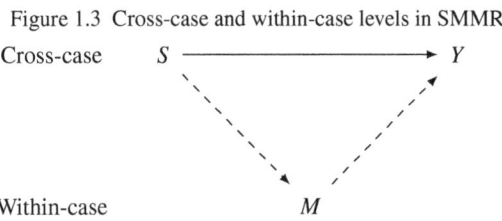

Figure 1.3 Cross-case and within-case levels in SMMR

S = sufficient term; M = mechanism; Y = outcome

Mechanism M is located at the within-case level. Within the SMMR framework, this comprises any form of mechanism that can be subjected to empirical scrutiny. The SMMR framework does not take any position on whether the cross-case expression causes, or triggers, the mechanism M or whether it simply provides the context within which M operates and unfolds its effect on the outcome.[5]

The empirical evidence for studying mechanisms in SMMR can vary, as long as the evidence is located at the within-case level. This means that M is not another condition to be added to the QCA model at the cross-case level. Although process tracing (Beach and Pedersen, 2019; Blatter and Haverland, 2012; George and Bennett, 2005) and qualitative evidence, in general, are the most likely candidates for framing the within-case empirical evidence, SMMR does not restrict the within-case phase to process tracing or qualitative data. Schneider and Makszin (2014; see also below), for instance, use aggregate numbers from large-N individual-level survey data to check if their postulated mechanisms are in place. Just like in QCA, also in SMMR any form of empirical evidence can be used for calibrating sets at the within-case level.[6]

What is required in SMMR is that mechanisms are perceived as sets in which cases hold membership (Mahoney, 2021; Mikkelsen, 2017). This is what makes SMMR a set-theoretic method: it is based on set membership scores and set relations not only at the cross-case (QCA) level, but also at

---

[5] For discussions on the various meanings of "mechanisms" in the social sciences, see, for instance, Beach and Rohlfing (2018, pp. 6ff.), Falleti and Lynch (2009), or Rutten (2022, pp. 6ff.).

[6] Pagliarin et al. (2023) spell out in useful detail how nonnumeric, qualitative information is gathered and then transformed into set membership scores (see in particular their figure 1). This applies not only to QCA, but also to SMMR and its within-case component. For further useful guidance on how to calibrate sets based on qualitative evidence, such as interviews or archival material, see de Block and Vis (2019) or Tóth et al. (2017).

the within-case (mechanism) level.This unifying framework (Rohlfing and Schneider, 2018) means that SMMR avoids many of the pitfalls that bedevil most other forms of multi-method research, such as the combination between regression and case studies (Chatterjee, 2013) or combining methods in general (Ahmed and Sil, 2012; Beach and Kaas, 2020).

There is nothing unusual about perceiving not only cross-case conditions, but also within-case mechanisms and its elements in terms of (fuzzy) sets. In fact, the in-depth focus on a case in SMMR should make the calibration of the mechanism M easier than it often is for conditions at the cross-case level (Schneider and Rohlfing, 2019, p. 268). The works of Ragin (2008), Goertz and Mahoney (2012), and in particular Mahoney (2021) rest on the position that concepts in social science research – including concepts that constitute mechanisms – are best captured via sets. Furthermore, it is important to reiterate that in SMMR any form of within-case evidence can be used for analyzing mechanisms, not just process tracing.

Even if in Figure 1.3 the mechanism is denoted as just M, it can be a placeholder for various different scenarios. All of them are compatible with the SMMR principles and practices explained in this book. For instance, M can be a chain of steps, as in $S \rightarrow M_1 \rightarrow M_2 \rightarrow M_x \rightarrow Y$. M can also be a conjunction, as in $S \rightarrow M_1 * M_2 \rightarrow Y$, or a disjunction, as in $S \rightarrow M_1 + M_2 \rightarrow Y$.[7] The SMMR framework remains agnostic as to whether there is such mechanismic complexity and/or heterogeneity across cases of the same kind (Beach, 2018; Beach and Siewert, 2019). This means SMMR can accommodate situations in which more than one mechanism M is linking the sufficient term S to outcome Y or when M consists of a sequence of steps. As we learn throughout the book, SMMR renders plausible the *assumption* of mechanistic homogeneity by restricting inference to cases of the same type (Schneider and Rohlfing, 2016). Pending evidence to the contrary, within-case findings from one case are assumed to hold for all cases of the same type (e.g. all typical cases). As with any assumption, this one can be wrong. It is precisely the set of SMMR principles, though, that increases the plausibility of the homogeneity assumption *and* enables researchers to detect mechanismic heterogeneity and complexity when it is there. But until empirically shown otherwise, mechanismic homogeneity across analytically similar cases is a plausible assumption on which SMMR-based inferences rest.

---

[7] See Goertz (2017, chap. 2) for equifinality and causal mechanisms and Beach and Rohlfing (2018, pp. 17ff.) for further forms of mechanismic heterogeneity.

1.4 The Elements of SMMR

1.4.2 Analytic Goals

There are two different analytic goals that one can pursue with SMMR. One consists in refining the model by identifying omitted conditions. By "model" I here refer to the QCA solution formula derived via the logical minimization of a truth table.[8] Such model refining can also be considered an improvement of the descriptive inference of a QCA study. This is why I label studies with this goal as *descriptive inference SMMR designs*. The goal of identifying omitted conditions from the cross-case model is pursued by focusing on the within-case level of deviant cases and the mechanisms that are found or not found in them.

The other goal consists in probing the causal properties of the model. SMMR rests on the claim that causal inference is enhanced if a cause makes a difference not only to the outcome at the cross-case level, but also to the mechanism at the within-case level. Studies with this goal are labeled *causal inference SMMR designs*.[9] They require the choice of at least one typical case.[10]

1.4.3 Types of Cases

The choice of cases for within-case analysis is determined by the goal of the analysis. One of the tricks of the trade in SMMR consists in first identifying and then choosing the right types of cases for the envisaged within-case analytic goal. Case types are defined based on their membership in the outcome and the conditions identified by the QCA at the cross-case level. There are four different main case types in SMMR: *typical* cases, *deviant consistency* cases, *deviant coverage* cases,[11] and *individually irrelevant* cases. For instance, in the example by Schneider and Makszin (2014), Norway 1995 is a typical case for the sufficient term "supportive welfare regime", whereas Austria 2005 a

---

[8] The conditions that constitute the truth table I refer to as the "truth table model".
[9] I prefer the terms descriptive inference and causal inference SMMR designs over condition-centered and mechanism-centered designs proposed by Beach and Rohlfing (2018). In both descriptive and causal inference designs both cross-case conditions and within-case mechanisms play a crucial role – a fact also acknowledged in Beach and Rohlfing (2018).
[10] The distinction between descriptive and causal SMMR designs is not identical to the distinction between theory-testing and theory-building within-case analyses (Beach and Pedersen, 2013, pp. 11ff.). While for causal inference SMMR designs it is more likely to already have a theory on the within-case mechanism that can be tested, this does not have to be the case; furthermore, theory-building within-case analyses are, in principle, compatible with causal inference SMMR designs. Likewise, while there is an elective affinity between descriptive inference SMMR designs and exploratory, theory-building within-case analyses, there could also be existing theories on within-case mechanisms in so-called deviant cases.
[11] For necessity claims, they are called deviant relevance cases (see Chapter 6).

deviant consistency case (see Figure 1.2). When it comes to case types, SMMR is far from reinventing the wheel. Many types of cases in SMMR are based on the classic case study literature (e.g. Eckstein, 1975; Lijphart, 1971).

Later in the book, I introduce more sub-types that are needed for appropriate case selection in SMMR when the QCA solution formulas display causal complexity (a disjunction, conjunctions, or both), which they usually do. A constitutive part of SMMR is sorting all cases under study into one of the mutually exclusive and jointly exhaustive case types and to select the best available instance for within-case analysis on the mechanism for either descriptive or causal inference. One of the central goals in this book is to explain how the types are distinguished from each other, which case type is good for which within-case analysis, and how to identify the best available case in one's own data.

1.4.4 Single and Comparative Within-Case Designs

The within-case element of SMMR can be performed as single-case or comparative within-case studies. Single-case studies can make valuable contributions to integrated inferences and I show how to choose the best available single cases in a given dataset. Wherever possible and feasible, comparative within-case studies should be the preferred choice of SMMR design, though. Building on the extensive work on case comparisons (e.g. Goertz, 2017; Lijphart, 1971; Rohlfing, 2012, chaps. 4 and 5), I explain which forms of comparative SMMR designs are available, which analytic goals can be pursued by each of them, and how to identify the best-matching pairs of cases for SMMR.

1.4.5 Types of Sets

The distinction between types of cases and comparisons applies to all three types of sets: *crisp*, *fuzzy*, and *multi-value*. I usually first introduce a topic based on crisp sets and then extend to fuzzy sets. Crisp sets are more intuitive and are still used in applied QCA at least as often as fuzzy sets (Rihoux et al., 2013). Since crisp sets are a special case of fuzzy sets, all SMMR principles that hold for crisp sets also apply to fuzzy sets. Some principles, however, make use of the additional information about cases' degree of membership and thus apply only to fuzzy sets. More specifically, with fuzzy sets and their differences in degree, one can distinguish between cases of the same type. For this, I will introduce *formulas* for identifying the best available cases of the same type.

Multi-value sets are similar to crisp sets because cases are either fully in or fully out of a set.[12] Even though multi-value sets are useful for adding multinomial concepts to an analysis, they still have not gained traction in applied research (Thiem, 2013). I therefore only briefly reflect on multi-value-based SMMR in Chapter 7 and focus instead on crisp and fuzzy sets as the ubiquitous set types in applied QCA and, by extension, SMMR.

1.4.6 Types of QCA Solution Formulas and Regularity Theory of Causation

In QCA, there are three types of solution formulas: (enhanced) *conservative*, (enhanced) *intermediate*, and (enhanced) *most parsimonious* (Ragin, 2008; Schneider and Wagemann, 2012). In SMMR, any solution type can be used and be causally interpreted, provided the within-case empirical evidence points in this direction. In other words, in SMMR token-level causality at the within-case level trumps type-level causality at the cross-case level. In Chapter 5, once we have all SMMR tools in our hand, I will return to this point.

SMMR is fully in line with a *regularity theory of causality* put forward by Mahoney (2021) and Mahoney and Acosta (2022). According to this interpretation, causal inference requires meeting three criteria: The cause must (1) begin before the outcome, (2) have spatiotemporal contact with the outcome, and (3) be in constant conjunction with the outcome. Criterion 1 is relatively uncontested and simply means that a cause must occur before the effect. Criterion 2 is crucial for SMMR: spatiotemporal contact mandates the specification of a mechanism that links the cause and the outcome. This is precisely what SMMR is about and makes this regularity theory of causality the most plausible choice for SMMR. As Mahoney (2021, p. 98) states: "Of the different approaches to causality [counterfactual, causal power, regularity], only regularity models view connecting mechanisms as a part of causation itself."[13]

Criterion 3 "[...] links causality to sufficiency rather than necessity: a cause is something that is always followed by the outcome but is not required for the outcome." (Mahoney and Acosta, 2022, p. 7). This "sufficiency bias" in QCA has already been diagnosed earlier by Schneider and Wagemann (2012, chap. 9) and, accordingly, most of this book will be about statements of sufficiency. Yet, the notion of necessity does play an important role in SMMR and is discussed on several occasions in this book. As I explain in Chapter 4, whenever a sufficiency claim is made about conjunctions, so-called INUS

---

[12] Assigning fuzzy set membership scores to the various categories of a multi-value set is possible in principle (Thiem, 2014), but not achieved in practice yet.

[13] "Scholars must [...] analyze the causal sequence, or chain of intermediary events, through which the initial causal event makes spatiotemporal contact with the outcome of interest. The analysis of this sequence is required for the demonstration of causality." (Mahoney, 2021, p. 105).

conditions are created. Such INUS conditions, in turn, imply that each single conjunct in a conjunction is a *necessary* element of the sufficient conjunction (the "N" in INUS). In other words, in the context of a sufficient term, each conjunct is necessary for the outcome to occur in cases that are (only) typical for a specific sufficient conjunction. Necessity claims and their consequences for combining QCA with within-case analyses will therefore play a role in this book. And Chapter 6 is exclusively dedicated to SMMR designs based on necessity claims at the cross-case level.

1.4.7 SMMR in a Nutshell

All in all, SMMR can be seen as a detailed specification of Ragin's core dictum for QCA as a dialogue between ideas and evidence (Ragin, 2000, p. 317). SMMR focuses on the model-related aspect of this dialogue. Other elements, such as the content-valid calibration of conditions and the outcome, or the definition of the population, are not explicitly addressed. Yet, performing SMMR certainly also fosters pursuing these important goals.

SMMR puts back on the agenda of QCA researchers the importance of case-based evidence. One reason for why the "Q" in QCA stands for "qualitative" is that it requires and enables the use of case knowledge when performing QCA, interpreting its results, and linking it back to within-case analyses. Critics and proponents of QCA alike have pointed out that case knowledge often seems to be taking a back seat in applied QCA (Collier, 2014). SMMR can be seen as a tool in not only reversing this trend, but also enhancing the use of case knowledge in QCA-based research. SMMR specifies the principles and research-practical tools for identifying the best available cases for within-case analysis with the goal of descriptive and causal inference.

Figure 1.4 visualizes the process of performing SMMR. It starts with the cross-case analysis using QCA. The choice of the SMMR design – descriptive or causal – depends on whether or not the parameters of fit (consistency and coverage) are deemed as satisfactory. If they are not considered high enough[14] and/or if important cases remain unexplained, researchers should choose a descriptive SMMR design. These can be further subdivided. If the coverage of the QCA solution formula is too low, a within-case analysis of deviant coverage cases is warranted. As I explain in this book, the analytic leverage is increased if the within-case analysis of this case is performed in comparison with an iir case. Here the analytic goal consists in identifying an entire new

---

[14] What is deemed as high enough, in turn, partially depends on the research goal. For instance, if fully contradiction-free descriptive inference is the goal, then very high, if not perfect, parameters of fit are needed.

1.5 Structure of the Book

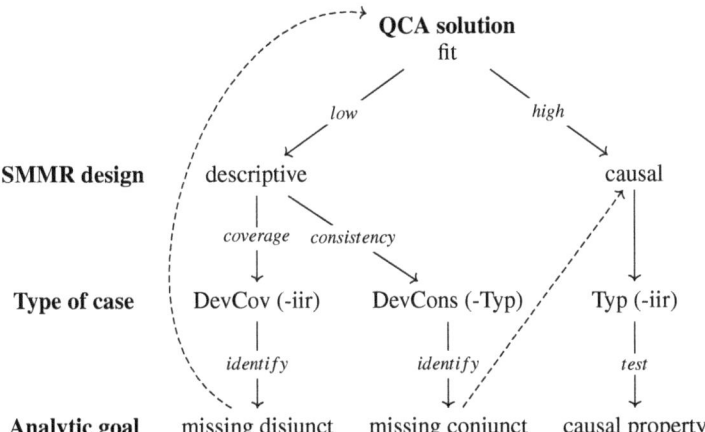

Figure 1.4 Flow chart of SMMR designs

term that is omitted from the QCA solution. This requires going back to the drawing board, adding condition(s) to the truth table, and rerunning the QCA based on the updated set of conditions. If, in contrast, the consistency level of one or more sufficient terms is too low, researchers should perform within-case analyses involving deviant consistency cases, best in comparison with a typical case. Here the goal is to identify a conjunct that is missing from the known sufficient term. No re-specification of the entire truth table is needed because this omitted conjunct is missing only from the already identified sufficient term. Finally, for all sufficient terms with high-enough consistency, a causal inference SMMR design can be chosen. This requires within-case analysis of typical cases, preferably in comparison with an iir case, and the goal consists in probing the difference-making properties of the sufficient term for the within-case mechanism.

1.5 Structure of the Book

The sequence of the chapters is straightforward and moves from simple to more complex scenarios that applied researchers might encounter. "Complexity" refers to the shape of the QCA solution – that is, whether it is a disjunction and/or contains conjunctions. I distinguish four different levels of complexity that I address one after another to climb the ladder of solution complexity. At each level additional challenges arise to which SMMR responds with additional sub-types of cases and principles for identifying the best available (pairs of) cases for model refinement and causal inference.

$$A \Rightarrow Y \tag{1.1}$$

The simplest solution consists of one sufficient condition. Expression 1.1 represents such a situation. In Chapter 2, I use it to introduce the four main types of cases – typical, deviant consistency, deviant coverage, and individually irrelevant (iir) cases – and the different single-case and comparative SMMR designs that one can choose to pursue one of the two main analytic goals: model refinement and causal inference. A first set of basic SMMR principles is introduced that govern each SMMR design.

$$A + B \Rightarrow Y \tag{1.2}$$

In Chapter 3, I add one layer of complexity by introducing disjunctions (Expression 1.2). The logical operator (+) is a nonexclusive "OR". This means, one and the same case can be a member of, that is, "explained by", more than one disjunct. To avoid problems of overdetermination in the within-case analysis, we first need to introduce additional subtypes of cases: the uniquely covered typical case and the globally uncovered iir case. I further explain that when confronted with a disjunction, users of SMMR need to follow the *focal disjunct principle*, *uniquely covered principle*, and the *globally uncovered principle* when implementing the SMMR design of their choice.

$$A * B \Rightarrow Y \tag{1.3}$$

Chapter 4 introduces a different element of complexity by turning to solutions that contain a conjunction (Expression 1.3). Conjunctions essentially have two implications for SMMR. First, they introduce heterogeneity among the cases that are nonmembers of a conjunctural solution formula. For instance, cases that are not members of the solution $A * B$ can be cases of $\sim A * B$, of $A * \sim B$, or of $\sim A * \sim B$. I explain in detail why and how this heterogeneity must be taken into account when matching members and nonmembers of a conjunction for within-case analysis. Second, ideally empirical researchers perform as many comparisons as there are conjuncts in a conjunction because for each conjunct one needs to analyze whether it is really needed (i.e. is necessary) for triggering the mechanism that links conjunction $A * B$ to outcome Y. Conjunctions affect only those SMMR designs whose goal is to draw causal inference, not the SMMR designs aiming at model-refining, descriptive inference. Four additional principles are needed to handle conjunctions in SMMR: the *focal conjunct principle*, the *iir focal conjunct unique* *nonmembership principle*, the *attribution principle*, and the *clean corridor principle*.

$$A * B + \sim C \Rightarrow Y \tag{1.4}$$

In Chapter 5, we reach the highest form of solution complexity: a disjunction that consists of conjunctions (Expression 1.4). Such solution formulas are by far the most common in applied QCA. All the (sub-)types of cases and principles that govern SMMR based on such solutions will have been already introduced in the previous chapters. Chapter 5 serves the purpose of further demonstrating how SMMR is implemented in applied QCA. In particular, I provide illustrative data on within-case mechanisms. It is also here where I return to the question of type- and token-level causality and how the latter takes primacy over the former in causal inference SMMR designs.

In Chapter 6, I show that all elements of SMMR – case types, principles, formulas – travel from QCA formulas of sufficiency to claims of necessity with only minor modifications. In this chapter, I follow the same structure of increasing complexity, from simple necessity claims ($A \Leftarrow Y$) to disjunctive ($A + B \Leftarrow Y$) and conjunctive ($A * B \Leftarrow Y$) necessity claims. For the highest form of complexity – a necessary disjunction of conjunctions – virtually no example exists. Instead, I discuss the implications for SMMR if a disjunction of conjunctions is both necessary and sufficient ($A * B + C * D \Leftrightarrow Y$). Along the way, three existing principles require minor changes to also apply to SMMR designs on necessity claims.

Chapter 7 reflects on SMMR more generally. I detail various issues of practical feasibility of SMMR and where, in my view, the direction in which SMMR should and could be developed. I also further reflect on the relation of SMMR to established case selection approaches.

I recommend reading this book in the order in which the chapters are arranged. Concepts that I introduce in earlier chapters will be needed for better understanding further down the road. In the spirit of the book as a tool for applied researchers and instructors of QCA, I am using data from published research for explaining and illustrating SMMR. I recommend running the R code at the end of each chapter and engaging with the output it produces before moving on to the next chapter.

1.6 SMMR and Related Case-Oriented Approaches

In this section, I relate SMMR to similar approaches to combining cross-case and within-case analyses. I explain what SMMR contributes to these long-standing debates. Broadly speaking, the contribution consists in the full treatment of causal complexity at the cross-case level and its consequences for choosing cases for within-case analysis; the requirement that not only the cross-case, but also the within-case analysis is designed based on sets and set relations; and the implementation of the SMMR principles in the dedicated R software package `SetMethods`. Unavoidably, the discussion in this section anticipates several of the points I will explain in detail in the chapters to come. Readers are therefore invited to first skim through this section and then return to it after having finished reading the entire book.

SMMR is fully inserted in, and compatible with, the general social science methodology literature on selecting cases for within-case analysis. As will become clear, the SMMR principles[15] and types of cases resonate with existing definitions and practices as they have been spelled out by leading scholars, such as Eckstein (1975), Lijphart (1971, 1975), Mill (1874), and Przeworski and Teune (1970). In many senses, SMMR can be seen as a translation into the language of set theory of these known and approved principles of comparative social research at large. On several occasions, this translation amounts to not only an adaptation, but also an inferential improvement. Where well-known approaches, such as Mill's methods, have long-acknowledged shortcomings (e.g. see Rohlfing, 2012, chap. 4), SMMR tackles those head-on and proposes strategies to, for instance, handle equifinal and conjunctural causal claims (see in particular Section 4.3). In Section 7.1, I return to the topic of how SMMR principles integrate and enhance established case selection strategies. What this book adds to the literature is detail and depths, combined with the technical implementation of guidelines via a dedicated R software package.

Over the past years, several authors have approached the specific question of how to combine QCA with within-case analyses. Many of them explicitly refer to the SMMR framework as outlined in this book. In the following, I discuss the differences and similarities between SMMR and these authors' approaches.

***

Above, I have already mentioned Goertz (2017) as one prominent approach to multi-method research and pointed out that the ambition of his book is broader than mine. Goertz (2017) does, however, also discuss in detail the combination of QCA and within-case studies. Several important similarities and differences between his approach and SMMR as developed in this book exist.

Let us start with the similarities. First, we agree that causal analysis requires the identification of a cross-case causal effect and of a within-case causal

---

[15] See Table A.1 in the Appendix for a list of all SMMR principles.

1.6 SMMR and Related Case-Oriented Approaches

mechanism.[16] Second, for both, mechanism M is a placeholder for potentially complex mechanisms. Third, both books are not about discussing how to best perform either the cross-case or the within-case analysis. Instead, and finally, both books are about how to select cases for within-case analysis based on findings from the cross-case analysis.

Beyond these important, basic agreements, there are some points in which the approach by Goertz (2017) differs from SMMR. First, and as already mentioned, at the cross-case level, I consider QCA only as a method, whereas Goertz (2017) takes a broader methodological perspective. Likewise, at the within-case level, I restrict the mechanism to be perceived in terms of set relations. Goertz (2017), in contrast, does not require the mechanisms to be captured via sets. Second, as mentioned, readers get a more comprehensive overview in Goertz (2017). In exchange, in my book I provide readers with a more detailed and practice-oriented discussion of SMMR. One aspect of this greater detail consists in the careful discussion of the consequences of causal complexity at the cross-case level for case selection. Another aspect is the operationalization of SMMR in the form of the dedicated R package SetMethods.

There also exist some conceptual differences. As I explain in all subsequent chapters, in SMMR, the use of iir cases is very important for causal inference SMMR design. For Goertz (2017), in contrast, cases in the 0, 0 cell have little to no role to play – at least when focusing on sufficiency statements. For SMMR designs based on necessity claims, Goertz's and my positions on the role of iir cases seem to differ, but they do not, a point that I elaborate in Chapter 6.[17]

Throughout the book, I frequently refer back to Goertz (2017) to detail further similarities and differences between our two approaches on how to combine QCA with within-case analyses.

---

[16] Goertz expresses it succinctly: "The purpose of case studies is to explore causal mechanisms at the heart of theories. One does case studies because cross-case methods give little purchase on the causal mechanisms (M_i) by which X produces Y. For multimethod researchers, showing a significant causal effect in a cross-case analysis is not sufficient; one needs to provide a causal mechanism and evidence for it. Demonstrating a causal effect is only half the job; the second half involves specifying the causal mechanism and empirically examining it, usually through case studies." (Goertz, 2017, p. 1).

[17] Beyond this, two more subtle and inconsequential differences between Goertz (2017) and my vision for SMMR seem to exist. For Goertz (2017), the goal of the cross-case analysis is about generalization, whereas for SMMR it is primarily about detecting the causal effect. In addition, for Goertz (2017), the mechanism includes the cross-case causes and the outcome, whereas in SMMR it does not. As a consequence, in Goertz (2017), the within-case analysis does not seem to be equivalent to studying the causal mechanism (see his figure 1.1), whereas in SMMR it is (see my Figure 1.2). As another consequence, in Goertz, a "configurational path in QCA" can be the mechanism. In SMMR, the QCA solution formula and the mechanism are two different things that manifest themselves at distinct levels of analysis (cross-case and within-case, respectively).

***

The approach by Beach and Pedersen (2018) to multi-method research rests on some basic assumptions that are identical to, or at least compatible with, those that underpin SMMR. "Causation is viewed in deterministic and asymmetric terms, the focus is ensuring causal homogeneity in case-based research to enable cross-case inferences to be made, and ... mechanisms are understood as more than just intervening variables ...." (Beach and Pedersen, 2018, p. 837). Furthermore, their "mapping" or categorization of cases into typical and deviant cases, based on their membership in cross-case conditions and the outcome, is virtually identical to that of Schneider and Rohlfing (2013), which, in turn, is a core building block of SMMR as envisaged in my book. Several important differences exist, though, mainly with regard to selecting among typical cases.

Just like in SMMR, Beach and Pedersen (2018) hold that to study the causal mechanism one must choose cases that are typical for a cross-case relation of sufficiency (or necessity), that is, cases that are members of both the cause X and the outcome Y. Furthermore, both Beach and Pedersen (2018, pp. 860f) and I agree that typical cases should be selected such that it is plausible to assume causal homogeneity at the within-case level, that is, such that it is plausible to assume that they all follow the same causal mechanism. SMMR is increasing the plausibility of the causal homogeneity assumption by a series of case selection principles that I explain in the next chapters. It turns out that several suggestions by Beach and Pedersen (2018) run counter to these SMMR principles.

First, as I explain in Chapter 2, one principle for strengthening the assumption of causal homogeneity among typical cases requires to contrast the most typical case with a just-so typical case – a case that has the lowest possible fuzzy set membership scores in the condition X and the outcome Y. Beach and Pedersen (2018, pp. 549f.), in contrast, advise against the use of cases close to the 0.5 membership anchor, arguing that they might be misclassified due to conceptual ambiguity or poor empirical evidence (see also Beach, 2018). I agree that just-so typical cases should not be the first choice for within-case analysis and the most typical cases should be chosen instead. However, in comparative within-case SMMR designs, matching a just-so with the most-typical case has two merits: it provides the best setup for investigating whether the same mechanism operates in all typical cases. And it provides empirical evidence on whether the classification of the just-so typical case as typical is appropriate (Rohlfing and Schneider, 2013).

Second, Beach and Pedersen (2018), instead, suggest choosing a typical case in which most potential background conditions are present. In practice, this translates to selecting typical cases based on the truth table row to which

1.6 SMMR and Related Case-Oriented Approaches

they belong. I do not find this convincing because it means that no information from the QCA cross-case analysis is taken into account. SMMR, instead, relies on the logical minimization of the truth table using QCA. Conditions that are in the truth table but not part of a sufficient term are deemed irrelevant for producing the within-case mechanism and the outcome. Of course, this inference could be wrong, but in SMMR-based research this would become visible during the within-case analysis in the form of mechanismic heterogeneity.[18]

Third, Beach and Pedersen (2018) see no point in selecting typical cases such that other causes for the outcome can be ruled out (see also Beach, 2018). In SMMR, instead, it is strongly advised to choose so-called uniquely covered typical cases, that is, cases that are typical for only one sufficient term – a point I elaborate in Chapter 3 when I introduce disjunctive QCA solutions.[19] As we will see, SMMR goes even further and stipulates the choice of cases that are typical not only for just one sufficient conjunction, but also for only one conjunct within the conjunction. This point I elaborate in Chapter 4 when introducing conjunctive QCA solutions.

Third, in SMMR, scholars are advised to match the typical case with appropriate iir cases, that is, cases that are members of neither X nor Y. According to Beach and Pedersen, in contrast, these cases do "not tell us anything about how causal mechanism actually works because [it is] not present" (Beach and Pedersen, 2018, p. 850). This is true but from an SMMR perspective misses the point: iir cases are analytically relevant for empirically testing whether the absence of the cause leads to the absence of the mechanism. Only if this is the case is the condition causal. We therefore need to perform within-case analysis in iir cases to corroborate whether the mechanism is absent.[20] Declaring iir cases analytically useful follows from the fact that SMMR rests on a clearly defined regularity theory of causation. This theory is able to connect the cross-case and within-case elements of a causal explanation.[21]

Fewer differences exist in the treatment of deviant cases. The analytic role of deviant cases in Beach and Pedersen (2018) is largely identical to how I present SMMR in this book. According to Beach and Pedersen (2018), the study of both types of deviant cases are condition-centered designs, that

---

[18] As I explain in Chapter 2, the selection of cases based on their truth table membership is recommended only for cases that cannot be explained by the QCA solution formula, the so-called deviant coverage cases.
[19] Goertz (2017) agrees with this and also recommends the choice of so-called uniquely covered typical cases.
[20] The alternative is to perform counterfactual thought experiments, as suggested below or by Nielsen (2016).
[21] Beach and Pedersen (2018), instead, contrast difference-making evidence with mechanismic evidence and restrict the former to "variance-based, experimental designs" (p. 838). This seems counterintuitive because the regularity theory of causation that underpins SMMR as envisaged in this book is doing both: it connects mechanismic evidence with difference-making evidence and is firmly rooted in qualitative methods via its set-theoretic logic.

is, they contribute to identifying omitted conditions. Just like Schneider and Rohlfing (2013) before them and like SMMR in this book, Beach and Pedersen (2018) contend that deviant consistency cases help identify omitted conjuncts (or a contextual condition) from a known cause, whereas deviant coverage cases contribute to identifying an entire new disjunctive cause. Beach and Pedersen (2018) even suggest the same comparison between a typical and deviant consistency case as I do in this book and as Schneider and Rohlfing (2013) do. Beach and Pedersen (2018), however, leave unaddressed how to adequately choose deviant coverage cases and how to increase analytic leverage by comparing them to iir cases. Both topics will be addressed in the following chapters.[22]

***

In his overview article, Rihoux (2020) stipulates five different uses of QCA. In one of them, QCA as an approach is used to explore and discover hitherto overlooked patterns by investigating truth tables without, however, proceeding to the analytic moment of logically minimizing the truth table (QCA as a technique or "QCA proper" as Rihoux (2020, pp. 7ff) calls it). Another use is based on "contradictory evidence". In the SMMR terminology applied in this book, this corresponds to the selection of deviant cases, that is, cases that contradict a claim of necessity or sufficiency or remain unexplained by them. Unlike Rihoux (2020), in SMMR deviant consistency cases are not selected based on the truth table but, instead, based on the QCA solution formula (i.e. the result of a logical minimization of a truth table). That is, SMMR kicks in after the analytic moment.

Further, unlike for Rihoux (2020), in SMMR, contradictory, or deviant, cases are primarily used for discovering model-related reasons for deviance, that is, deviance due to the omission of conditions from the QCA solution formula. Other reasons for deviance, such as faulty scope conditions, calibration decisions, or plain "measurement error", as listed by Rihoux (2020), remain, of course, possible reasons for deviance and the application of SMMR increases the chances of spotting such problems. Fixing them, however, belongs more to the phase prior to the analytic moment and is not the primary focus in SMMR.

The usage of QCA mentioned by Rihoux (2020) that is most in line with the gist of SMMR is that of establishing causality. For this, according to Rihoux (2020, p. 7), a case-based interpretation is needed. SMMR does exactly that: after the formulation of a causal effect at the cross-case level, "establishing causality", or completing the causal analysis, requires the investigation of a

---

[22] Further, more nuanced, similarities and differences between SMMR and Beach and Pedersen (2018) will be mentioned throughout the book.

1.6 SMMR and Related Case-Oriented Approaches

causal mechanism at the within-case level. SMMR specifies which cases to select for this purpose.

∗∗∗

Rihoux et al. (2021) take a much broader perspective on the question of how to combine QCA with other approaches in one research design than I do with SMMR. In their framework, there are not only the two sequences of either going first with the cross-case QCA followed by the within-case analysis or vice versa. Instead, their conceptualization on using both QCA and case studies is based on the distinction between the type of evidence (qualitative vs. quantitative) and the uncontestable insight that any good QCA, understood as a research approach, is an iterative process that goes back and forth between ideas and evidence (Ragin, 2008, p. 78), that is, from preliminary QCA back to empirical cases (qualitative or quantitative, cross-case or within case). This leads them to identify five strategies, or forms of combining QCA and case studies (see especially their table 17.1). This makes perfect sense but addresses a broader topic than I do in this book. They take into account also the research stage prior to the analytic moment (Oana et al., 2021; Rihoux and Lobe, 2009), that is, prior to having produced those results with QCA that provide the basis for substantive interpretation. In my book, by contrast, I assume that all the back and forth between ideas and evidence has taken place, using the strategies outlined by Rihoux et al. (2021) – except their strategy 4. That strategy is, in essence, SMMR as described in this book. In other words, in this book SMMR assumes that a high-quality QCA has already been produced – following the standards of good practice as depicted in, among others, the strategies by Rihoux et al. (2021) or Schneider and Wagemann (2010). The challenge solved by SMMR consists in identifying the best available cases for within-case analysis on the mechanism once a high-standard QCA has been implemented.

∗∗∗

Pattyn et al. (2022) discuss the explicit combination of QCA and process tracing for policy evaluation. Much of their framework is fully in line with SMMR. First, they require the identification of both cross-case conditions and within-case mechanisms for a complete causal analysis.[23] Second, Pattyn et al. (2022) see multi-method approaches combining QCA and process tracing as adequate tools for strengthening causal inference. Third, they use QCA results for selecting cases for within-case analysis. And, fourth, they see sets and

---

[23] They call it "CMO configurations, i.e. contexts (C) and mechanisms (M) that account for outcomes (O)" (Pattyn et al., 2022, p. 36).

set theory as the unifying framework for uniting QCA and process tracing analyses.

Their approach differs from SMMR in only some respects. First and most important, in SMMR the within-case analysis can be performed by whatever methodological approach is most adequate for analyzing the mechanism. Process tracing is but one such approach. Second, Pattyn et al. (2022) postulate that by selecting cases based on their membership in conjunctions, mechanismic heterogeneity is ruled out. In SMMR the almost exact opposite is suggested. To increase the plausibility of mechanismic homogeneity, cases should be selected not only based on their membership in a disjunction (see Chapter 3), but, beyond that, based on membership in the conjunct (see Chapter 4). Third, Pattyn et al. (2022) claim that for QCA and process tracing to be compatible, in the former researchers must declare – based on theory rather than empirical evidence – some INUS conditions as contextual conditions, whereas others are causal conditions. This is not in line with what is proposed in SMMR where all conditions are treated prima facie as equal. Nothing, however, in the tool set of SMMR prevents researchers from applying the notion of contextual and causal INUS conditions. All it requires is applying the protocol for selecting cases based only on those INUS conditions that are defined as causal and to disregard those declared as contextual. Furthermore, the discussions on necessary conditions and necessary INUS conditions in Section 4.4 and Chapter 6, respectively, do provide some guidance on how to treat conceptually different conditions differently when selecting cases for within-case analysis.

***

Kahwati and Kane (2019) provide a book-length treatment of QCA in "mixed" methods research.[24] Their framework is strongly rooted in Schneider and Rohlfing (2013) and is, thus, very much aligned with what is presented in this book. In my book, I go into much greater detail regarding types of cases and their roles in meaningful case selection in SMMR. One difference and, I think shortcoming, in Kahwati and Kane (2019) is that they treat the within-case analysis as an "interpretation of the results". In my view, SMMR is an integrated analysis in which the cross-case QCA is only one part. The within-case analysis does not "interpret" the QCA results. Instead, it provides the second necessary element for causal inference: the within-case causal mechanism. Furthermore, Kahwati and Kane (2019) discuss three within-case analytic approaches: process tracing, pattern matching, and data matrices and

---

[24] See Section 1.7.3 on why SMMR is "multi-method" and not "mixed method".

displays. In my book, I do not restrict the within-case analysis to these three approaches. Instead, any method (and data, for that matter) can be used at the within-case analysis level. The only aspect that matters in SMMR is that also the evidence at the within-case level is transferred into set membership scores.

***

In their book, Gerrits and Verweij (2018) provide an insightful discussion of using QCA for the study of large infrastructure projects. Their main focus is on the pre-analytic moment of QCA, that is, the careful definition and selection of cases, conditions, and calibration anchors based on intimate knowledge of (some) cases. Less attention is paid to the post-analytic moment when the QCA solution formula, obtained during the analytic moment of a truth table analysis, is used for selecting cases for follow-up within-case analysis of the causal mechanism. This is precisely what SMMR is about. Gerrits and Verweij (2018) can therefore be seen as a complementary reading to my book that illustrates how case knowledge informs QCA prior to the logical minimization of truth tables.

1.7 How to Use This Book

This book is written for researchers and practitioners who seek to enhance the descriptive and causal inference of their QCA results by implementing a set-theoretic multi-method research (SMMR) design. Because of the focus on the novel and unique elements of this design and for the sake of striking the right balance between depth and breadth, this book will leave out several aspects that are either related to, or part of, SMMR. In exchange, it provides several resources for users of SMMR. In the following, I give more detail on those resources and highlight key terminology. I start with a list of prerequisites for reading this book with most success and, hopefully, also pleasure.

1.7.1 Prerequisites

As already mentioned, I will not engage in a discussion of the case study first SMMR design. This book discusses the principles and practices to be applied in the crucial moment *after* QCA and *before* within-case analyses.[25]

---

[25] Rihoux and Lobe (2009) use the distinction of prior, during, and after the analytic moment, that is, the analysis of a truth table that produced the QCA solution formula (see also Oana et al. (2021) for the same distinction). In this book, I largely skip any considerations regarding the important stage prior to the analytic moment and assume that the QCA result produced during the analytic moment is based on the sound application of standards of good practice.

In other words, my book focuses on the second half of QCA as an approach (Berg-Schlosser et al., 2009; Rihoux, 2020): the phase after the analytic moment and here, more specifically, the step of going back to cases based on rigorous methodological principles. All good practices for the period prior to the analytic moment – the iterative specification of concepts, calibration, conditions, scope, cases, and "casing" (Ragin and Becker, 1992) – remain untouched and are fully compatible with SMMR as envisaged in this book. SMMR, thus, can very much be seen as a further specification and detailed set of instructions on the dialogue between ideas and evidence, as aptly captured by the nature of QCA as a research approach.

In general, I assume that users of SMMR apply both the cross-case QCA and within-case analyses according to existing standards of best practices. It is beyond the scope of this book to provide introductions to either QCA or within-case analytic techniques.[26] This book also does not spell out any practical guidelines on how to collect the data for QCA or within-case analyses.[27] This will not prevent me, of course, from discussing aspects of these techniques if and when this becomes necessary for explaining aspects of SMMR.

For reasons of clarity, I also do not engage in systematic discussions on possible reasons for less-than-perfect set relations (i.e. consistency and coverage lower than 1) other than model-related reasons, that is, the suboptimal choice of conditions. In applied QCA, such other reasons could be measurement errors, invalid calibration decisions, or wrongly specified scope conditions. In applied research, these sources of deviance are always to be kept in mind. In fact, SMMR with its insistence on in-depth case studies provides ample opportunities not only to improve the model, but also to detect other sources of deviance. Such discoveries would be a side effect of a researcher's goal to refine the model or to probe its causal properties, the two analytic goals of SMMR.

The implementation of an SMMR design requires the use of dedicated software. Both the truth table analysis and the identification of adequate cases for within-case analysis easily become too demanding to be done "by hand". The software that offers the most for empirical researchers, by a wide margin, is the R software environment. Within the limited space of this book, I cannot provide a general introduction to the use of R. I again refer the uninitiated user to the vast amount of excellent introductory material to R, in general,

---

[26] On QCA, readers can consult, for instance, Mello (2021), Oana et al. (2021), Ragin (1987, 2008), or Schneider and Wagemann (2012). For case studies, I suggest, for instance, Beach and Pedersen (2019), Bennett and Checkel (2014), Blatter and Haverland (2012), or Rohlfing (2012).

[27] On principles and practices of doing field research, see, for instance, Kapiszewski (2015). On how to turn qualitative data into set membership scores, see de Block and Vis (2019), Pagliarin et al. (2023), and Tóth et al. (2017).

or, even more helpful, to two recent books on the use of R for QCA: Dusa (2019) and Oana et al. (2021). What is offered in this book, though, are detailed explanations and documentation of all the steps that are necessary for performing SMMR by using function `smmr()` in the R package `SetMethods`. In the book, I display all of the relevant R code and the output that is produced. Supplementary information is made available in the online Appendix. The decisive advantage of using R is its flexibility, which, in theory, is limitless and allows more experienced R users to customize their own analysis. Readers who are R beginners find in this book everything that is required for performing SMMR according to the current standards. For this, I mainly use two R packages: `QCA` (Dusa, 2019) and `SetMethods` (Oana and Schneider, 2018).

1.7.2 Data and Resources

Each chapter starts with a box spelling out the *Learning Goals* and ends with a box summarizing the *Core Points* explained in the chapter. In each chapter, I use data from published QCA articles. Their core attributes are summarized in *Empirical Example* boxes. In line with QCA's rising popularity in different disciplines (Oana et al., 2021, chap. 1.3; Rihoux et al., 2013), I select examples from various social science fields, with a slight overrepresentation of examples from political science broadly understood. Where necessary for didactic purposes, I take the liberty to alter the original data and the analytic setup. It is not the goal in any of these examples to contribute to the substantive literature or to try and improve the analyses.

All chapters end with a section entitled *Applying SMMR*. It shows the use of the `smmr()` function in the R package `SetMethods`. These sections contain boxes with R *Code* and *Output*. Readers can directly copy and paste the R code and apply it to the data that I provide, together with the R code, in the book's online Appendix.[28] Function `smmr()` in package `SetMethods` is specifically tailored to this book and the SMMR designs explained in it. In fact, the book and the package have co-evolved over the past years.

The book's online Appendix contains various forms of supportive material, all in machine-readable formats. I provide data files of all the empirical examples that are used in the book. These files are available in .csv format. All analytic steps explained and performed in this book are documented in a commented R script delivered in an R Markdown and an HTLM file. Together with the data files, these scripts allow for a complete replication by the reader of all the analyses that I perform in the book.

[28] This online Appendix can be found at https://doi.org/10.7910/DVN/URMOVC.

Throughout the book, I introduce *SMMR Principles*. They provide the guidelines for selecting cases for within-case analysis based on information generated at the cross-case level. The more complex the cross-case QCA solution formula, the more principles are needed for analytically meaningful case selection. All principles are collected for a better overview in Table A.1 in the Appendix. In addition, the Core Points at the end of each chapter list the principles introduced in that chapter. In the concluding Chapter 7, I also provide an overview table of all principles and discuss which of them apply only to fuzzy sets, which ones only for causal inference SMMR designs, and which ones only when the QCA solution consists of disjuncts or conjuncts. Last but not least, the book also contains both an *Index* and a *Glossary* that defines key terms in SMMR. This is very useful because throughout the book several new concepts and terms will need to be introduced and properly defined.

1.7.3 Some Terminology

SMMR rests on set theory and Boolean algebra. For a full understanding of how case types are defined and then selected for within-case analysis in SMMR, we need to clarify and define some key terms right at the beginning. For this, consider Expression 1.5. It illustrates the result of a truth table analysis that virtually all applied QCA researchers encounter in their work.

$$A * B + \sim C \Rightarrow Y \tag{1.5}$$

The entire expression is a *solution formula*, sometimes also referred to as simply *solution* or *model*.[29] In this example, the solution is a *disjunction*, as indicated by the logical "OR" operator (+). A disjunction implies *equifinality*. In the example, the disjunction consists of the two *disjuncts* $A * B$ and $\sim C$. The disjunct $A * B$ is a *conjunction*, or *configuration*, that consists of the two *conjuncts* A and B that are combined by the logical "AND" operator (*).[30] The second disjunct is the single *condition* $\sim C$, with the logical operator for *negation* ($\sim$). Both $A * B$ and $\sim C$, respectively, are also referred to as sufficient *terms*.

The *implication* symbol $\Rightarrow$ denotes that the expression to the left is sufficient for the outcome Y on the right or, in set-relational terms, that it is a subset

---

[29] If the truth table analysis produces multiple solution formulas, we are confronted with *model ambiguity* (Baumgartner and Thiem, 2017). I do not further discuss model ambiguity because SMMR is based on the use of a single solution formula and the assumption is that the choice of this one model is based on current standards of best practice.

[30] Whenever possible, I leave out the logical "AND" operator (*).

1.7 How to Use This Book

of the outcome. It follows that the condition $\sim C$ is sufficient for Y and that the conjuncts A and B are each *INUS conditions* (Mackie, 1965). This means each conjunct is an **I**nsufficient and **N**ecessary element of a conjunction that is **U**nnecessary and **S**ufficient.

If the implication symbol points in the other direction ($\Leftarrow$), the convention in QCA is that this denotes a relation of necessity: the condition set on the left is necessary for the outcome set to the right. In applied QCA, statements of necessity are most often about single conditions. In Chapter 6, I will nevertheless spell out SMMR principles and practices in the presence of conjunctive and disjunctive claims of necessity. They give rise to so-called SUIN (Mahoney et al., 2009) and ININ[31] causes.

In applied QCA, a solution sometimes is not only sufficient, but also necessary. If so, the *equivalence* operator $\Leftrightarrow$ is used. Virtually everything we have to say about SMMR applies to solutions that are sufficient and to those that are necessary and sufficient.[32]

For the analysis of evidence on the mechanism at the within-case level, a wide range of methods can be used. SMMR, thus, does not require process tracing in all circumstances. I therefore use the generic term *within-case analysis* when referring to the study of mechanisms. For the definition of all these and many more key terms in SMMR, I direct the reader to the Glossary at the end of this book.

SMMR is called *multi-method* and not mixed method. Multi-method designs are integrative designs "[...] in which two or more methods are carefully combined to support a single, unified causal inference." (Seawright, 2016, p. 8). Mixed method designs, instead, engage in triangulation which "... involve[s] asking the same question of causal inference using two different methods, and checking that the same substantive conclusions are produced by both." (Seawright, 2016, p. 4).[33] In SMMR, the goal is to draw *one* causal (or descriptive) inference. For that one inference, two levels – cross-case and within-case – need to be addressed. This is done by combining QCA at the cross-case level and whatever other method of data analysis is adequate for studying the mechanism at the within-case level.

---

[31] I introduce ININ causes in Chapter 6.
[32] In Chapter 7, I briefly discuss the implications of necesssary and sufficient conditions for SMMR.
[33] Another, in my opinion less convincing, distinction is offered by, for instance, Rihoux et al. (2021, p. 186) or Kahwati and Kane (2019, chap. 1), who separate between multi- and mixed-method approaches based on whether qualitative and quantitative methods and data are used in one research (mixed methods) or whether two or more methods from only one of the two camps are used (multi-method).

2
Basics of SMMR
$A \Rightarrow Y$

Set-theoretic multi-method research (SMMR) is the integrated, sequential analysis of truth tables followed by the within-case analysis of selected cases. SMMR rests on the idea that studying different *types* of cases is useful for achieving different research *goals*. The implementation of a coherent research strategy therefore requires an understanding of which types of cases there are in SMMR and which ones we can use for which analytic purpose. The result of a truth table analysis, that is, the QCA solution formula, determines to which type of case each empirical case belongs. My goal in this chapter is to introduce the different types of cases and to identify the rationales for selecting and studying them in a single-case or comparative case study design. I develop the arguments based on the simplest solution formula that there can be: a single sufficient condition. This empirical result is rare in applied QCA, but it works best for introducing the basic notions of SMMR. We can set aside for a moment the challenges created by disjunctions, conjunctions, and INUS conditions.

2.1 Empirical Example

For illustration, I use the study by Vis (2009), which aims at identifying the factors that lead governments in Western Europe to implement unpopular reforms of the welfare state. The fuzzy-set QCA consists of 25 cases and analyzes three conditions.

The most parsimonious solution (consistency threshold: 0.8) reveals that S alone is sufficient for U ($S \Rightarrow U$). Table 2.1 displays the parameters of fit: both consistency (0.901) and solution coverage (0.878) are relatively high, which means that there are only few cases that empirically contradict this sufficiency claim and most cases that implemented unpopular reforms are covered, or explained, by condition S.[1]

---

[1] Unique coverage is not reported because the solution is not equifinal.

2.1 Empirical Example

Empirical Example 2.1: Governments and unpopular social policy reform: Biting the bullet or steering clear? (Vis, 2009)

- *Research question*: What are the factors for implementing unpopular welfare state reforms?
- *Cases*: 25 governments in Western Europe
- *Set type*: Fuzzy
- *Outcome*: Unpopular welfare state reforms (U)
- *Conditions*: Weak political position (P), weak socio-economic position (S), right-leaning government (R)

Table 2.1 *Most parsimonious solution for outcome "unpopular reforms" U*

	inclS	PRI[a]	covS	covU
S	0.901	0.787	0.878	
Solution	0.901	0.787	0.878	

condition S: weak socio-enonemic situation; outcome U: unpopular Welfare state reform

[a] PRI, introduced by Charles Ragin, stands for proportional reduction in inconsistency. It expresses the degree to which a set (here S) is a subset not only of the outcome (here U) but also its negation $\sim U$ (Schneider and Wagemann, 2012, pp. 237–244).

Figure 2.1 XY plot: sufficient term for outcome "unpopular reforms" U

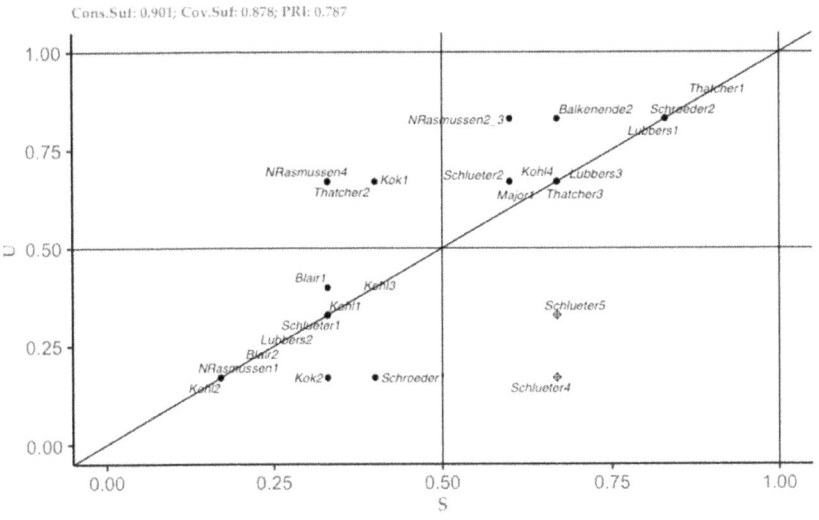

> **Learning Goals 2.1: Basics of SMMR**
>
> - Understand how membership of cases in the QCA solution and the outcome is used for sorting cases into one of the four basic case types: typical, deviant consistency, deviant coverage, and individual irrelevant (iir)
> - Learn about the first set of SMMR principles that guide the selection of cases for within-case analyses on the mechanism linking the condition to the outcome
> - Get acquainted with the seven possible SMMR designs: three single-case and four comparative SMMR designs
> - Become familiar with the basic logic of the smmr() function and the interpretation of the output it produces
> - Learn about how information on differences in degree contained in fuzzy (but not crisp) sets is used for distinguishing between better and worse choices of cases of the same type
> - Understand the different scenarios in which a typical and an iir case can hold membership in the condition, the outcome, and the mechanism, and the implications of these scenarios for causal inference

The solution can be visualized with an enhanced XY plot (Schneider and Rohlfing, 2013), as shown in Figure 2.1. It reveals which cases have high membership in both S and U (upper-right quadrant, e.g. Balkenende2), which ones only in S (lower-right quadrant, e.g. Schlueter4), which ones only in U (upper-left quadrant, e.g. Kok1), and which ones in none of the two sets (lower-left quadrant, e.g. Blair1). The XY plot also shows which cases have membership in S smaller than or equal to that in U (above or on the main diagonal), as required by the sufficiency statement $S \Rightarrow U$, and which ones do not (below the diagonal).

What is the within-case mechanism that underpins the cross-case pattern of the sufficiency statement $S \Rightarrow Y$? For illustrative purposes, let us hypothesize that a deteriorating socio-economic situation (S) makes incumbents worry about both their own future in government and the financial viability of their country. These concerns are the mechanism (C_M) that leads governments to implement unpopular reforms (U). Figure 2.2 graphically depicts the logic of the argument.

In the remainder of the chapter, I explain which area in an XY plot denotes which type of case in SMMR, which analytic goals can be pursued via within-case analysis of a given case type, and how to select the best available case in the data for each type of case.

2.2 Types of Cases in SMMR

Figure 2.2 Cross-case condition and within-case level mechanism for outcome "unpopular reforms"

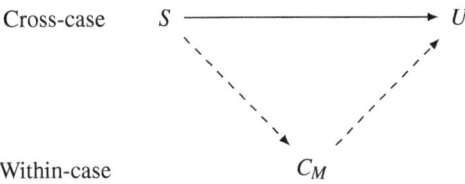

S = socio-economic trouble; C_M = concerns for future; U = unpopular reforms

2.2 Types of Cases in SMMR

Types of cases are fundamental for SMMR. The QCA solution formula determines to which type each empirical case belongs. And each analytic goal of SMMR – descriptive inference (model refinement) and causal inference – requires the selection of specific types of cases.

2.2.1 Crisp Sets

Suppose we are interested in the conditions under which governments pass unpopular welfare state reforms (Vis, 2009). As shown above, the most parsimonious solution for outcome U, unpopular reforms, displays a weak socio-economic environment as the single sufficient condition (S): $S \Rightarrow U$. If we disregard for a moment the differences in degree among cases on the same side of the 0.5 qualitative anchors in S and U, respectively, then we can display the result as shown in the 2×2 table in Figure 2.3.

I summarize this solution in a 2×2 table because it is the most intuitive way to understand what types of cases we can identify based on a QCA solution. The 2×2 table in Figure 2.4 captures each possible combination of membership and nonmembership in the condition and the outcome and provides the labels for the types of cases in each of the four basic constellations.

Whenever QCA yields a solution, the upper-right cell must contain at least one case. This so-called 1, 1 cell, or causal mechanism cell (Goertz, 2017, chap. 3) contains the cases that are *typical* for the finding that S is sufficient for U. Every member of both S and U represents the sufficiency relation and corresponding theoretical argument. That is, each case in the upper-right cell is as typical as any other for the statement of sufficiency, because all cases from the same cell are qualitative identical. In Vis (2009), there are ten such cases,

Figure 2.3 2 × 2 table: sufficient term for outcome *U*

Sufficiency Plot
Cons.Suf: 0.901; Cov.Suf: 0.878; PRI: 0.787
U
1
0
3
10
10
2
0
1
solution_formula

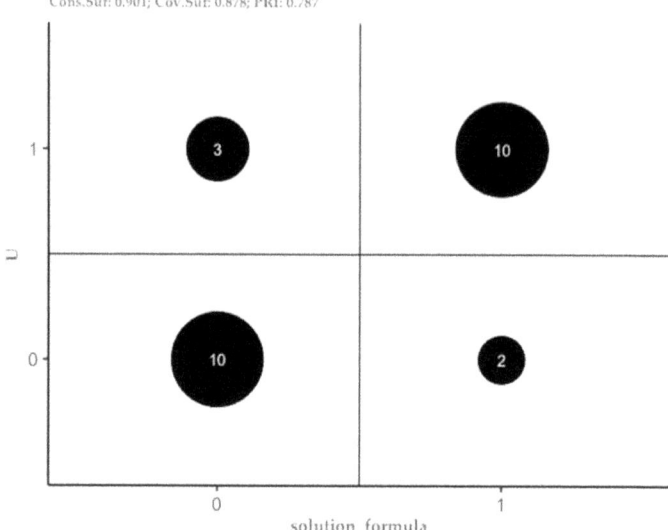

Figure 2.4 Types of cases, crisp-set SMMR

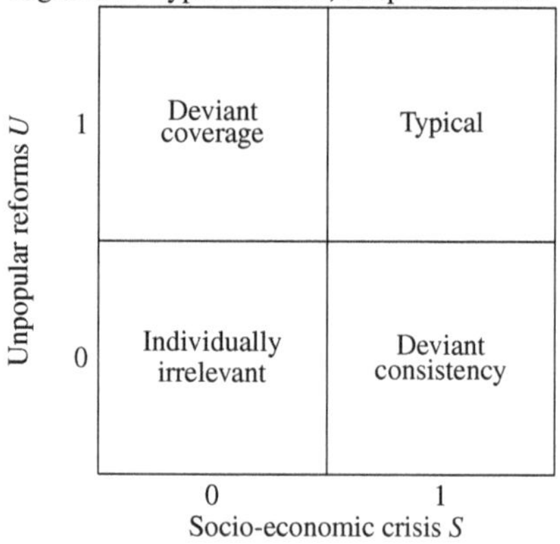

Unpopular reforms U
1
0
Deviant coverage
Typical
Individually irrelevant
Deviant consistency
0
1
Socio-economic crisis S

among them, for instance, several governments led by Thatcher or Lubbers (see Figure 2.1).

Cases in the lower-right cell are puzzling because despite being members of the known sufficient condition, they fail to display the outcome. We label such instances of socio-economic crisis (*S*) paired with the *absence* of unpopular reforms ($U = 0$) as *deviant consistency cases*.[2] The more cases of this type exist, the lower the consistency of the sufficient term. In our example, the fourth and fifth governments by Schlueter are such deviant consistency cases.

Cases in the cells where the condition is absent ($S = 0$) are not directly relevant for assessing the empirical consistency of the sufficiency statement $S \Rightarrow U$. However, as we will see, in SMMR they do play a role and thus deserve their own label. Cases in the upper-left quadrant are puzzling because they do show the outcome for reasons yet unknown to the researcher. For QCA researchers, who tend to be Y-oriented, this is a problem: the more *deviant coverage cases*[3] there are, the less empirically important the findings. In our example on the causes for unpopular reforms (U), for instance, there are three cases that are members of U but not of condition S. The reasons why the governments by NRasmussen4, Kok1, and Thatcher2 implemented unpopular reforms are left unexplained by the QCA solution formula $S \Rightarrow U$.

Cases in the lower-left quadrant are cases that are neither members of the outcome, nor of any of the known conditions for it. As such, they, in and of themselves, are not relevant for assessing the statement $S \Rightarrow U$. As I explain later, they do play a crucial role in *comparative* within-case analysis when trying to assess the causal status of the sufficiency statement $S \Rightarrow U$ and to discover causes that are omitted from the solution formula. This is why they are labeled individually irrelevant cases (*iir*). In the present example, there are ten such iir cases, for instance, Blair1 or Kok2 (see, again, Figure 2.1).

2.2.2 Fuzzy Sets

Do these types of cases also exist with fuzzy sets? Yes, they do – with only one minor, for SMMR inconsequential, amendment. Consider Figure 2.5. It is an XY plot with a 2 × 2 table superimposed. As mentioned, we call this an enhanced XY plot because it captures both the difference in *degree* and difference in *kind* between cases. The diagonal denotes where a case i holds equal membership in condition S and outcome U, that is where $S_i = U_i$. Cases above the diagonal are consistent with the sufficiency statement $S \Rightarrow U$, because for all of those cases $S_i \leq U_i$ holds.[4] In contrast, cases below are inconsistent with the sufficiency statement because they hold higher membership in S than in U ($S_i > U_i$).

---

[2] Goertz (2017, chap. 3) calls it the falsification-scope cell. This is in line with the role of these cases in SMMR: to refine the original sufficiency statement by identifying a missing conjunct.

[3] Goertz (2017, chap. 3) labels it the equifinality cell because these cases indicate the existence of an alternative path toward the outcome.

[4] A statement of sufficiency entails that condition S is a subset of outcome U. In other words, all cases' membership in S must be smaller than or equal to their membership in U.

For performing SMMR, both groups of cases need to be further divided. For this, we make use of the qualitative distinction imposed by the qualitative anchor at 0.5 in the condition and the outcome. Cases inside the same quadrant are qualitatively identical but they differ in the degree to which they belong to sets S and U. Cases in different quadrants are deemed as qualitatively different, regardless of how close they are to the 0.5 qualitative anchors.

The distinction of cases based on their degrees of membership in fuzzy sets is limited by an important principle.

Principle of differences in kind and degree: Differences in degree should be established only among cases that are similar in kind and located on the same side of the secondary diagonal.

Put differently, only among the same type of case can fuzzy sets establish differences in degree. Graphically speaking, this means that cases must be located in the same area of an enhanced XY plot, like in Figure 2.5, before differences in degree can be established. Differences in kind trump differences in degree.

With fuzzy sets, it is not enough to be in the upper-right quadrant. In addition, their fuzzy set membership scores must be consistent, that is, their membership in S must be smaller than or equal to their membership in U ($S \leq U$). This is area 1 in Figure 2.5. Among these qualitatively identical typical cases, we can establish differences in degree (see below).

Cases in the lower triangle in the upper-right quadrant are *inconsistent* and are labeled *deviant consistency cases in degree* (area 2b). This is the only type of case that has no correspondence in crisp-set QCA. In our example on unpopular reforms, no deviant consistency cases in degree exist (see Figure 2.1). All cases in the upper-right quadrant are also above the diagonal and thus are typical cases for the sufficiency claim $S \Rightarrow U$. The use of deviant consistency cases in degree for within-case analysis in SMMR is not encouraged.[5]

Instead, *deviant consistency cases in kind* (lower-right quadrant, area 2) are always to be preferred. Among those, we have the sub-type of the ideal deviant consistency cases in kind (2a). It sits in the lower-right corner and displays the maximum possible difference in set membership scores in S and U. In the example by Vis (2009), the fourth and fifth governments of Schlueter are deviant consistency cases in kind. While both cases are qualitatively identical (they are in the same lower-right quadrant of the XY plot), Schlueter4 is more

---

[5] Beach (2018) classifies deviance consistency cases in degree as typical cases. This amounts to ignoring information on differences in degree provided by fuzzy sets and, as a consequence, the various SMMR principles and formulas that are based on such differences and that I introduce in this book.

2.2 Types of Cases in SMMR

deviant than Schlueter5 (it is closer to the ideal-typical deviant consistency case in the lower-right corner).

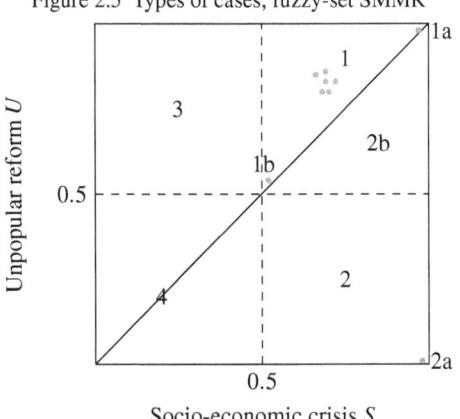

Figure 2.5 Types of cases, fuzzy-set SMMR

1 = typical; 1a = ideal typical; 1b = just-so typical; 2 = deviant consistency in kind; 2a = ideal deviant consistency; 2b = deviant consistency in degree; 3 = deviant coverage; 4 = individually irrelevant

Both deviant coverage cases (area 3 in Figure 2.5) and iir cases (area 4) are defined in the same way in crisp- and fuzzy-set QCA. Note that Figure 2.5 does not display an ideal deviant coverage case, which, analogous to the ideal deviant consistency case, one would expect to be located in the upper-left corner of Figure 2.5. However, the reason why this case is not displayed is because in SMMR, for cases that are *not* members of the sufficient term of interest (here "socio-economic crisis", S), we need to select based on their membership in the truth table row. When selecting cases for within-case analysis, it is not enough to select based on what they are *not* (here: "not members of S"), but on what they *are*. And the most detailed description of deviant coverage cases is the truth table row to which they belong. This logic is distilled in a principle:

Truth table row principle: For SMMR designs involving cases that are members of the outcome but not members of any term in the QCA solution formula, choose based on the membership in the truth table row to which this case belongs.

This principle is also one reason why the diagonal in area 4 is not relevant, that is, why the diagonal in the lower-left quadrant in Figure 2.5 is not separating different types of iir cases. Whether or not an iir case is consistent or not with the sufficiency claim $S \Rightarrow U$ is irrelevant. What matters for selecting iir cases for comparative within-case analysis (see below) is their membership in their truth table row (comparison with deviant coverage case) or the so-called focal conjunct of the focal disjunct, two concepts that I introduce in Chapters 3 and 4 when the solution formula consists of a disjunction and a conjunction, respectively.[6]

Table 2.2 *Types of cases and analytic goals of within-case analysis* $(S \Rightarrow U)$

Type of case	Condition S	Outcome U		Goal of single within-case analysis
			Causal inference	
(1) Typical	>0.5	>0.5	$S \leq U$	Test mechanism M
(4) iir	<0.5	<0.5		None
			Descriptive inference	
(2) Dev cons (kind)	>0.5	<0.5		Identify omitted conjunct
(2b) Dev cons (degree)	>0.5	>0.5	$S > U$	Not recommended
(3) Dev cov	<0.5	>0.5		Identify omitted disjunct

Source: adapted from Schneider and Rohlfing (2019).

Table 2.2 summarizes the definitions of the types of cases that are created when performing a fuzzy-set QCA. While the types of cases are the same as in crisp-set QCA, fuzzy sets do add information for distinguishing between cases *of the same type*. This difference is captured with dedicated formulas, a topic that I address in the next section. In SMMR, it is important that the type of case chosen matches the analytic goal pursued. Based on Table 2.2, two additional principles can be derived. Both principles apply to single-case and comparative SMMR designs, to which I turn below.

Causal inference selection principle: A causal inference SMMR design must include a typical case.[7]

Descriptive inference selection principle: A descriptive inference SMMR design must include a deviant case.

---

[6] In the special scenario of a single set being the only sufficient term, that term S is automatically also the focal disjunct and the focal conjunct. Only in this specific circumstance is the diagonal in the lower-left quadrant of an XY plot like the one shown in Figure 2.1 meaningful and distinguishes consistent (above the diagonal) from inconsistent iir cases. That distinction is relevant for the comparison of iir cases with typical cases (see below).

[7] This principle is in line with suggestions by Goertz (2017), who postulates that, for causal process tracing, at least one case must be typical for the causal claim under investigation.

2.3 Single-Case SMMR

According to the principle of differences in kind and in degree, with fuzzy sets, it is possible to distinguish between cases that fall into the same area of an enhanced XY plot. In the following, I first discuss the rationales for identifying the best available cases for each of the two types of deviant cases. Then I turn to identifying the best available typical cases. The latter are involved in all causal inference SMMR designs (single and comparative), whereas the former are involved in all descriptive inference SMMR designs.

2.3.1 Descriptive Inference SMMR

Deviant coverage cases are puzzling because, like typical cases, they are members of U but, unlike typical cases, they are not members of S. In our example from Vis (2009), NRasmussen4, Thatcher2, and Kok1 are such unexplained cases of governments that implemented unpopular reforms for reasons not captured by the QCA solution formula. Within-case analysis in such cases aims at identifying a hitherto overlooked disjunct, that is, a new sufficient term. Following the truth table row principle (see above), the omitted disjunct might consists of the case's truth table row plus a hitherto overlooked condition.

For instance, both NRasmussen4 and Kok1 are located in truth table row $\sim P * \sim S * \sim R$. Without signs of political and socio-economic crises and not being a right-of-center government, they implemented unpopular reforms. Within-case analysis should reveal which functionally equivalent mechanism to reelection concerns (C_M) operates in these cases that triggers the outcome and which hitherto overlooked cross-case condition triggers this alternative mechanism in combination with $\sim P * \sim S * \sim R$. The same logic is applied in the within-case analysis of the third deviant coverage case, Thatcher2, which is located in truth table row $\sim P * \sim S * R$. In general, cases located in separate truth table rows require separate within-case analyses. Each truth table row is qualitatively distinct and might trigger a different within-case mechanism (Beach and Siewert, 2019).

The best available deviant coverage case is identified by Formula (2.1). The higher a case's membership in the truth table row (TT), the more adequate it is for within-case analysis with the goal of identifying the missing sufficient disjunct.[8] For this and the numerous other SMMR formulas that I will introduce in this book, it holds that smaller values indicate better choices of

---

[8] In addition, membership in the truth table row should be smaller than in the outcome, else it would not be consistent with the sufficiency claim $TT \Rightarrow Y$. The R output does provide this information (see Section 2.6).

(pairs of) cases. This and all other formulas are implemented in the smmr() function of the R package SetMethods (Oana and Schneider, 2018). At the end of each chapter, I demonstrate the use of the smmr() function for identifying the best available cases for within-case analysis.

$$DCOV = 1 - TT \quad \text{\small large membership in truth table row} \quad (2.1)$$

$DCOV$ = deviant coverage case; TT = truth table row

If coverage of the QCA solution is considered low, then the advice is to add the omitted condition to the truth table and run a QCA based on that refined truth table. As Figure 1.4 shows, this would mean a return to the pre-analytic moment (Schneider and Rohlfing, 2013). If, however, the solution coverage of the initial QCA is deemed high enough, then the disjunct that is formed by the deviant coverage case's truth table row plus the omitted condition might be added to that QCA solution, that is, without the need to add the omitted condition to the truth table and thus the need return to the pre-analytic moment. All this implies that all the following SMMR designs should be applied only to QCA solution formulas that display a high-enough solution coverage.[9]

With fuzzy sets we can identify the most *deviant consistency case*. They are puzzling because, like typical cases, they are members of the sufficient term S, but, unlike typical cases, they are *not* members of the outcome U. The goal of the within-case analysis consists in finding out why mechanism C_M is not triggered in the deviant consistency case. The only model-related reason is that in this case a hitherto overlooked condition is needed, in conjunction with S, for triggering the mechanism C_M. In other words, the goal when analyzing a deviant consistency case consists in unraveling a conjunct that has been omitted from a known sufficient term. The goal, thus, is to make a known sufficient term more precise by adding to it an overlooked conjunct. That condition is usually not added to the truth table and no new truth table analysis is needed because the within-case evidence is exclusively related to those cases that are members of the known sufficient term. The omitted conjunct is not expected to be missing from any other sufficient term.[10]

The most puzzling case is the one that deviates most from a consistent sufficiency pattern (i.e. that is farthest below the main diagonal in Figure 2.5). A case located at $S = 1, U = 0$ in Figure 2.5 is the ideal deviant consistency

---
[9] In the concluding chapter, once we have all SMMR tools at hand, I return to the question of how to choose among and sequence the different SMMR designs (see Section 7.2.4).
[10] Researchers who have strong reasons to suspect that the omitted condition could be relevant for other sufficient terms as well can add that condition to the truth table and rerun their QCA.

case. The closer empirical cases come to this ideal type, the more deviant they are. This can be condensed into the following principle.

Principle of maximum set membership difference: The most deviant consistency case displays maximum difference in its set membership in the condition and the outcome.

The principle is captured by Formula 2.2. The case of Schlueter4 comes closer to the ideal deviant case consistency than Schlueter5 (see Figure 2.1).

$$DCON = \underbrace{[1-(S-Y)]}_{\text{far from diagonal}} + \underbrace{(1-S)}_{\text{large membership in sufficient term}} \quad (2.2)$$

DCON = deviant consistency case; S = sufficient term of interest; Y = outcome

Within-case analysis of the Schlueter4 government should focus on why socio-economic crisis S did not trigger the mechanism reelection concern (C_M) in this case. For the sake of illustration, let us assume that during Schlueter's fourth government the socio-economic crisis occurred at the very beginning of the government's tenure. There was, thus, no reason to fear not being reelected simply because no elections were scheduled in the near future. Timing of elections is thus identified as a relevant but so far overlooked conjunct. At the cross-case level, it is not a socio-economic crisis (S) alone that triggers unpopular reforms (U); it must be combined with elections being imminent (E). The new cross-case condition is then $S*E \Rightarrow U$. Since Schlueter4 is not a member of E, it is also not a member of $S*E$ and therefore turns from a deviant consistency case into an individually irrelevant (iir) case with regard to the sufficiency claim $S*E \Rightarrow U$.[11] The hitherto overlooked conjunct E would not have been discovered without within-case analysis on the mechanism that failed to be triggered by S alone. It is also important to point out that adding the omitted conjunct E at the cross-case level is not the same as specifying a within-case mechanism C_M.

2.3.2 Causal Inference SMMR

As shown in Table 2.2, when analyzing a typical case, the goal consists in identifying or testing the presence of the within-case mechanism M that links

---

[11] Whether or not condition E turns all deviant consistency cases into iir cases is an empirical question: If it does, then there is causal homogeneity among cases in socio-economic trouble (S). If it does not, then there is causal heterogeneity among them and there is yet another omitted condition with which S must be combined to resolve the puzzle of other deviant consistency cases, such as Schlueter5 in our example.

the cross-case condition S to the outcome U. In our example, a weak socio-economic situation (S) might trigger heightened concerns about reelection and the future of the country (C_M), which, in turn, leads them to propose welfare state reforms (U) as a way out of the socio-economic crisis because it enhances the chances for reelection. A case's membership in the mechanism set "reelection concern" C_M could be determined in manifold ways, for instance via interviews with core governmental actors, archival research of party documents, or content analyses of press news. The cross-case–within-case argument can be written as $S \Rightarrow C_M \Rightarrow U$, where the subscript "$_M$" indicates a within-case mechanism as opposed to a cross-case condition.

The goal of identifying or testing the causal mechanism is best achieved in cases that have maximum membership in both S and U and, by virtue of this, are located on the diagonal ($S = U$). In other words, the ideal typical case is located in the upper-right corner of the XY plot in Figure 2.5. Short of this ideal, all other typical cases in area 1 fulfill these two criteria – high membership in S and being close to the diagonal – to different degrees. We define as the *best available typical case* the one that best maximizes these two criteria (high on S and U, and close to the diagonal). This can be condensed in two principles. The first one reads as follows:

Principle of maximum set membership: The most typical case displays maximum set membership scores in the condition and the outcome.

The criterion of high membership in the sufficient condition of interest seems straightforward. The higher the membership, the better a case represents the set of interest, that is, it becomes more typical for the set. This, in turn, means that the expectation is that it should also be more typical for the mechanism, that is, it should also hold a high membership score in the mechanism set.

Why, however, is it important to choose cases close to the diagonal? Why does it strengthen the within-case analysis if a typical case is chosen that holds as similar as possible membership scores in the condition S and outcome U? Why is Lubbers3, located on the diagonal (see Figure 2.1) a better choice than Balkenende2, which has a similar membership in S but much higher membership in U and is thus located far above the diagonal?

To answer these questions, let us remember what the goal of within-case analysis in a typical case is. We aim at analyzing (either discovering or testing) the mechanism C_M that links condition S to outcome U. It is important to spell out what is meant by "link". We mean that S triggers C_M, which, in turn, triggers U. The term trigger can be translated as "is sufficient for".[12]

---

[12] See Mikkelsen (2017) for a detailed explanation of why mechanism arguments denote chains of sufficiency. Nonsufficient elements in a mechanism argument would lead to a breakdown of

We, thus, have the following chain of sufficiency: the cross-case condition socio-economic crisis (S) is sufficient for triggering the within-case mechanism reelection concern (C_M), which, in turn, is sufficient for triggering the outcome unpopular reforms (U):

$$S \Rightarrow C_M \Rightarrow U \tag{2.3}$$

From the cross-case QCA, we know that S is sufficient for U ($S \Rightarrow U$). The within-case analysis is performed to empirically test whether the other two elements of the "sufficiency chain" in Expression 2.3 also hold. The only possibility for this to be the case is when S is a subset of C_M (the $S \Rightarrow C_M$ part) and, at the same time, C_M is a subset of U (the $C_M \Rightarrow U$ part). This means, the case's membership in C_M must fall between its values in S and in U. This corridor of membership values for C_M has as its floor the membership in S and as its ceiling the membership in U. The smaller this corridor (i.e. the closer the membership scores of a case in S and U), the more difficult it is to find that the case's membership in C_M falls within that corridor. Harder tests are preferred over easier tests. The smallest corridor exists when $S = U$. The only possible membership in C_M that leaves the chain $S \Rightarrow C_M \Rightarrow U$ empirically consistent is $S = C_M = U$.

I condense this important insight into the following principle. We will encounter this principle several times in the following chapters because it is relevant for case selection for all those single-case and comparative SMMR designs that seek causal inference. It applies to the choice of a typical case and to the comparison between two typical cases and a typical and an iir case.

Test corridor principle: For causal inference SMMR designs, choose cases that hold membership scores in the set of interest[13] and the outcome set that are as similar as possible.

Figure 2.6 graphically illustrates the idea of a test corridor. Case$_1$ is closer to the diagonal than Case$_2$. The horizontal lines depict the size of the corridor and thus the test strictness for each of the two cases. For Case$_1$, the line is short and with this the range of possible membership values for C_M. For Case$_2$,

---

"[...] the productive relation between start-up conditions and outcome [...]" (Mikkelsen, 2017, p. 431). In Sections 2.4 and 4.4, I discuss various other possible and plausible forms of connections between cross-case conditions, within-case mechanisms, and cross-case outcomes.

[13] In subsequent chapters, when I introduce the elements of causal complexity (equifinality in Chapter 3 and conjunctural causation in Chapter 4), further specification is needed as to what "the set of interest" in the test corridor principle is referring to. In the current example with only one sufficient condition S, it refers to membership in S.

this range of values, the corridor, for C_M is much larger and the test for C_M in $Case_2$ is more likely to be successful than in $Case_1$. The test in $Case_1$ is more severe, or strict, than in $Case_2$. Applied to the example by Vis (2009) displayed in Figure 2.1, for the typical case of Thatcher1 on the diagonal, with memberships $S = U = 0.83$, the only membership in C_M that passes the test is 0.83. In contrast, for Balkendende2, located above the diagonal, with $S = 0.67$ and $U = 0.83$, membership in C_M can range between 0.67 and 0.83 for the mechanism test to pass.

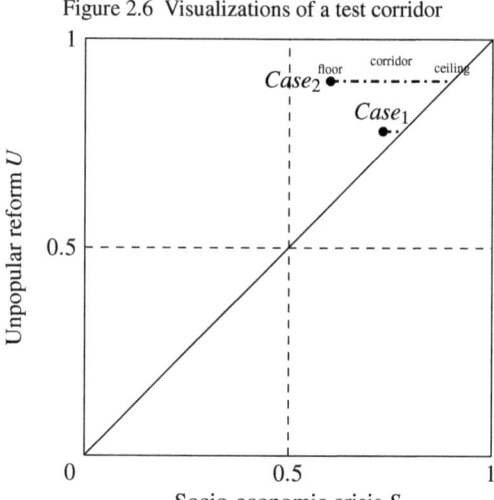

Figure 2.6 Visualizations of a test corridor

Needless to say, the test corridor principle applies only when fuzzy sets are used for all sets at the cross-case and the within-case levels. However, even if only the sets at the cross-case level are fuzzy, but the mechanism is calibrated as a crisp set, it is still advised to choose cases that adhere to the test corridor principle. The principle ensures that cases close to the diagonal are chosen and those cases display membership in the outcome that one expects given their membership in sufficient condition.

The two principles specifying good choices for typical cases are captured by Formula 2.4.[14] The smaller the formula value, the more a case approaches the ideal case. As mentioned, this feature holds for all formulas that are relevant for identifying best available cases in SMMR: the smaller the value, the better

---

[14] I point out that in Chapter 4 another formula will be introduced that should be used for identifying typical cases when confronting conjunctions.

2.3 Single-Case SMMR

the case or pair of cases. For Vis (2009), the cases of Lubbers1, Schroeder2, and Thatcher1 come closest to the ideal typical case (see Figure 2.1).

$$TYP = 2*(Y-S) \quad \text{\scriptsize strictness}$$
$$+ (1-S) \quad \text{\scriptsize large membership in term} \quad (2.4)$$

TYP = typical case; S = sufficient term of interest; Y = outcome

Choosing cases close to, or on, the diagonal might sound like a hazardous strategy because only a minor change in a case's membership in either the condition or the outcome would change the case's status from a typical to a deviant consistency in degree case. It is a general insight that if the precision of the data is low, drawing inference is more difficult. It is, however, the very nature of the within-case analysis for which cases on the diagonal are chosen that enables researchers to detect any misclassification of the case under study.[15] To minimize this possibility, researchers can limit their choice of typical cases to robust typical cases, that is, those that withstand alternative plausible analytic setups for the cross-case QCA (Oana and Schneider, 2021), a topic I elaborate in further detail in Section 7.3.2.[16]

Before turning to comparative SMMR designs, let me introduce another subtype among typical cases: the just-so typical case. It sits in the lower-left corner of the triangle denoting typical cases in Figure 2.5. It is the typical case with the lowest possible membership scores in S and U. In the example from Vis (2009), Major1 and Schlueter2 are the best empirical representation of the just-so typical case. Just-so typical cases play a role when later I introduce the comparative SMMR design that matches two typical cases with the goal of generalizing the causal mechanism to all typical cases for a sufficient term.

Just one last word on different notions of "typicalness" and why the one I chose is appropriate in SMMR. When looking at the distribution of typical cases in area 1 of Figure 2.5, one might be tempted to argue that the most typical case should be the one that is closest to most other typical cases. This would be appropriate if the meaning of typicalness was to identify the case that best represents *all the other cases*. With sets and set relations, however, we are interested in which case best represents *the set(s) in question*. Put differently, when asked "typical for what?", in set-theoretic methods the answer is "for the

---

[15] Even though, in this book, I focus mostly on model-related issues (Does the model have a causal interpretation and does it omit conditions?), SMMR with its strong reliance on within-case evidence is certainly helpful in gauging whether a given case has been placed on the "right" side of the 0.5 anchor (Rohlfing and Schneider, 2013).

[16] One might, in addition, restrict the choice to "most likely typical cases", identified based on the set-theoretic theory evaluation approach (Schneider and Wagemann, 2012, chap. 11.3), an argument I elaborate in further detail in Section 7.3.1.

set(s)", whereas in non-set-theoretic methods the answer tends to be "for the other cases".

Single iir cases in and of themselves are not puzzling. They neither confirm nor contradict the statement of sufficiency. Given their individual irrelevance, there is, thus, no need to identify the most irrelevant case. They do play a role, though, in comparative SMMR design, a topic to which I turn after an excursus on so-called broken sufficiency corridors.

2.4 Excursus: Forms of Broken Sufficiency Corridors

Sufficiency chains ($X \Rightarrow M \Rightarrow Y$) are probably the most common form of linking cross-case conditions and outcomes via within-case mechanisms.[17] Other forms are possible, though. With a sufficiency relation at the cross-case level ($X \Rightarrow Y$), three alternatives to a sufficiency chain can occur in a typical and in an iir case. Provided there is adequate substantive theorizing, two of them can be causally interpreted, whereas one constitutes empirical evidence that the $X \Rightarrow Y$ relation is not causal. Figure 2.7 graphically depicts the four possible locations of M in relation to X and Y in a typical case (upper-part of Figure 2.7).[18]

In a sufficiency statement, the floor of the test corridor is provided by a case's membership in condition X. Hence, a broken floor means that a case's membership in mechanism M_2 is smaller than in X. If, and only if, there are plausible theoretical arguments in favor of claiming that X is a necessary condition for M_2, then the empirical pattern $X > M_2$ can be interpreted as a necessity relation $X \Leftarrow M_2$. The location of M_2 would then provide evidence for the "nec-suf chain" $X \Leftarrow M_2 \Rightarrow Y$.[19] Sufficient condition X is necessary for mechanism M, which, in turn, is sufficient for outcome Y.

In a broken ceiling chain, in contrast, the case's membership in M_3 exceeds that in outcome Y ($M_3 > Y$). Such an empirical pattern is in line with theoretical arguments of M_3 being necessary for the occurrence of outcome Y ($M_3 \Leftarrow Y$). The location of M_3 would then provide evidence for the "suf-nec chain" $X \Rightarrow M_3 \Leftarrow Y$.[20] The sufficient condition X is sufficient for mechanism M, which, in turn, is necessary for outcome Y.

---

[17] For some important examples in applied research, see Mahoney (2021, p. 128 and appendix).
[18] Figure 2.7 displays the locations of M for not only the typical case, but also the iir case (see below) in the lower-left half of the plot.
[19] By pure logic, if $X > M_2$ and $X < Y$, membership in M_2 must also be smaller than in Y ($M_2 < Y$). In other words, in a broken floor, or "nec-suf chain", M_2 is a subset of, or sufficient for, Y.
[20] By pure logic, if $M_3 > Y$ and $X < Y$, membership in M_3 must be bigger than in X. In other words, in a broken ceiling, or also "suf-nec chain", X is a subset of, or sufficient for, M_3.

2.4 Excursus: Forms of Broken Sufficiency Corridors

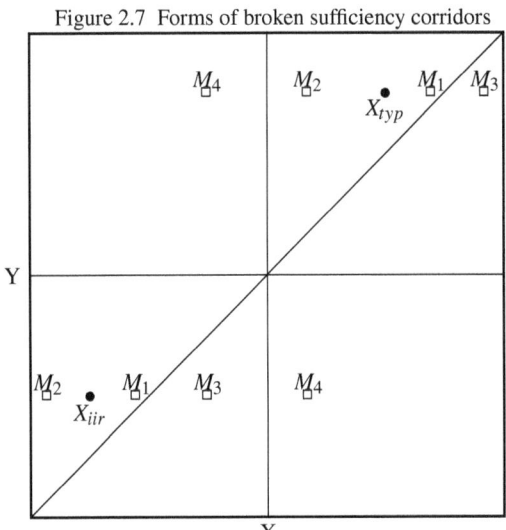

Figure 2.7 Forms of broken sufficiency corridors

- Cross-case condition
- □ Within-case mechanisms:
  M_1 sufficiency chain; M_2 "broken floor" (nec-suf chain); M_3 "broken ceiling" (suf-nec chain); M_4 noncausal

As mentioned, both broken floor and broken ceiling chains are empirically possible and do reveal causally interpretable patterns, provided strong theoretical arguments exist for either a nec-suf or a suf-nec chain.[21] Only if the within-case analysis reveals that the case is *not* a member of M, that is, its membership is below 0.5, as depicted by M_4, can that mechanism be dismissed as being the causal mechanism that underpins the cross-case sufficiency relation $X \Rightarrow Y$.[22]

Perhaps somewhat surprisingly, even for the two broken corridor scenarios, it is recommended to choose cases with membership in X and Y as similar as possible, that is, to follow the test corridor principle. The reason for this cannot be, of course, to make the space for M in between X and Y small because, by definition, in the two broken corridor scenarios M is located *outside* the space between X and Y. The reason, instead, is the following: as Mahoney et al. (2009) argue, the importance of a condition (be it sufficient or necessary) increases the closer it is in size to the outcome. The closer M is to its nearest

---

[21] Mahoney et al. (2009) discuss "sequence elaboration" – conceptually similar to my discussion of mechanisms here – and argue that the $X \Rightarrow Y$ relation at the cross-case level is *contextualized* by both broken corridor scenarios and *diminished* by the intact test corridor scenario.

[22] This inference is further strengthened if the iir case holds a membership *above* 0.5 in M_4.

cross-case set (X in the nec-suf chain and Y in the suf-nec chain), the more important M becomes. Now, the more similar membership in X and Y are (i.e. the smaller the test corridor), the higher the importance of M for *both* cross-case sets X and Y.

I mention only in passing that both broken corridor scenarios could have at their root also mechanismic heterogeneity. For broken floors, where membership in M_2 is lower than that in X, it could be that M_2 is underspecified and, in fact consists of the disjunction $M_2 + M_d$. If the case's membership in M_d is higher than in X, then the floor would not be broken anymore. Similarly, for a broken ceiling, where membership in M_3 exceeds that in Y, it could be that M_3 is under-specified and, in fact, consists of the conjunction $M_3 * M_c$. If the case's membership in M_C is lower than in Y, then the ceiling would not be broken anymore. In short, just as at the cross-case level deviant cases might be an indication for model underspecification, broken corridors could be a sign of mechanism underspecification.[23]

In Section 4.4, once I have introduced conjunctions as sufficient terms, I will come back to the issue of broken corridors and refine the scenarios depicted here.

2.5 Comparative SMMR

Single-case SMMR designs have their merits. Almost always, they rely on an implicit comparison, though. For instance, when trying to identify a missing conjunct during the within-case analysis of a deviant consistency case, this case is counterfactually contrasted to a hypothetical typical case. Similarly, in the analysis of a typical case, the question of what happens to the mechanism if the sufficient condition was taken away can be answered only by counterfactually contrasting the typical case to a case that looks similar except for its membership in the condition of interest.

Comparative SMMR designs aim at strengthening the descriptive or causal inference goal by substituting a counterfactual with an empirical comparison. Which within-case comparisons between the four main types of cases are meaningful and which ones are futile? Some comparative designs can be ruled out by remembering that the goal of any within-case analysis is to learn something about the outcome. Either we want to know the mechanism that produces it or we want to identify omitted conditions whose absence prevent the mechanism from producing the outcome. From this, it follows that a

---

[23] I thank Ingo Rohlfing (personal communication) for bringing up this argument.

2.5 Comparative SMMR

feasible SMMR comparison must include at least one case that is a member of the outcome.

Positive outcome principle: At least one case must be a member of the outcome in comparative SMMR designs.

This principle renders a comparison between a deviant consistency case and an iir case fruitless, such as between Kohl2 and Schlueter4 in Figure 2.1. Both are nonmembers of the outcome. Furthermore, a comparison of the two types of deviant cases – consistency (e.g. Schlueter4) and coverage (e.g. Thatcher2) – is futile. While in line with the positive outcome principle, there is nothing puzzling about such case pairs because they differ in *both* their condition and outcome memberships. The deviant consistency case has the known cause but not the outcome, whereas the deviant coverage case shows the outcome but is a nonmember of any known cause. A last futile comparative SMMR design consists of matching typical cases (e.g. Lubbers1) with deviant coverage cases (e.g. Thatcher2). While both share the same membership in the outcome, they differ in their membership in the known cause for the outcome. In a sense, a comparison between these two case types mimics the logical minimization of the truth table that has produced the QCA solution formula based on which cases are classified as typical and deviant coverage. This design would thus second-guess this logical minimization by aiming at identifying redundant conjuncts in the known sufficient term. Since any redundancies have already been eliminated by the cross-case QCA, such a comparison would be futile.[24]

This leaves us with the four feasible within-case comparisons in SMMR, depicted in Figure 2.8. The two comparisons "along the diagonal" aim at probing the causal properties of the sufficient term, whereas the two comparisons in vertical direction aim at uncovering omitted conditions. Table 2.3 summarizes the four designs and the analytic goals that are pursued with each.

2.5.1 Descriptive Inference SMMR

The goal of improving a QCA model makes sense only if there is room for improvement. A QCA solution that perfectly describes the data cannot be improved, at least not based on empirical grounds. Only if there are cases that either contradict the QCA solution or that are left unexplained is there a reason

---

[24] This holds true regardless of the QCA solution type – conservative, intermediate, or most parsimonious. All solution types define the same cases as typical and the same as deviant coverage.

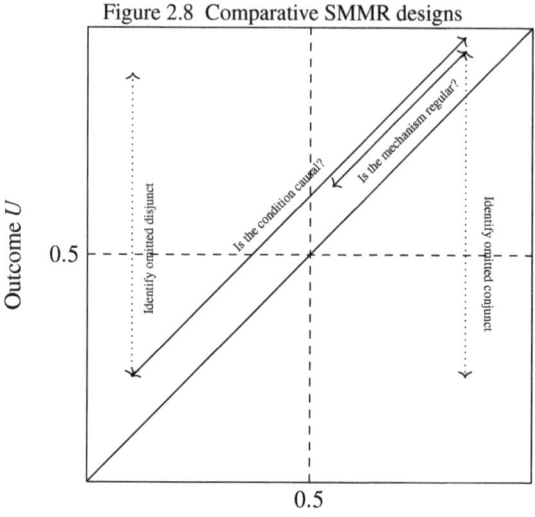

Figure 2.8 Comparative SMMR designs

Dotted line: model specification; solid line: causal inference

Table 2.3 *Comparative SMMR designs and their goals*

Comparison	Inferential goal
Causal inference	
Typical – iir	Causal properties of mechanism
Typical – typical	Generalizability of mechanism
Descriptive inference	
Typical – deviant consistency	Identify omitted conjunct
iir – deviant coverage	Identify omitted disjunct

Source: adapted from Schneider and Rohlfing (2019, table 3) and Oana et al. (2021, table 6.4).

to engage in model-refining SMMR. In addition, the information on how to improve the model can be found in such deviant cases.

When performing within-case analyses in a *typical and a deviant consistency case*, the goal is to solve the puzzle: why does the outcome occur in the former but not in the latter, despite them holding qualitatively identical membership in the sufficient term? Put differently, why does S trigger mechanism C_M trigger U in the typical case ($S \Rightarrow C_M \Rightarrow U$) but not in the deviant consistency case? The comparative within-case analysis can solve this puzzle by identifying what, in conjunction with condition S, triggers C_M in the

2.5 Comparative SMMR

typical case but is missing in the deviant consistency case. Adding this omitted conjunct, let us call it E for "elections are imminent", to stay in the example from above, to the known sufficient term S solves the puzzle. The typical case is now typical for the new sufficient term $S*E$, whereas the former deviant consistency case turns into an iir case vis-à-vis term $S*E$. For instance, the comparative within-case analysis of Lubbers1 (typical case) and Schlueter4 (deviant consistency case, see Figure 2.1) might reveal that in the latter the mechanism "reelection concern" (C_M) was not triggered because, for this, the joint presence of a weak socio-economic situation and imminent elections ($S*E$) is needed and Schlueter4 lacked the latter, that is, elections were not imminent ($S*\sim E$). This is why no reelection concerns were triggered ($\sim C_M$) and no unpopular reforms ($\sim U$) were implemented ($S*\sim E \Rightarrow \sim C_M \Rightarrow \sim U$).

Table 2.4 depicts the logic of this comparison. The values in normal font indicate the membership scores of cases known from the cross-case analysis and used for case selection. The values in bold font are membership scores not known prior to the within-case analysis and indicate the ideal-typical result of this analysis.

Table 2.4 *Matching of typical and deviant consistency cases*

Cross-case: Within-case:	Known **Expected**	S	$\Rightarrow$ C_M	U
	Typical	1	**1**	**1**
	Dev$_{cons}$	1	**0**	**0**
	Expected	$S*E$	C_M	U
	Typical	1	**1**	**1**
	Dev$_{cons}$	**0**	**0**	**0**

Nonbold font: findings from QCA; bold font: target of within-case analysis

With crisp sets, any typical case can be matched with any deviant consistency case for sufficient term S. With fuzzy sets, we have the possibility to distinguish better from less good pairs for comparison. First of all, among the two types of deviant consistency cases – in degree and in kind – the latter are to be preferred.

Principle of deviance in kind: Choose deviant consistency cases that are qualitatively different from typical cases in their membership in the outcome.

Among deviant consistency cases in kind, further distinctions are possible. The max–min difference principle governs this distinction. This principle also applies to the second model-refining comparative SMMR design that matches a deviant coverage case and an iir case.

Principle of max–min difference: In model-refining comparative SMMR designs, maximize the difference of the cases' set membership in the outcome and minimize the difference in the condition.

Just imagine a typical and deviant consistency pair of cases being close to each other and just divided by the horizontal line at $Y = 0.5$. Such a pair is clearly inferior to a pair where the two cases are far apart, with the typical case close to $U = 1$ and the deviant consistency case close to $U = 0$, while both holding high membership in S. The best available pair of cases maximizes the membership difference in the outcome, membership similarity in the condition, and high membership in the condition. Formula 2.5 captures these criteria and yields a numerical value for each pair of typical and deviant consistency cases in a given data set. As before, smaller values indicate better pairs of cases.

$$\begin{aligned} TYP - DCON = &[(1 - S_{TYP}) + (1 - S_{DCON})] && \text{Large membership in term} \\ &+ [1 - (Y_{TYP} - Y_{DCON})] && \text{Large difference in outcome} \\ &+ |S_{TYP} - S_{DCON}| && \text{Similar membership in term} \end{aligned} \quad (2.5)$$

TYP = typical case; $DCON$ = deviant consistency case; S_{TYP} and S_{DCON} = membership in sufficient term of typical and deviant consistency case, respectively; Y_{TYP} and Y_{DCON} = membership in outcome of typical and deviant consistency case, respectively

The second within-case comparison aiming at improving the cross-case model and thus enhancing descriptive inference is the one between a *deviant coverage case and an iir case*. Unlike with the previous comparison, the goal cannot be to identify a missing conjunct from the known term S, though. The reason is simple. By adding a conjunct to S, we create a subset of S. But because deviant coverage cases are, by definition, not members of S, they cannot be members of any subset of S, either. This means any conjunction that contains in it condition S will never be able to capture, or explain, deviant coverage cases. For instance, Thatcher2 is a case of not being in a socio-economically weak position ($\sim S$). Any further specifying condition S cannot explain why Thatcher2 did implement unpopular reforms (U). To find an explanation as to why deviant coverage cases display the outcome, we have to turn to hitherto unknown factors unrelated to S. We need to add a separate disjunct to the solution formula $S \Rightarrow U$.

This search is facilitated by contrasting deviant coverage cases with cases that are qualitatively identical except for their membership in the outcome.

2.5 Comparative SMMR

Identical is defined as "being member of the same truth table row", as stipulated by the truth table row principle (see Section 2.2.2). In other words, we need to match a deviant coverage case with an iir case from the same truth table row. Both are instances of $\sim S$ but qualitatively differ in their membership in U. The puzzle is now similar to that between a typical and a deviant consistency case. We are looking for an analytically relevant difference between the deviant coverage case and the iir case, let us call it X, that can explain why in the former a mechanism M is triggered, which in turn produces U. The omitted condition X is added to the truth table row to which the deviant coverage case and the iir case belong. Since the iir case is not member of X, it is not a member of the new truth table row $TT * X$ to which the deviant coverage case belongs. This solves the puzzle why the deviant coverage case does and the iir case does not display M and, in turn, also U. Table 2.5 displays the logic of the comparison between a deviant coverage case and an iir case.

Table 2.5 *Matching of deviant coverage and iir cases*

Cross-case:	Known	TT	$\Rightarrow$	U
Within-case:	**Expected**		**M**	
	Dev$_{cov}$	1	**1**	1
	iir	1	**0**	0
	Expected	$TT * X$	**M**	**U**
	Dev$_{cov}$	1	**1**	1
	iir	**0**	**0**	0

Nonbold font: findings from QCA; bold font: target of within-case analysis

With fuzzy sets, we can further rank all possible case pairs according to how well they maximize the criteria for this comparison. Analogous to the within-case comparison of a typical with a deviant consistency case, the goal is to maximize both cases' membership and their similarity in the truth table row TT and their difference in the outcome Y. Formula 2.6 achieves this. It is applied separately to each truth table row that contains at least one deviant coverage and one iir case.

$$\begin{aligned} DCOV - IIR = &[(1-(TT_{DCOV})+(1-TT_{iir})] \quad \text{\small Large membership in truth table row} \\ &+ [1-(Y_{DCOV}-Y_{iir})] \quad \text{\small Large difference in outcome} \quad (2.6)\\ &+ |TT_{DCOV}-TT_{iir}| \quad \text{\small Similar membership in truth table row} \end{aligned}$$

$DCOV$ = deviant coverage case; *iir* = individually irrelevant case; TT_{DCOV} and TT_{IIR} = membership in truth table row of deviant coverage and individually irrelevant case, respectively; Y_{DCOV} and Y_{iir} = membership in outcome of deviant coverage and individually irrelevant case, respectively

2.5.2 Causal Inference SMMR

There are two within-case comparisons that focus on the causal properties of the sufficient term. Following the causal inference selection principle, both involve at least one typical case. Furthermore, for both designs the test corridor principle is applicable. This means that this principle also applies to iir cases in the comparison with typical cases. Beyond this, with fuzzy sets, better from worse pairs can be distinguished by following the principle of max–max difference.

Principle of max–max difference: In causal inference comparative SMMR designs, maximize the differences of the cases' set membership in the set of interest and the outcome.

Let us start with the comparison between a typical case and an iir case (see Figure 2.8).[25] In order for term S to be causal, it must make a difference to outcome U. From our QCA, we do know that this is the case at the *cross-case* level because S has survived the logical minimization of the truth table as a nonredundant condition, that is, cases with $\sim S$ also have $\sim U$.[26] What we do not know from the QCA is whether S is also a difference maker for mechanism C_M at the *within-case* level. If within-case level analysis reveals that a typical case is also member of mechanism C_M, whereas an iir case is not, we can infer that condition S is causal because at the cross-case level it makes a difference for U via being a difference maker to C_M at the within-case level.

Table 2.6 displays the logic and analytic goal of this within-comparative analysis. We match a typical and an iir case based on their qualitative differences in membership in both S and U. Since only S is identified as analytically relevant for explaining U, this comparison matches two cases

---

[25] On the surface, it might seem that Goertz (2017) and I differ in assessing the analytic role of cases in the 0, 0 cell when he states that "[f]or investigating causal mechanisms, cases in cell (0, 0) have little or no role to play." (Goertz, 2017, p. 70). In SMMR, instead, iir cases in the 0, 0 are crucial for establishing the difference-making properties of the cross-case causes on the within-case mechanisms. Goertz seems to acknowledge this role by pointing out the counterfactual qualities of cases in the 0, 0 cell (see his tables 3.2 and 3.3), but he holds that "... we do not have to choose a separate case of (0, 0) because counterfactual analysis generates these cases from the (1, 1) cell. The (0, 0) cell is critical to case study methodology, but not as a separate cross-case case study." (Goertz, 2017, p. 77). In SMMR, instead, choosing an empirical case from the 0, 0 cell is superior to performing a counterfactual.

[26] Two caveats are needed. First, it would be better to write "tend to have $\sim U$" in order to acknowledge the presence of deviant consistency cases. Second, unless it is the most parsimonious solution, QCA solutions can also contain elements that are not difference makers at the cross-case level. They nevertheless could still be difference makers at the within-case levels – just as difference makers at the cross-case levels could fail to be so at the within-case level. It requires the implementation of an SMMR design to find out whether or not a condition is a difference maker for the mechanism. If the within-case evidence and cross-case evidence point in different directions, it is the former that overrides the latter. For a detailed discussion of QCA solution types in SMMR, see Section 5.4.

2.5 Comparative SMMR

Table 2.6 *Matching of a typical case and an iir case*

Cross-case: Within-case:	Known **Expected**	S	$\Rightarrow$ C_M	U
	Typical case	1	**1**	1
	iir case	0	**0**	0

Nonbold font: findings from QCA; bold font: target of within-case analysis

that differ in only one relevant condition. Any other potential difference is deemed irrelevant. The motivation for the within-case analysis is to empirically establish whether they also qualitatively differ in their membership in C_M. If yes, it provides evidence for the causal properties of S at the within-case level; if no, it calls the causal properties of S into question, despite it being a difference maker at the cross-case level.

For instance, we can match the typical case Schroeder2 with the iir case Kohl2. If we find empirical evidence for the mechanism "concerns for the future" (C_M) in Schroeder2 but not in Kohl2, it contributes to our inference that a 'difficult socio-economic situation' (S) is causal for implementing unpopular reforms (U) because it is a difference maker not only at the cross-case level, but also at the within-case level.

With crisp sets, any pair of typical and iir cases is as good as any other. With fuzzy sets we can rank case pairs according to the degree to which they maximize the criteria for the best-matching pair. Formula 2.7 captures the various criteria.[27]

$$\begin{aligned}TYP-IIR = &\left[1-(S_{TYP}-S_{iir})\right] &\text{\small Large difference in term}\\ &+\left[1-(Y_{TYP}-Y_{iir})\right] &\text{\small Large difference in outcome}\\ &+2*|Y_{TYP}-S_{TYP}| &\text{\small Strictness for typical case}\\ &+2*|Y_{iir}-S_{iir}| &\text{\small Strictness for iir case}\end{aligned} \quad (2.7)$$

TYP = typical case; iir = individually irrelevant case; S_{TYP} and S_{iir} = membership in sufficient term of typical and individually irrelevant case, respectively; Y_{TYP} and Y_{iir} = membership in outcome of typical and individually irrelevant case, respectively

The second comparison that focuses on the mechanism underlying the cross-case model is the one between *two typical cases*. The logic is this: if mechanism C_M can be found in not just one typical case but two or more, then our inference that C_M operates in *all* typical cases is strengthened. Ideally, of course, one would want to perform within-case analyses in all typical cases to

---

[27] In Chapter 4, another formula will be introduced, which should be used when confronting conjunctions, because for causal inference, conjunctions create an additional layer of requirements that will need to be captured in an updated formula.

know if C_M really operates in all of them. Apart from this being practically unfeasible in most applied research, it also means that in such a scenario there would be no need to *infer* anything anymore, for we then *know* whether C_M operates in all typical cases or not.

To make the most of limited resources, the suggestion is to compare two typical cases that are as different from each other as possible with regard to their memberships in the term and the outcome. Obviously, this can be done only with fuzzy sets, not crisp sets. Table 2.7 depicts the logic of the comparison between two typical cases.

Table 2.7 *Matching of two typical cases*

Cross-case: Within-case:	Known **Expected**	S	$\Rightarrow$ C_M	U
	Most typical case$_1$	0.98	**0.98**	0.98
	Just-so typical case$_2$	0.51	**0.51**	0.51

Nonbold font: findings from QCA; bold font: target of within-case analysis

The selection rationale is as follows: if mechanism C_M can be shown to be operative in the two typical cases that are farthest apart, then we have good reason to infer that C_M also operates in all the other typical cases that fall in between these two. In other words, if C_M is found in typical cases that are far apart, we infer that C_M is the regular mechanism underlying the cross-case sufficiency relation $S \Rightarrow U$ in all typical cases. Ideally, then, one matches the ideal typical case at $S = 1$, $U = 1$ with a just-so typical case that barely passes the qualitative anchors in S and U, say a case at $S = 0.51$, $U = 0.51$. Any possible pair between two typical cases approaches this ideal comparison to different degrees and can be ranked using Formula 2.8.[28]

$$TYP_1 - TYP_2 = [0.5 - (S_{TYP_1} - S_{TYP_2})] \quad \text{\small Large difference in term}$$
$$+ [0.5 - (Y_{TYP_1} - Y_{TYP_2})] \quad \text{\small Large difference in outcome}$$
$$+ 2 * (Y_{TYP_1} - S_{TYP_1}) \quad \text{\small Strictness for typical case}_1$$
$$+ 2 * (Y_{TYP_2} - S_{TYP_2}) \quad \text{\small Strictness for typical case}_2$$
(2.8)

TYP_1 = typical case$_1$; TYP_2 = typical case$_2$; S_{TYP_1} and S_{TYP_2} = membership in sufficient term of typical cases 1 and 2, respectively; Y_{TYP_1} and Y_{TYP_2} = membership in outcome of typical cases 1 and 2, respectively

---

[28] As with the formulas for the best available typical case and the best-matching pair of a typical and an iir case, this formula will also be updated in Chapter 4 when discussing conjunctions and their consequences for causal inference designs in SMMR.

2.5 Comparative SMMR

The SMMR design of comparing two typical cases is in line with extant case selection strategies that propose to select diverse cases (e.g. Seawright and Gerring, 2008; Rohlfing, 2012).

Core Points 2.1: Basics of SMMR

- A QCA solution formula is used to sort each case into one type of case
- The four main case types are typical, deviant consistency, deviant coverage, and individually irrelevant
- With crisp sets, all cases within one type are qualitatively identical and indistinguishable when selecting for within-case analysis
- With fuzzy sets, all cases within one type are qualitatively identical but their differences in degrees can be used to identify better from worse instances when selecting for within-case analysis
- Differences in degree are captured by formulas. For all of them, the following holds: smaller values indicate better choice of cases for within-case analysis
- Each type of case is useful for some analytic goals but not for others
- Causal inference SMMR designs must involve a typical case. Descriptive inference SMMR designs must involve a deviant case
- There are three single-case and four comparative SMMR designs
- In typical and iir cases, membership in mechanisms M can be situated in four different locations vis-à-vis the case's membership in the condition X and outcome Y, respectively. Only for one location can the causal effect of the condition be ruled out per se. In the other locations, causal inference is possible, provided sound theoretical reasoning is offered for either a sufficiency chain, nec-suf chain, or a suf-nec chain
- The smmr() function can be used to identify the best-available case or pair of cases for descriptive of causal inference SMMR designs
- The following SMMR principles are relevant regardless of the level of complexity of the QCA solution formula: principle of difference in kind and degree, truth table row principle, causal inference selection principle, descriptive inference selection principle, principle of maximum set membership difference, principle of maximum set membership, test corridor principle, positive outcome principle, principle of deviance in kind, principle of max–min difference, and principle of max–max difference

2.6 Applying SMMR

With the basic concepts, types of cases, principles, and formulas in place, I now demonstrate, with the example by Vis (2009), how applied researchers can sort all their cases into the respective types of cases and, based on this, select the best available cases for either single-case or comparative within-case analysis. Code box C 2.1 produces the finding that S is sufficient for U, shown in the output box O 2.1.

C 2.1

```
VIS_fs <- read.csv("Vis_09_fs.csv", row.names = 1)
VIS_fs

tt_fy <- truthTable(data = VIS_fs,
  outcome = "U",
  conditions = "P, S, R",
  incl.cut = 0.8,
  sort.by = "incl",
  complete = TRUE)

sol_fyp <- minimize(tt_fy,
                    include = "?",
                    details = TRUE)
sol_fyp
```

O 2.1

M1: S -> U

		inclS	PRI	covS	covU
1	S	0.901	0.787	0.878	–
	M1	0.901	0.787	0.878	

2.6.1 The smmr() Function

Applied researchers can use the function `smmr()` in package `SetMethods` (Oana and Schneider, 2018) for this task. Because this command is at the core of performing SMMR, let us have a look at its structure in some detail. The function requires four basic pieces of information.[29] First, what is the QCA result based on which cases are selected? This information is provided via the argument `results` and it expects an object created by function `minimize()` from R package `QCA` (Dusa, 2019). Second, with argument `outcome`, the name of the outcome of the analysis is provided and needs to be put in quotation marks (" "). Third, argument `match` determines whether single-case (`match = FALSE`) or comparative SMMR (`match = TRUE`) is performed.

---

[29] Additional arguments will be introduced in the following chapters.

C 2.2

```
smmr(results = ,
     outcome = ,
     match = ,
     cases = )
```

Fourth, with `cases`, one specifies which (single-case or comparative case) SMMR design is implemented. The numeric code for specifying single cases or pairs of cases is displayed in Table 2.8. For instance, if a researcher wants the list of best available deviant consistency cases, she needs to set arguments `match = FALSE` and `cases = 3`. If she wants the list of best-matching pairs of typical and deviant consistency cases, arguments `match = TRUE` and `cases = 3` must be specified. Code box C 2.2 shows the template code for the `smmr()` function and the four main arguments that need to be specified: what is the QCA solution (`result`); what is the outcome (`outcome`); do you perform a single-case or comparative design (`match`); and which SMMR design do you perform (`cases`).

Table 2.8 *Function* smmr(), *argument* case *for SMMR on sufficiency*

	For single-case studies (`match = FALSE`):
1	Typical cases for each term
2	Typical cases for each focal conjunct in a sufficient term*
3	Deviant consistency
4	Deviant coverage
5	Individually irrelevant
6	All of the above
	For comparative case studies (`match = TRUE`):
1	Typical-typical for each focal conjunct in a sufficient term*
2	Typical-iir for each focal conjunct in a sufficient term*
3	Typical-deviant consistency
4	Deviant coverage-iir
5	Typical-typical for each term
6	Typical-iir for each term
7	All of the above

* Applicable only when the QCA solution contains conjunctions; see Chapter 4

The `smmr()` function accepts several more arguments that are needed when the QCA solution formula is more complex (equifinal and conjunctural) and when the cross-case claim is a statement of necessity rather than sufficiency. I introduce them in the following chapters.

2.6.2 Single-Case SMMR

With such a simple example of just one single-condition sufficient term, some of the best available cases can be identified with a look at an XY plot like the one in Figure 2.1, at least for single-case SMMR designs. As soon as the QCA solution gets more complex or when there are more cases, visual inspection is not enough, especially for comparative SMMR designs. It is therefore recommended to make use of the smmr() function.

Model-Refining SMMR

Even with a simple example such as the present one, just looking at an XY plot is not enough to identify the best available *deviant coverage case*. The truth table row principle (see Section 2.2.2) requires that, for nonmembers of any sufficient term, the choice must be based on these cases' membership in their truth table row.

From Figure 2.1 we learn which cases are deviant coverage, but not which truth table row describes them best. In Figure 2.1, the cases Rassmussen4 and Thatcher4 share the same nonmembership in S and U. However, as output O 2.2, produced with code C 2.3, shows, they belong to two different truth table rows and therefore need to be subjected to two separate within-case analyses. Column $TT <= Y$ in output O 2.2 indicates whether a case's membership in the truth table row is smaller than its membership in the outcome and thus in line with the sufficiency statement $TT \Rightarrow Y$. Such cases are to be preferred even if their value in column "Best" is higher (i.e. worse). Values in column "Best" are calculated based on Formula 2.1.

C 2.3

```
dcov <- smmr(results = sol_fyp,
             outcome = "U",
             match = FALSE,
             cases = 4)
dcov
```

O 2.2

Deviant Coverage Cases :

	Case	Sol	TT_P	TT_S	TT_R	TT_row	Outcome	TT<=Y	Best	MostDCOV
2	NRasmussen4	0.33	0	0	0	0.67	0.67	TRUE	0.33	TRUE
1	Kok1	0.40	0	0	0	0.60	0.67	TRUE	0.40	FALSE
3	Thatcher2	0.33	0	0	1	0.67	0.67	TRUE	0.33	TRUE

The same holds for iir cases, which in an XY plot look similar, or even identical, but are different in ways that analytically matter. Since iir cases are not a target for single within-case analyses, I show only the R command (C 2.4) and do not display the output.

2.6 Applying SMMR

C 2.4

```
iir <- smmr(results = sol_fyp,
            outcome = "U",
            match = FALSE,
            cases = 5)
iir
```

From Figure 2.1, we see that there are only two *deviant consistency cases* in kind, the fourth and fifth governments of Schlueter. As output 2.3, produced by code 2.5, confirms, Schlueter4 is the best available deviant consistency case, because it has a larger difference in S and U than Schlueter5 while sharing the same membership in S. This is why its value in column "Best" – calculated based on Formula 2.2 – is smaller. Column "MostDCONS" simply reports whether a case displays the smallest value in column "Best" or not. In the case of identical values in column "Best", cases with higher membership in the sufficient term are preferred and ranked higher in the output.

C 2.5

```
dcons <- smmr(results = sol_fyp,
              outcome = "U",
              match = FALSE,
              cases = 3)
dcons
```

O 2.3

Deviant Consistency Cases :

	Cases	Term	TermMemb	Outcome	Best	MostDCONS
1	Schlueter4	S	0.67	0.17	0.83	TRUE
2	Schlueter5	S	0.67	0.33	0.99	FALSE

Causal Inference SMMR

All SMMR designs aiming at causal inference – single-case or comparative – are subject to a set of principles that kick in if and when the sufficient term of interest consists of a conjunction. So far, we have dealt only with single-set sufficient terms. The following scripts and outputs (and the formulas introduced above) therefore apply only to the specific situation of a sufficient term that consists of a single set. In Chapter 4, I further refine the selection of best available cases for causal inference in the presence of conjunctions.

As shown in the XY plot in Figure 2.1, the typical cases Thatcher1, Schroeder2, and Lubbers1 all hold the same membership in S and U and those membership scores maximize the criteria for the best available typical case: high and similar memberships in S and Y.

As shown in output O 2.4, this is why function smmr() identifies them as the best available typical cases for analyzing the mechanism M that links the sufficient term S to outcome U. All three have the lowest value in column "Best" whose values are calculated based on Formula 2.4. In addition, the output displays each case's membership in the term of interest (S), the outcome (U), and whether, according to its value in column "Best", it is the most typical case. The meaning of column "UniqCov" will become clear when in Chapter 3 I discuss QCA solution formulas that display equifinality, that is, when there is more than one sufficient term. The ordering of cases from better to worse is as follows: uniquely covered cases are preferred over jointly covered cases. Among them, cases with lower (i.e. better) values in column "Best" are preferred. And if two or more cases display identical values in "Best", the informal rule is that those with higher membership in the term are preferred.

C 2.6

```
typ_term <- smmr(results = sol_fyp,
                 outcome = "U",
                 match = FALSE,
                 cases = 1)
typ_term
```

O 2.4

Typical Cases :

	Case	Term	TermMemb	Outcome	UniqCov	Best	MostTyp
1	Lubbers1	S	0.83	0.83	TRUE	0.17	TRUE
5	Schroeder2	S	0.83	0.83	TRUE	0.17	TRUE
8	Thatcher1	S	0.83	0.83	TRUE	0.17	TRUE
2	Lubbers3	S	0.67	0.67	TRUE	0.33	FALSE
4	Kohl4	S	0.67	0.67	TRUE	0.33	FALSE
9	Thatcher3	S	0.67	0.67	TRUE	0.33	FALSE
6	Schlueter2	S	0.60	0.67	TRUE	0.54	FALSE
10	Major1	S	0.60	0.67	TRUE	0.54	FALSE
3	Balkenende2	S	0.67	0.83	TRUE	0.65	FALSE
7	NRasmussen2_3	S	0.60	0.83	TRUE	0.86	FALSE

2.6.3 Comparative SMMR

Identifying the best-matching pairs of cases for comparative within-case analyses via visual inspection becomes close to impossible even in the current simple example; therefore, the use of the dedicated smmr() function becomes indispensable.

Model-Refining SMMR

The two forms of comparison with the goal of refining the QCA model are implemented in R as displayed in codes C 2.7 and C 2.8 and their results are shown in outputs O 2.5 and O 2.6.

2.6 Applying SMMR

For the comparison between a *deviant coverage case and an iir case*, we see that there are several pairs in each of the two truth table rows (000 and 001) that are populated by both types of cases (output O 2.5). For truth table row 000, all pairs are equally good: their formula value "Best"[30] is the same and all deviant coverage cases' membership in the truth table is smaller than in the outcome (column "TT_DCV<=Y").[31] For truth table row 001, the pair Thatcher2–Kohl2 ranks slightly better ("Best" = 1.16) than the other pairs that all involve Thatcher2 ("Best" = 1.32). Such small differences in the formula values should, however, not be overinterpreted. If other, research-practical and nonmethodological criteria speak in favor of selecting a pair other than Thatcher2–Kohl2, it can be done without much loss of methodological rigor.

C 2.7

```
dcoviir <- smmr( results = sol_fyp,
                 outcome = "U",
                 match = TRUE,
                 cases = 4)
dcoviir
```

O 2.5

Matching Deviant Coverage–IIR Cases :

	DCOV	IIR	TT_P	TT_S	TT_R	TT_DCV<=Y	Best
1	Kok1	Schroeder1	0	0	0	TRUE	1.30
2	Kok1	Kok2	0	0	0	TRUE	1.30
3	Kok1	NRasmussen1	0	0	0	TRUE	1.30
4	NRasmussen4	Kok2	0	0	0	TRUE	1.30
5	NRasmussen4	NRasmussen1	0	0	0	TRUE	1.30
6	Thatcher2	Kohl2	0	0	1	TRUE	1.16
7	Thatcher2	Lubbers2	0	0	1	TRUE	1.32
8	Thatcher2	Kohl3	0	0	1	TRUE	1.32
9	Thatcher2	Kohl1	0	0	1	TRUE	1.32
10	Thatcher2	Schlueter1	0	0	1	TRUE	1.32

Matching a *typical and a deviant consistency case*, we see in output 2.6 that three typical cases with identical membership scores in S and U (Lubbers1, Schroeder2, and Thatcher1; see Figure 2.1) each form a best available pair with deviant consistency case Schlueter4. In addition, typical case Balkenende2 forms an equally good pair with Schlueter4. The lower membership in S of Balkenende2 than the other three typical cases just mentioned is counterbalanced by the greater similarity of Balkenende2's membership in S to that of Schlueter4, compared with the other three typical cases. Output O 2.6 also shows for each case if it is the most typical or the most deviant consistency case, using the Formulas 2.2 and 2.4, respectively. In applied SMMR, it is not always the case that the most typical and deviant cases also form the

---
[30] Calculated based on Formula 2.6.
[31] The ordering of pairs is based first on ConsTT_DCV = TRUE and then on the values in "Best".

64   *Basics of SMMR* $A \Rightarrow Y$

best matching pair. Plenty of further examples in the remainder of this book will illustrate this point. The ordering of best available case pairs is based on values in the column "Best".[32] If two or more case pairs hold the same value in "Best", then pairs including the most typical case are preferred. If there are two or more cases also ticking this box, then the ones involving the most deviant consistency case are preferred.

C 2.8

```
typdcons <- smmr(results = sol_fyp,
                 outcome = "U",
                 match = TRUE,
                 cases = 3)
typdcons
```

O 2.6

Term S :

	TYP	DCONS	Best	MostTypTerm	MostDCONS
1	Lubbers1	Schlueter4	1.00	TRUE	TRUE
3	Schroeder2	Schlueter4	1.00	TRUE	TRUE
4	Thatcher1	Schlueter4	1.00	TRUE	TRUE
2	Balkenende2	Schlueter4	1.00	FALSE	TRUE
5	NRasmussen2_3	Schlueter4	1.14	FALSE	TRUE

Causal Inference SMMR

The two forms of comparison with the goal of drawing causal inference are implemented in R as displayed in codes C 2.9 and 2.10 and their results are shown in outputs O 2.7 and 2.8.

Output O 2.7 shows that the best available pair of a *typical and an iir case* matches the iir cases of Kohl2 or NRasmussen1 with various typical cases that all hold the same membership in the term and the outcome and thus all show the same smallest value in the column "Best".[33] Matches with iir cases Kohl3 or Schlueter1 lead to slightly worse values in "Best". Output O 2.7 further indicates whether the typical case is uniquely covered (column "UniqCov") and whether it is the most typical (column "MostTyp", based on Formula 2.4). In addition, it is reported whether the iir case is globally uncovered (column "GlobUnvoc") and whether its membership scores are consistent with the statement of sufficiency (column "ConsIIR").[34] The ordering of case pairs from best to worst available is based on the following hierarchy of criteria: uniquely covered typical cases, consistent iir case, globally uncovered iir case,

---

[32] Calculated based on Formula 2.5.
[33] Calculated based on Formula 2.7.
[34] Uniquely covered and globally uncovered are two concepts that I explain in Chapter 3 when we deal with the analytic consequences triggered by equifinality. If there is no equifinality, as in the current example, by definition all typical cases are uniquely covered and all iir cases globally uncovered.

2.6 Applying SMMR

lowest value in the column "Best", and then whether the typical case is the most typical case.[35]

C 2.9

```
typiir_term <- smmr(results = sol_fyp,
                    outcome = "U",
                    match = TRUE,
                    cases = 6,
                    max_pairs = 10)
typiir_term
```

O 2.7

Term S :

	TYP	IIR	UniqCov	ConsIIR	GlobUncov	Best	MostTyp
1	Lubbers1	Kohl2	TRUE	TRUE	TRUE	0.68	TRUE
2	Schroeder2	Kohl2	TRUE	TRUE	TRUE	0.68	TRUE
3	Thatcher1	Kohl2	TRUE	TRUE	TRUE	0.68	TRUE
4	Lubbers1	NRasmussen1	TRUE	TRUE	TRUE	0.68	TRUE
5	Schroeder2	NRasmussen1	TRUE	TRUE	TRUE	0.68	TRUE
6	Thatcher1	NRasmussen1	TRUE	TRUE	TRUE	0.68	TRUE
16	Lubbers1	Kohl3	TRUE	TRUE	TRUE	1.00	TRUE
17	Schroeder2	Kohl3	TRUE	TRUE	TRUE	1.00	TRUE
18	Thatcher1	Kohl3	TRUE	TRUE	TRUE	1.00	TRUE
19	Lubbers1	Schlueter1	TRUE	TRUE	TRUE	1.00	TRUE

Matching *two typical cases* reveals several pairs that are equally good, a direct consequence of the fact that several cases share identical scores in the sufficient term and the outcome (output O 2.8). Obviously, in the absence of equifinality, in all pairs, both cases are uniquely covered (column "UniCov"). And as column "MostTyp" indicates, in all pairs the more typical of the cases qualifies as the most typical case in the data set. The pair Thatcher1–Major1 shows a slightly worse value in "Best".[36] Major1 is not located on the diagonal, but above it, and therefore adheres less to the test corridor principle. The ordering of pairs of two typical cases is based on unique coverage (both cases are better than only the first typical being uniquely covered, which is better than only the second typical case being uniquely covered, which is better than none of them); lowest value in "Best"; and most typical (both cases better than the first better than the second better than none of them).

C 2.10

```
typtyp_term <- smmr(results = sol_fyp,
                    outcome = "U",
                    match = TRUE,
                    cases = 5,
                    max_pairs = 10)
typtyp_term
```

---

[35] With argument max_pairs, one can determine the number of pairs that are shown in the output.
[36] Calculated based on Formula 2.8.

O 2.8

Term S :

	TYP1	TYP2	UniqCov	Best	MostTyp
3	Schroeder2	Kohl4	both	0.68	typ1
17	Schroeder2	Lubbers3	both	0.68	typ1
21	Thatcher1	Kohl4	both	0.68	typ1
25	Lubbers1	Thatcher3	both	0.68	typ1
26	Thatcher1	Thatcher3	both	0.68	typ1
46	Lubbers1	Kohl4	both	0.68	typ1
65	Schroeder2	Thatcher3	both	0.68	typ1
75	Lubbers1	Lubbers3	both	0.68	typ1
81	Thatcher1	Lubbers3	both	0.68	typ1
10	Thatcher1	Major1	both	0.75	typ1

2.7 Conclusion

Set-theoretic multi-method research provides a framework for integrating QCA with case studies. Based on QCA solution formulas, each case can be attributed to a specific type of case: typical, deviant (consistency or coverage) and individually irrelevant. The within-case analysis can either serve the purpose of further improving the QCA solution formula or can probe its causal properties – both done based on within-case evidence on the mechanisms. Depending on which goal is pursued, a specific type of case or pair of cases must be chosen. If fuzzy sets are used, it is possible to identify the best available single case or pair of cases. This case selection for within-case analysis is governed by a series of principles that are implemented in the R function smmr() of the SetMethods package.

Causal inference designs should be used only in situations in which descriptive inference is satisfactory, that is, if the parameters of fit (the consistency of the sufficient term and the coverage of the solution formula) are high enough and no important cases contradict the findings or are left unexplained. This implies that one should engage first in model-refining SMMR designs if and when consistency or coverage are too low. Within-case analyses on deviant coverage cases, either alone or in comparison with iir cases, are advisable only if the QCA solution coverage is too low because results from these SMMR designs most likely suggest an update and thus reanalysis of the entire truth table.

As a rule, findings from one case or pair of cases travel to all the other cases or pairs of cases that are qualitatively identical, that is, to the same type of case. Graphically speaking, then, findings from one case or pair of cases travel to all cases that are in the same area(s) of an XY plot.

2.7 Conclusion

The scenario we have encountered so far – a QCA solution with a single sufficient term that consists of a single set – has been chosen because it has allowed me to introduce the fundamental building blocks of SMMR. Such a scenario is very unusual in applied QCA, though. To make SMMR work in applied research, we must adapt it to the presence of disjunctions (equifinality) and conjunctions (conjunctural causation). As we will learn in the following chapters, this requires the introduction of further sub-types of cases, additional principles, and refined formulas. Most of these changes relate only to causal inference SMMR designs. We start with discussing the analytic consequences of disjunctions (Chapter 3) and then continue with conjunctions (Chapter 4). In both chapters, I describe the challenges and present solutions, and how to implement them in applied SMMR using R.

3

Disjunctions
$A + B \Rightarrow Y$

Equifinality is one core feature of causal complexity. In applied QCA, almost all solution formulas show that two or more terms are individually sufficient for an outcome. Whenever there is a logical OR in the solution formula, a claim of equifinality is made. Even though "equifinality" is the more commonly known term, I prefer the term "disjunction" because the latter concept is the proper term used in logic and "equifinality" is a feature of disjunctions. A disjunction includes at least two disjuncts, that is, at least two individually sufficient terms. In Empirical Example 3.1 $LD + LH$ is the disjunction that consists of the two disjuncts LD and LH. In this chapter, after introducing the empirical example, I first spell out the analytic challenges posed by disjunctions and then provide solutions. The latter requires the introduction of additional sub-types of cases and three more SMMR principles. The chapter concludes by empirically illustrating the output of the smmr() function in the presence of equifinality.

Learning Goals 3.1: Disjunctions

- Understand the inferential challenges triggered by disjunctions (equifinality)
- Get acquainted with the additional sub-types of cases produced by disjunctive solution formulas
- Understand how additional principles guide case selection in the presence of disjunctions
- Understand if and how moving up the ladder of generality can be used to theorize away disjunctions and the inferential challenges it poses
- Become familiar with the smmr() function and the interpretation of its output in the presence of disjunctions

---

3.1 Empirical Example

> **Empirical Example 3.1: Configurations of corruption: A cross-national qualitative comparative analysis of levels of perceived corruption (Stevens, 2016)**
>
> - *Research question*: What are the factors for high perceived corruption?
> - *Cases:*[a] 77 countries
> - *Set type:* Fuzzy
> - *Outcome*: High perceived corruption (*HC*)
> - *Conditions:*[b] Low democracy (*LD*), high rational secular orientation (*HR*), high self expression orientation (*HS*), low human development (*LH*), high income inequality (*HI*)
>
> a For didactical reasons the scores of some cases in some sets have been altered
> b For didactical reasons conditions *LD* and *LH* have been inverted

I use the study by Stevens (2016) to illustrate the implications of disjunctions for SMMR. The outcome of interest is high perceived corruption (*HC*) in 77 countries. The most parsimonious solution (consistency threshold: 0.85; frequency threshold: 2) states that either "low democracy" (*LD*) or "low human development" (*LH*) are sufficient for "high perceived corruption" (*LD+LH* ⇒ *HC*).

Table 3.1 *Most parsimonious solution, outcome "high perceived corruption"* HC

	inclS	PRI	covS	covU
LD	0.872	0.823	0.564	0.138
LH	0.914	0.871	0.610	0.184
Solution	0.866	0.813	0.748	

LD: low democracy; *LH*: low human development

Table 3.1 displays the parameters of fit. Both terms show high consistency scores (0.872 and 0.914) and the solution coverage of 0.748 indicates that about three-quarters of the outcome is jointly covered by these two disjuncts. The big difference between each term's raw coverage (covS) and unique coverage (covU) indicates a large empirical overlap between the two terms. This means that many cases have membership in both disjuncts. For instance, we see in Figures 3.1 and 3.2 that Bangladesh is a typical case for both *LD* and

LH. As I discuss in this chapter, this is the challenge that disjunctions pose for SMMR: the effect of disjuncts on the outcome in specific cases needs to be disentangled.

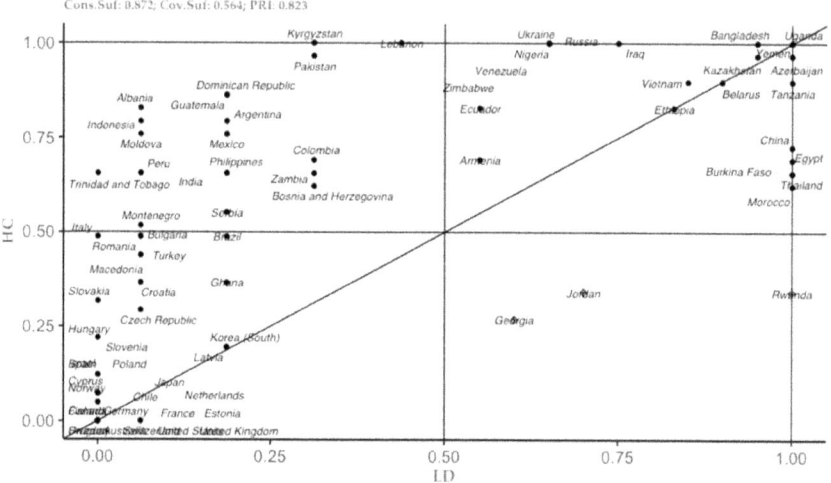

Figure 3.1 XY plot: sufficient term LD, outcome HC

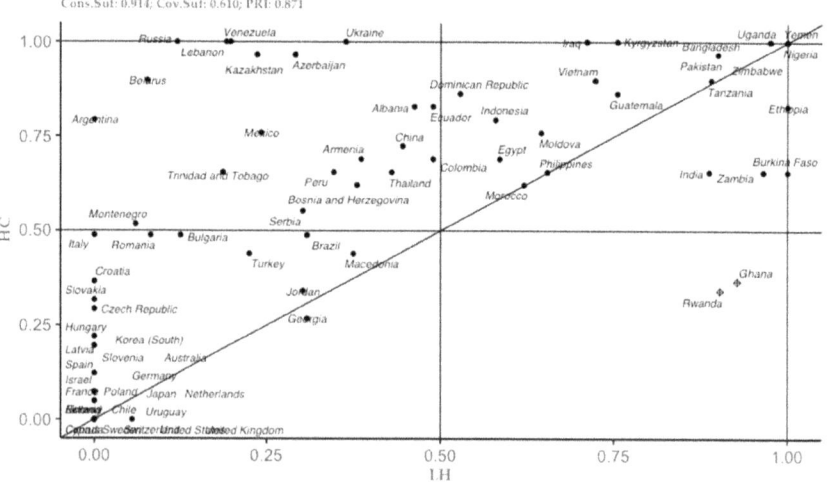

Figure 3.2 XY plot: sufficient term LH, outcome HC

3.1 Empirical Example

Figure 3.3 XY plot: solution formula $LD + LH$, outcome HC

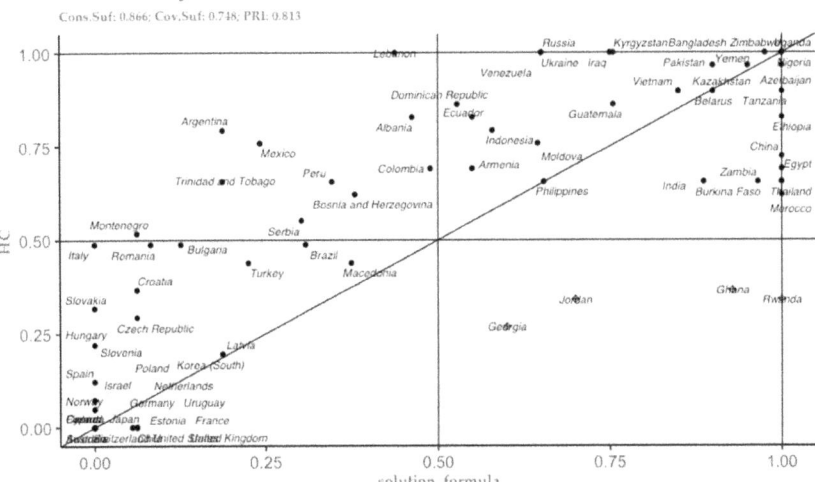

Figure 3.4 graphically displays the cross-case – within-case structure of the argument why perception of corruption is high in some countries. Each of the two sufficient disjuncts LD and LH triggers a separate mechanism, M_{LD} and M_{LH}, respectively. Low democracy (LD) can be hypothesized to provide evidence to citizens that many deeds go unpunished due to lack of proper accountability mechanisms via free media and meaningful elections (M_{LD}), which, in turn, increases perceived corruption (HC). Sufficient term low human capital (LH), in contrast, can be expected to trigger difficulties in satisfying basic needs of large segments of the population – needs that often can be fulfilled only for some and only by violating formal rules and procedures. This mechanism M_{LH} then leads to outcome HC.

In this scenario, there is, thus, equifinality at both the cross-case and the within-case levels. This is different if and when the researcher uses theoretical arguments and subsumes both disjuncts LD and LH under one higher-order concept. For instance, in the example by Stevens (2016), a researcher might argue that low democracy (LD) and low human development (LH) are functional equivalents of the higher-order concept "low modernization" (LM). Low modernization is then conceptualized as: $LM = LD + LH$. The solution formula for the outcome "high perceived corruption" HC would then be $LM \Rightarrow HC$.[1]

---

[1] Schneider and Makszin (2014) (discussed in further detail in Chapters 1 and 5), for instance, find two disjuncts, which they label coordinated and protective welfare regimes and unite those under the higher-order concept "supportive welfare regime".

Figure 3.4 Cross-case and within-case levels for outcome "high perceived corruption"

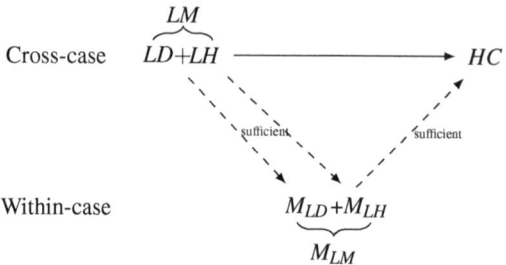

LD: Low democracy; LH: low human development; HC: high perceived corruption
M_{LD}: low accountability; M_{LH}: rule-breaking incentives
M_{LM}: conducive opportunity structure for rule breaking

Correspondingly, *LM* then could be expected to trigger *one* mechanism that we could label "conducive opportunity structure for corruption" (M_{LM}).

3.2 The Challenge

The main challenge for SMMR that a disjunction poses is that, on the one hand, the different disjuncts are postulated to trigger separate mechanisms and outcomes independent of each other. The equifinal claim that different roads are leading to Rome entails that these different terms follow a separate causal logic and trigger different mechanisms.[2] On the other hand, sufficient terms can, and usually do, empirically overlap. The logical OR (+) operator is nonexclusive.[3] This means that a given case can be typical for more than one sufficient term, such as Bangladesh in our current example. This is a problem in SMMR because the outcome in such cases is overdetermined. For within-case analysis in overdetermined cases it is difficult to disentangle which of the sufficient terms triggers which mechanism. This means that case choice for within-case analysis needs to reflect this separation; we need to analyze each disjunct separately. I will explain now that this implies that cases are typical with regard to a disjunct, not the entire disjunction. Likewise, cases are deviant consistency cases with regard to single disjuncts, not the entire

---

[2] Treating disjuncts as qualitatively different causal terms is the default option. As mentioned, it can be overwritten if a researcher moves up the ladder of generality (Adcock and Collier, 2001; Sartori, 1970) and treats two or more disjuncts as functional equivalents of a higher-order concept Z (see Section 3.3.1).

[3] The operator for an exclusive disjunction is XOR. See Hackett (2016) for its potential use in fuzzy-set analyses.

disjunction. At the same time, by definition, cases are deviant coverage and individually irrelevant with regard to the entire disjunctive solution formula, not single disjuncts.

3.3 The Solutions

The inferential problems triggered by disjunctions can be tackled by formulating additional SMMR principles. For those principles, in turn, we first need to introduce additional sub-types of cases. In a nutshell, the additional sub-types reflect how many terms a case is a member of. The additional principles govern which of those sub-types to focus on for the within-case analysis. Overall, in the presence of a disjunction, the goal of SMMR is "to turn equifinality off" via purposeful choice of cases for within-case analysis.

3.3.1 Climbing the Ladder of Generality

One possible way to turn off equifinality could be to theorize it away. If a researcher finds reasons to interpret two (or more) disjuncts as functional equivalents of a higher-order concept LM, then LM is the *single* sufficient cause. This is done under the assumption that the different disjuncts all trigger the same mechanism. LD and LH could be labeled as SUSU conditions: sufficient but unnecessary elements of a condition (here LM), which itself is sufficient but unnecessary for the outcome (here HC). None of the principles that I introduce in this chapter would be needed.

As any form of aggregation, though, this merging of two (or more) disjuncts into one new single set comes with loss of information. The difference in cases in terms of membership in one or the other disjunct is assumed to be irrelevant and in all cases the same mechanism M_{LM} is assumed to be triggered. For instance, Kazhakstan is a low democracy ($LD = 0.95$) but does not feature low human development ($LH = 0.236$). For Pakistan it is the inverse ($LD = 0.312$ and $LH = 0.9$). Merging LD and LH into LM assumes that in both types of cases the same mechanism triggers the outcome high perceived corruption, HC. If this assumption of the same mechanism being triggered by LD and LH turns out to be wrong upon empirical evidence gathered during the within-case analysis, the merging of disjuncts into one single set should be reversed and, instead, each disjunct be treated as a sufficient cause of its own. For this, the following sub-types and principles are needed.

3.3.2 Additional Sub-Types of Cases

There are four new sub-types of cases when a solution formula consists of disjuncts: *uniquely covered typical, jointly covered typical, globally uncovered iir*, and *globally uncovered deviant coverage*. Table 3.2 displays the features of these new sub-types of cases. Just as all the other types of cases introduced in Chapter 1, they are also defined by their membership in the terms X_i and outcome Y. In the presence of a disjunction, though, we need to take into account in how many of the terms, or disjuncts, a given case holds membership of higher than 0.5: it can be none, one, or more than one.

Typical cases are, by definition, members of at least one term.[4] If it is a member of just one term, then it is called a uniquely covered typical case. For instance, Kazakhstan is such a case. It is a member of *LD* but not of *LH* (see XY plots in Figures 3.1 and 3.2). If a case is typical for more than one term, then it is a jointly covered typical case. For instance, Uganda fits in this category as it is typical for both *LD* and *LH*.

Table 3.2 *Uniquely covered, jointly covered, and globally uncovered cases*

Y	globally uncovered deviant coverage	deviant coverage or uniquely covered typical[a]	jointly covered typical[a]
$\sim Y$	globally uncovered iir	deviant consistency or iir	
	0	1	>1
		Member in how many sufficient terms X_i	

[a] $X_i \leq Y$, new case types in italics

The definition of additional sub-types reveals that, in the presence of an equifinal solution formula, it is crucial to distinguish between sufficient terms (a disjunct) and the sufficient solution formula (the disjunction). Typical and deviant consistency cases are defined by their membership in each disjunct. They must be members of a disjunct to be either typical or deviant consistency cases. For instance, Georgia is a deviant consistency case with regard to disjunct *LD* and Ghana for disjunct *LH*. Rwanda is a deviant consistency case for both *LD* and *LH*.[5] In contrast, deviant coverage and iir cases are defined by their membership in the disjunction. They must be nonmembers

---

[4] And, as explained in the previous chapter, with fuzzy sets their membership in the term must be smaller than or equal to their membership in the outcome.

[5] None of the SMMR principles requires a distinction between deviant consistency cases such as Rwanda, on the one hand, and Ghana and Georgia, on the other. In other words, for within-case analyses of deviant consistency cases, it is of no major importance whether they are deviant for only one or more than one sufficient term. Researchers may nevertheless want

of the disjunction to qualify as deviant coverage or iir cases, that is, they must be nonmembers of all known sufficient terms. For instance, Russia is left unexplained by the sufficient term *LH* (it is located in the upper-left corner of the XY plot for *LH* in Figure 3.2) but it is explained by the other sufficient term *LD* (see Figure 3.1). This makes Russia a deviant coverage case with regard to sufficient term *LH*, but not a globally uncovered deviant coverage case.

Globally uncovered deviant coverage and globally uncovered iir cases are visualized when plotting the solution formula (the disjunction) against the outcome. The XY plot in Figure 3.3 shows deviant coverage cases, such as Argentina or Colombia, in the upper-left quadrant. In Chapter 1, we learned that an iir case is a case that is not a member of either the term or the outcome. In the presence of more than one sufficient term in a QCA solution, we need to further specify this definition and distinguish between iir cases that are not members of any term and those that are only nonmembers of some. The former we label as globally uncovered iir cases and the latter simply iir cases. In the example by Stevens (2016), we can see from the XY plot displaying the solution formula in Figure 3.3 that, for instance, Latvia and Hungary are two of the many globally uncovered iir cases. Georgia, instead, is an iir case only with regard to term *LH*. For term *LD* it is a deviant consistency case.

3.3.3 Additional Principles

Coping with a disjunction in SMMR is achieved by applying three principles in addition to the ones already introduced in the previous chapter. The first principle requires that we analyze each disjunct, or sufficient term, in separation.

Focal disjunct principle: For each term separately perform descriptive and causal inference SMMR designs.

The focal disjunct principle applies to any form of single and comparative SMMR design that involves either a typical or a deviant consistency case.

One implication of this principle for applied SMMR is that QCA solution formulas with more sufficient terms require, in principle, more within-case analyses. This makes sense because each sufficient term represents a separate descriptive or causal claim, including a claim on the presence of an underlying mechanism. Depending on the complexity of a solution and resources available

to make use of the information that a given case contradicts more than one, or even all, statements of sufficiency. One model-unrelated reason for this could be measurement error and/or miscalibration of the case's membership in the outcome.

to empirical researchers, it might be infeasible to implement a sufficiently detailed within-case analysis on each disjunct. In the face of resource constraints, I find it justified to choose cases for a subset of disjuncts and to use theoretical and practical reasons for selecting the disjuncts to focus on. If empirical work is interested only in selected sufficient terms – something we could call term-centered analysis – limiting the focus to selected terms is justified. QCA work has traditionally taken an outcome-centered perspective, though (Marx et al., 2014). For this perspective, SMMR requirements are higher because the goal is to explain for *each* disjunct how it is linked to the outcome. Plus, an outcome-centered perspective requires that jointly the disjuncts explain enough, preferably all, of the outcome. That means solution coverage should be high enough. If it is not, within-case analyses on deviant coverage cases are also needed. Only insights from SMMR designs involving deviant coverage cases can increase solution coverage by revealing hitherto overlooked disjuncts.[6]

The second additional principle aims at tackling the problem of overdetermined typical cases. It stipulates that only so-called uniquely covered typical cases should be chosen. These are cases that are typical for just one of the two or more sufficient terms in the QCA solution formula.

Uniquely covered principle: Choose typical cases that are members of just one term.

Compliance with the uniquely covered principle allows empirical researchers to avoid the problem that is known as *overdetermination* or *redundant causation* (Paul and Hall, 2013, chap. 2). Overdetermination is the problem of having too many potential causes present in a single case to make determinate inferences. Therefore the selection of uniquely covered typical cases is recommended in causal inference SMMR designs (Schneider and Rohlfing, 2013; Goertz, 2017).[7]

For illustration, let us focus on the disjunct *LD*. We call it the *focal disjunct* of our analysis and hypothesize that low levels of democracy lead to more freedom for politicians to engage in illicit activities, such as corruption, because they lack control via independent media and courts and sanctioning by voters via free and fair elections. This is our mechanism M_{LD}. In a country with low democracy (*LD*), say Kazakhstan, we expect to observe both the mechanism

---

[6] In Section 7.2, I discuss in more detail further research-practical aspects of applied SMMR.
[7] Beach and Pedersen (2018) recommend the use of jointly covered typical cases to see if other conditions activate the mechanism. I do not find this strategy convincing because the question of other conditions activating the mechanism is better answered by choosing cases that are uniquely covered by those other conditions. Even if applied readers do not follow this line of reasoning, the tool set provided by SMMR allows for the identification of jointly covered cases and researchers are at liberty to choose those for within-case analysis.

3.3 The Solutions

M_{LD} and outcome HC, whereas in a country with not-low democracy ($\sim LD$), say Latvia, we expect to observe the opposite, that is, $\sim M_{LD}$ and $\sim HC$. However, this expectation applies only to typical cases that are uniquely covered by LD. For cases that are jointly covered by both LD and LH, such as Uganda, the outcome "high perceived corruption" (HC) remains present even if we take away condition LD (counterfactually or by empirical comparison with an iir case).[8] And this continued presence of an alternative sufficient term can also trigger the presence of the mechanism M_{LD}. If we find M_{LD} in jointly covered typical cases such as Uganda we cannot disentangle whether it is low democracy (LD) or low human development (LH) that triggers M_{LD}.

We would have to conclude that the presence and absence of LD and the attached mechanism do not make a difference to outcome "high perceived corruption" and that the relationship is not causal. This conclusion would be entirely driven by inadequate case selection that ignores the uniquely covered principle and leads to the choice of a jointly covered typical case instead. The fallacy of selecting joint members becomes fully apparent by recognizing that we would have to conclude the same in an analysis on the second term LH. If in a jointly covered typical case we take away disjunct LH (again, by counterfactual or comparison with an iir case), LD is still present and we still observe high perceived corruption (HC). We would need to conclude that LH is not making a difference to HC and is therefore not causal, in particular if we also find the mechanism M_{LD} present in this case. Taken together, neither of the two terms in the solution would be inferred to be causal. Assuming that we have a strong design and at least one term must be causal, this finding would not make sense and reflects the perils of choosing joint members and ignoring the problems of redundant causation (Paul and Hall, 2013, chap. 2).

A third principle that is needed if and when we confront a disjunction is that deviant coverage cases and iir cases must be globally uncovered. As shown in Table 3.2, deviant coverage and iir cases can be globally uncovered or not globally uncovered. The globally uncovered principle dictates that only globally uncovered deviant coverage and iir cases should be chosen. This means that when analyzing the causal properties of focal disjunct LD by matching a typical and an iir case, the latter should not be a member of – and thus a deviant consistency case for – any of the other disjuncts. Likewise, when matching a deviant coverage and an iir case, the former should not be a typical case for any other disjunct.

---

[8] Whether a unique member is available for analysis depends on the data set at hand. I do not discuss criteria for constructing good counterfactuals in qualitative research and refer to the existing work on this topic (e.g. Bunzl, 2004; Emmenegger, 2011; Fearon, 1991; Lebow, 2010).

78   Disjunctions $A + B \Rightarrow Y$

Globally uncovered principle: Choose deviant coverage and iir cases that are not members of any term.

Hungary, for instance, is a globally uncovered iir case; Georgia is not. The latter is an iir case with regard to *LH*, but a deviant consistency case with regard to *LD*. Choosing Georgia would mean the same case is counted as two different types of cases and thus potentially used in two different SMMR designs with different analytic goals. Georgia would be counted as a deviant consistency case and could be used in a comparison with a typical case with the goal of refining a disjunct. But Georgia would also be counted as an iir case and could be used in a comparison with a deviant coverage case with the goal of refining the disjunction. Counting the same empirical case as more than one type of case and using it for different analytic purposes sounds problematic. The globally uncovered principle prevents this pitfall.

The globally uncovered principle is also automatically adhered to in the comparison between deviant coverage and iir cases. The truth table row principle requires that both case types must be located in the same truth table row. By definition, this truth table row cannot be part of the QCA solution formula. From this it follows that neither the iir case nor the deviant coverage case can be covered by any of the known sufficient terms of the QCA solution formula, that is, they are globally uncovered. For comparisons between a typical and an iir case, however, the globally uncovered principle is needed to avoid the choice of a case that is deviant consistent with regard to one or more sufficient terms.

***

All forms of single-case and comparative within-case analyses in SMMR are affected by one, more, or even all three additional principles. Table 3.3 focuses on the comparison of a typical case and an iir case and displays various scenarios in which both case types can differ from each other vis-à-vis their membership in the focal disjunct and the complementary disjuncts. The distinction between focal and complementary disjuncts means the focal disjunct principle is adhered to in all four scenarios. Based on the other two principles of uniquely covered and globally uncovered, we can distinguish which scenario is superior to others.

Scenario 1 is the best form of comparison between a typical case and an iir case. It adheres to the principles of uniquely covered and globally uncovered. This means the typical case is uniquely covered by focal disjunct *LD* (e.g. Kazakhstan) and the iir case is globally uncovered by the disjunction *LD* + *LH* (e.g. Australia). All remaining scenarios violate one or both principles.

Table 3.3 *Scenarios for comparison of typical and iir cases*

	Uniquely covered	Globally uncovered	Type	Membership in disjunct		Example
				Focal *LD*	Complementary *LH*	
1	✓		typical	1	0	Kazakhstan
		✓	iir	0	0	Australia
2	-		typical	1	1	Uganda
		✓	iir	0	0	Australia
3	✓		typical	1	0	Kazakhstan
		-	iir	0	1	Georgia
4	-		typical	1	1	Uganda
		-	iir	0	1	Georgia

In scenario 2, the iir case is globally uncovered but the typical case is jointly covered (e.g. Uganda). We therefore have the problem not only of overdetermination, but also of too many differences between the typical and the iir cases. They differ on *both* the focal and the complementary disjuncts. Similarly, in scenario 3, the typical case is uniquely covered, but the iir case is not globally uncovered because it is a member of the complementary disjunct *LH* (e.g. Georgia).

Scenario 4 violates both principles and matches a jointly covered typical case with a non-globally uncovered iir case. In SMMR, scenario 4 is clearly the least favored form of comparison. Note, however, that scenario 4 is fully in line with Mill's well-known method of difference (Mill, 1874). The reasons why scenario 4 is deemed inferior in SMMR are that the two cases differ in the wrong factor and that the outcome in the typical case is overdetermined.

3.4 Applying SMMR

The implementation of SMMR in the presence of disjunctions is based on the same R function smmr() from package SetMethods that I have already introduced in Chapter 2. I continue with the example by Stevens (2016) and first produce a truth table and derive the most parsimonious solution (code C 3.1) already shown in Table 3.1 and in output O 3.1. After this, I present first the code for model-refining and then for causal inference SMMR designs.

C 3.1

```
conds <- c("LD", "HR", "HS", "LH", "HI")

TT_y <- truthTable(data = STEV,
            outcome = "HC",
            conditions = conds,
            incl.cut = 0.85,
```

```
                show.cases = TRUE,
                n.cut = 2,
                sort.by = c("OUT", "incl"),
                complete = TRUE)
TT_y

sol_yp <- minimize(TT_y,
                   details = TRUE,
                   include = "?")
sol_yp
```

O 3.1

M1: LD + LH -> HC

		inclS	PRI	covS	covU
1	LD	0.872	0.823	0.564	0.138
2	LH	0.914	0.871	0.610	0.184
	M1	0.866	0.813	0.748	

Core Points 3.1: Disjunctions

- When a solution consists of a disjunction (equifinality), most SMMR designs require a focus on a sufficient term (disjunct). The descriptive inference SMMR designs with the goal of identifying a missing disjunct require a focus on the entire solution formula (disjunction)
- Case selection in the presence of disjunctions requires the introduction of four additional sub-types of case: uniquely covered typical, jointly covered typical, globally uncovered iir, and globally uncovered deviant coverage
- Case selection in the presence of disjunctions also requires three additional principles: focal disjunct principle, the uniquely covered principle, and the globally uncovered principle
- Causal inference SMMR designs require the selection of uniquely covered typical and of globally uncovered iir cases
- If convincing theoretical and conceptual arguments exist, equifinality can be theorized away by moving up the ladder of generality and thus subsuming multiple disjuncts under a single set

---

3.4.1 Descriptive Inference SMMR

Among the three single and four comparative SMMR designs, four aim at identifying factors that have been omitted from the analysis. The within-case analysis of a deviant coverage case and the comparison with an iir case both

3.4 Applying SMMR

aim at identifying a missing disjunct from the QCA solution, whereas the within-case analysis of a deviant consistency case and the comparison with a typical case aim at identifying an omitted conjunct from a known disjunct (see Chapter 2, in particular Table 2.2). The need for model refinement depends on the fit of the QCA model. The lower the solution coverage, the more reasons there are to identify a missing disjunct. Likewise, the lower the consistency of a given disjunct, the more reasons there are to identify a conjunct omitted from that disjunct. In our example, neither solution coverage (0.748), nor term consistencies (0.872 and 0.914) are particularly low. If researchers nevertheless aim at further refining the overall already well-fitting QCA solution, SMMR provides the following tools for identifying the best available (pairs of) cases in the data at hand.

Identifying Omitted Disjuncts

To identify an omitted disjunct, one needs to perform within-case analysis on a deviant coverage case. Two SMMR designs are available.

The best available deviant coverage case for a single case study is identified by setting the argument `cases` to 4 (see code C 3.2).[9] Cases are sorted by the truth table row to which they best belong. If there is more than one deviant coverage case in a truth table row, they are ranked from better to worse choices for within-case analysis on identifying the conjunct missing from the truth table row. For instance, in output O 3.2, Trinidad and Tobago is the only, and thus the best available, case in truth table row 00100. Truth table row 00101, instead, contains four deviant coverage cases. Among them Mexico is identified as the best available case: its membership in the truth table is smaller than in the outcome (column "TT<=Y") and it scores lowest in column "Best", calculated with Formula 2.1. Therefore, it is the most deviant coverage case (column "MostDevCov") for that row. As mentioned in Chapter 2, the ordering from best to worst available case within each truth table is based on whether the truth table membership is smaller than the outcome membership and then the lowest value in column "Best".

C 3.2

```
dcov <- smmr(results = sol_yp,
             outcome = "HC",
             match = FALSE,
             cases = 4)
dcov
```

---

[9] For an overview of the values in argument `cases`, see Table 2.8.

O 3.2

Deviant Coverage Cases :

	Case	Sol	TT_LD	TT_HR	TT_HS	TT_LH	TT_HI	TT_row	Outcome	TT<=Y	Best	MostDCOV
10	TRaTO	0.187	0	0	1	0	0	0.530	0.655	TRUE	0.470	TRUE
6	Mexico	0.242	0	0	1	0	1	0.748	0.759	TRUE	0.252	TRUE
8	Peru	0.346	0	0	1	0	1	0.586	0.655	TRUE	0.414	FALSE
4	Colombia	0.489	0	0	1	0	1	0.511	0.690	TRUE	0.489	FALSE
2	Argentina	0.187	0	0	1	0	1	0.502	0.793	TRUE	0.498	FALSE
3	BOaHE	0.379	0	1	0	0	0	0.621	0.621	TRUE	0.379	FALSE
1	Albania	0.462	0	1	0	0	0	0.538	0.828	TRUE	0.462	FALSE
7	Montenegro	0.062	0	1	0	0	0	0.838	0.517	FALSE	0.162	TRUE
5	Lebanon	0.437	0	1	0	0	0	0.563	1.000	TRUE	0.437	TRUE
9	Serbia	0.302	0	1	1	0	0	0.524	0.552	TRUE	0.476	TRUE

3.4 Applying SMMR

In single-case studies on deviant coverage cases, researchers need to use a counterfactual and ask: What if the case was not a member of the omitted conjunct that has just been discovered? Adding this conjunct to the truth table row is then justified only if the answer to this counterfactual is as follows: The case would then no longer be a member of the outcome, nor would the within-case mechanism be present anymore.

Rather than using counterfactuals, with SMMR researchers can also turn this into an empirical question. For this, we need to identify in our data the counterfactual case, that is, a case that is identical to the deviant coverage case except for its membership in the outcome. Function smmr() identifies such cases and reports the best-matching pairs of deviant coverage and iir cases. For this argument match is set to TRUE and argument cases to 4, as shown in code C 3.3.

C 3.3

```
dcoviir <- smmr(results = sol_yp,
                outcome = "HC",
                match = TRUE,
                cases = 4)
```

Output O 3.3 reveals, for instance, that Trinidad and Tobago is the only deviant coverage case in truth table row 00100, but there are two iir cases. Pairing Trinidad and Tobago with Cyprus is the best available pair for this truth table row, slightly better than pairing it with Poland, as indicated by the slightly lower value in "Best" (1.285 vs. 1.334), calculated with Formula 2.6. For truth table row 00101, the pair Mexico – Chile is the best available. The order in which pairs are ranked from best to worst available is identical to that for single deviant coverage cases: membership of the deviant coverage case in the truth table should be smaller than in the outcome and the pair should score lowest in column "Best".

O 3.3

Matching Deviant Coverage–IIR Cases :

	DCOV	IIR	TT_LD	TT_HR	TT_HS	TT_LH	TT_HI	TT_DCV<=Y	Best
1	TRaTO	Cyprus	0	0	1	0	0	TRUE	1.285
2	TRaTO	Poland	0	0	1	0	0	TRUE	1.334
3	Mexico	Chile	0	0	1	0	1	TRUE	0.889
4	Peru	Chile	0	0	1	0	1	TRUE	1.173
5	Argentina	Chile	0	0	1	0	1	TRUE	1.203
6	Colombia	Chile	0	0	1	0	1	TRUE	1.288
7	Mexico	Brazil	0	0	1	0	1	TRUE	1.345
8	Albania	Estonia	0	1	0	0	0	TRUE	1.096
9	BOaHE	Estonia	0	1	0	0	0	TRUE	1.209
10	Albania	Korea (South)	0	1	0	0	0	TRUE	1.291
11	Albania	Latvia	0	1	0	0	0	TRUE	1.291
12	BOaHE	Korea (South)	0	1	0	0	0	TRUE	1.332
13	Serbia	Australia	0	1	1	0	0	TRUE	1.400
14	Serbia	Sweden	0	1	1	0	0	TRUE	1.400
15	Serbia	Finland	0	1	1	0	0	TRUE	1.400
16	Serbia	France	0	1	1	0	0	TRUE	1.400
17	Serbia	Canada	0	1	1	0	0	TRUE	1.400

Identifying Omitted Conjuncts

To identify an omitted conjunct, one needs to perform within-case analysis on a deviant consistency case. Two SMMR designs are available.

The best available deviant consistency case for single-case analysis is revealed by setting argument cases in the smmr() function to 3 (see code C 3.4). The output automatically lists deviant consistency cases for each disjunct. For disjunct *LD*, Rwanda is the best available deviant consistency case, followed by Jordan and Georgia. For disjunct *LH*, in turn, Ghana is ranked slightly higher than Rwanda.[10] This result confirms the intuition one has when looking at the XY plots in Figures 3.1 and 3.2. In general, for each sufficient term the deviant consistency cases are ordered from best to worst based on the value in column "Best", calculated using Formula 2.2, and, if that value is identical, based on which case holds the highest membership in the sufficient term.

C 3.4

```
dcons <- smmr(results = sol_yp,
              outcome = "HC",
              match = FALSE,
              cases = 3)
dcons
```

O 3.4

Deviant Consistency Cases :

	Cases	Term	TermMemb	Outcome	Best	MostDCONS
3	Rwanda	LD	1.000	0.341	0.341	TRUE
2	Jordan	LD	0.700	0.341	0.941	FALSE
1	Georgia	LD	0.600	0.268	1.068	FALSE
11	Ghana	LH	0.928	0.366	0.510	TRUE
21	Rwanda	LH	0.903	0.341	0.535	FALSE

As mentioned in Chapter 2, the goal of within-case analysis in a deviant consistency case is to identify a conjunct missing from the sufficient term that is responsible for the mechanism *M not* being triggered in the deviant consistency case. This means that the goal is not only to identify an omitted condition in which the deviant consistency case is *not* a member. It also implies that researchers need to counterfactually argue that if the deviant case consistency was a member of this omitted conjunct, it would display the mechanism and the outcome.

Instead of a counterfactual, researchers could assess this claim empirically and match the deviant consistency case with a typical case that is identical

---

[10] Rwanda could be part of both comparisons on *LH* and *LD* because the uniquely covered principle applies only to causal inference SMMR designs, not descriptive inference designs.

3.4 Applying SMMR

(i.e. member of the same disjunct), except for the membership in the outcome. Identifying the best-matching pair of cases is done setting argument match to TRUE and argument cases to 3 (see code C 3.5). As shown in output O 3.5, the best-matching pair for focal disjunct *LD* consists of the deviant consistency case Rwanda and the typical cases Uganda or Yemen. For focal disjunct *LH*, it is the deviant consistency case Ghana matched with either one of the several typical cases that all share the same membership scores in *LH* and outcome *HC*. For both terms, the best available pairs match the most typical and the most deviant consistency cases, as indicated by columns "MostTypTerm" and "MostDevCons", respectively. For each term, the ordering of pairs is based on their values in column "Best", calculated using Formula 2.5, then whether the pair comprises the most typical case, and then whether it contains the most deviant consistency case.

C 3.5

```
typdcons <- smmr(results = sol_yp,
                 outcome = "HC",
                 match = TRUE,
                 cases = 3,
                 max_pairs = 10)
typdcons
```

O 3.5

Term LD :

	TYP	DCONS	Best	MostTypTerm	MostDCONS
1	Uganda	Rwanda	0.341	TRUE	TRUE
2	Yemen	Rwanda	0.341	TRUE	TRUE
3	Bangladesh	Rwanda	0.441	FALSE	TRUE
4	Kazakhstan	Rwanda	0.475	FALSE	TRUE
5	Vietnam	Rwanda	0.744	FALSE	TRUE
6	Iraq	Rwanda	0.841	FALSE	TRUE
9	Uganda	Jordan	0.941	TRUE	FALSE
10	Yemen	Jordan	0.941	TRUE	FALSE
7	Bangladesh	Jordan	0.941	FALSE	FALSE
8	Iraq	Jordan	0.941	FALSE	FALSE

Term LH :

	TYP	DCONS	Best	MostTypTerm	MostDCONS
2	Nigeria	Ghana	0.510	TRUE	TRUE
3	Uganda	Ghana	0.510	TRUE	TRUE
4	Yemen	Ghana	0.510	TRUE	TRUE
5	Zimbabwe	Ghana	0.510	TRUE	TRUE
1	Bangladesh	Ghana	0.510	FALSE	TRUE
7	Nigeria	Rwanda	0.535	TRUE	FALSE
8	Uganda	Rwanda	0.535	TRUE	FALSE
9	Yemen	Rwanda	0.535	TRUE	FALSE
10	Zimbabwe	Rwanda	0.535	TRUE	FALSE
6	Bangladesh	Rwanda	0.535	FALSE	FALSE

3.4.2 Causal Inference SMMR

There are three forms of within-case analysis that aim at probing the causal properties of the QCA solution formula. All involve at least one typical case.

Researchers can select a single typical case and investigate whether and which mechanism is present. Setting arguments `match` to FALSE and `cases` to 2 reveals the best available typical cases (see code C 3.6).

C 3.6

```
typ_term <- smmr(results = sol_yp,
                 outcome = "HC",
                 match = FALSE,
                 cases = 1)
typ_term
```

Output O 3.6 displays the ranking of the best available typical cases for focal disjunct *LD* and *LH*. For each typical case, in addition to the outcome, the output indicates whether the typical case is uniquely covered ("UniqCov"), its value in the formula for the best available case (see Formula 2.4) in column "Best", the membership in the sufficient term, and whether it is the most typical case ("MostTyp"). This is also the order of criteria based on which cases are ranked from best to worst available for within-case analyses.

The best available typical case for disjunct *LD* is Kazakhstan, followed by Armenia and Ecuador. If we look at the XY plot for term *LD* (see Figure 3.1), it might come as a surprise that these cases are ranked first. In particular the latter two cases display relatively low membership in *LD* and are far above the diagonal. Other typical cases, such as Yemen and Uganda, with their high and similar membership in both the term and the outcome, appear much more adequate. In fact, they score perfectly in column "Best" and are the most typical cases. However, they are jointly covered and are thus also typical cases for the other term *LH*. When selecting typical cases for within-case analysis, being uniquely covered trumps low values in "Best" and therefore puts Kazakhstan and other cases before Uganda and Yemen. It is only among uniquely covered cases that the lower value in column "Best" differentiates better from worse typical cases. A similar situation occurs with focal disjunct *LH*, for which Tanzania is identified as the best available typical case for within-case analysis. More typical, but jointly covered, cases, such as Uganda or Yemen, are ranked below more than a handful of other typical cases that have worse value in "Best" but that are uniquely covered by *LH*.

O 3.6

Typical Cases :

	Case	Term	TermMemb	Outcome	UniqCov	Best	MostTyp
5	Kazakhstan	LD	0.950	0.966	TRUE	0.082	FALSE
1	Armenia	LD	0.550	0.690	TRUE	0.730	FALSE
3	Ecuador	LD	0.550	0.828	TRUE	1.006	FALSE
7	Russia	LD	0.650	1.000	TRUE	1.050	FALSE
9	Ukraine	LD	0.650	1.000	TRUE	1.050	FALSE
10	Venezuela	LD	0.650	1.000	TRUE	1.050	FALSE
8	Uganda	LD	1.000	1.000	FALSE	0.000	TRUE
12	Yemen	LD	1.000	1.000	FALSE	0.000	TRUE
2	Bangladesh	LD	0.950	1.000	FALSE	0.150	FALSE
11	Vietnam	LD	0.850	0.897	FALSE	0.244	FALSE
[...]							
131	Tanzania	LH	0.890	0.897	TRUE	0.124	FALSE
111	Pakistan	LH	0.900	0.966	TRUE	0.232	FALSE
121	Philippines	LH	0.654	0.655	TRUE	0.348	FALSE
91	Morocco	LH	0.620	0.621	TRUE	0.382	FALSE
41	Guatemala	LH	0.755	0.862	TRUE	0.459	FALSE
81	Moldova	LH	0.645	0.759	TRUE	0.583	FALSE
31	Egypt	LH	0.585	0.690	TRUE	0.625	FALSE
71	Kyrgyzstan	LH	0.755	1.000	TRUE	0.735	FALSE
51	Indonesia	LH	0.579	0.793	TRUE	0.849	FALSE
21	Dominican Republic	LH	0.528	0.862	TRUE	1.140	FALSE
101	Nigeria	LH	1.000	1.000	FALSE	0.000	TRUE
14	Uganda	LH	1.000	1.000	FALSE	0.000	TRUE
[...]							

Within-case analysis of a single typical case needs to counterfactually ask: Would the mechanism and the outcome be absent if the case was not a member of the focal disjunct? For the disjunct to be causal, the answer to this question needs to be "yes". Rather than performing a counterfactual, researchers might choose to turn it into an empirical question. For this, they need to match a typical case with a case that is identical except for its membership in the disjunct and the outcome. In other words, a typical case needs to be matched with an appropriate globally uncovered iir case.

Setting arguments match to TRUE and cases to 6[11] achieves this (see code C 3.7). In addition, we can require the function to print a specific number of case pairs by using argument max_pairs. Let us set it to 10. Output O 3.7 displays the first ten best-matching pairs. Column "UniqCov" indicates whether the typical case is uniquely covered. Column "ConsIIR" reports whether the iir case's membership in the sufficient disjunct is consistent with the statement of sufficiency, that is, whether its membership in the disjunct is smaller than or equal to membership in the outcome. Column "GlobUncovIIR" reports whether the iir case is globally uncovered. Column "Best" reports the

---

[11] As I explain in the next chapter, when the QCA solution formula contains conjunctions, argument cases needs to be set to 2.

value calculated based on formula 2.7. And column "MostTyp" states whether the typical case involved in the pair is the most typical case according to formula 2.4. This is also the order of criteria in which case pairs are ranked from best to worst available for within-case analysis.

C 3.7
```
typiir_term <- smmr( results = sol_yp,
                     outcome = "HC",
                     match = TRUE,
                     cases = 6,
                     max_pairs = 10)
typiir_term
```

As output O 3.7 shows, for focal disjunct LD, the best available pair matches the typical case Kazakhstan with either of the several iir cases that all share the same membership in LD and outcome HC. Since Kazakhstan is uniquely covered and all these iir cases are globally uncovered and have consistent membership scores, all pairs are ranked equally high. Note that the best pair does not have to involve the most typical case. There are more typical cases for LD than Kazakhstan, for instance Yemen or Uganda (see Figure 3.1), but the last two are jointly covered, that is, they are also typical for LH, and therefore are inferior choices for within-case analysis. For focal disjunct LH, a similar pattern emerges. The typical case of Tanzania forms best-matching pairs with eight different iir cases without being the most typical case.

The fact that several pairs are identically well suited is rare in applied QCA. In the present example it is largely caused by the fact that the focal disjunct is a single set rather than a conjunction. Once there are several conjuncts in a disjunct, that is, once we confront INUS conditions, as we usually do in applied QCA, there will be more analytically relevant heterogeneity both among typical and iir cases. That, in turn, leads to more differentiation among case pairs. The examples in Chapters 4 and 5 will illustrate this point.

O 3.7

Term LD :

	TYP	IIR	UniqCov	ConsIIR	GlobUncov	Best	MostTyp
29	Kazakhstan	Australia	TRUE	TRUE	TRUE	0.116	FALSE
30	Kazakhstan	Canada	TRUE	TRUE	TRUE	0.116	FALSE
33	Kazakhstan	Finland	TRUE	TRUE	TRUE	0.116	FALSE
34	Kazakhstan	Germany	TRUE	TRUE	TRUE	0.116	FALSE
35	Kazakhstan	Japan	TRUE	TRUE	TRUE	0.116	FALSE
37	Kazakhstan	Norway	TRUE	TRUE	TRUE	0.116	FALSE
71	Kazakhstan	Israel	TRUE	TRUE	TRUE	0.335	FALSE
72	Kazakhstan	Spain	TRUE	TRUE	TRUE	0.335	FALSE
99	Kazakhstan	Korea (South)	TRUE	TRUE	TRUE	0.514	FALSE
134	Kazakhstan	Czech Republic	TRUE	TRUE	TRUE	0.933	FALSE

3.4 Applying SMMR

Term LH :

	TYP	IIR	UniqCov	ConsIIR	GlobUncov	Best	MostTyp
93	Tanzania	Australia	TRUE	TRUE	TRUE	0.227	FALSE
94	Tanzania	Canada	TRUE	TRUE	TRUE	0.227	FALSE
97	Tanzania	Estonia	TRUE	TRUE	TRUE	0.227	FALSE
98	Tanzania	Finland	TRUE	TRUE	TRUE	0.227	FALSE
100	Tanzania	Germany	TRUE	TRUE	TRUE	0.227	FALSE
101	Tanzania	Japan	TRUE	TRUE	TRUE	0.227	FALSE
102	Tanzania	Netherlands	TRUE	TRUE	TRUE	0.227	FALSE
105	Tanzania	Switzerland	TRUE	TRUE	TRUE	0.227	FALSE
109	Pakistan	Australia	TRUE	TRUE	TRUE	0.266	FALSE
110	Pakistan	Canada	TRUE	TRUE	TRUE	0.266	FALSE

The third within-case analysis with the goal of causal inference matches two typical cases. The question is whether mechanism M operates in all typical cases for a focal disjunct. The case selection logic is to match the most typical with a just-so typical case. Code C 3.8 identifies the best-matching pair of two typical cases by setting argument `cases` to 5.[12]

C 3.8

```
typtyp_term <- smmr(results = sol_yp,
                   outcome = "HC",
                   match = TRUE,
                   cases = 5,
                   max_pairs = 10)
typtyp_term
```

O 3.8

Term LD :

	TYP1	TYP2	UniqCov	Best	MostTyp
4	Kazakhstan	Armenia	both	0.636	none
2	Kazakhstan	Ecuador	both	1.050	none
92	Kazakhstan	Ukraine	both	1.466	none
97	Kazakhstan	Venezuela	both	1.466	none
128	Kazakhstan	Russia	both	1.466	none
64	Armenia	Ecuador	both	1.974	none
90	Armenia	Russia	both	2.390	none
95	Armenia	Venezuela	both	2.390	none
132	Armenia	Ukraine	both	2.390	none
21	Venezuela	Ukraine	both	2.400	none

Term LH :

	TYP1	TYP2	UniqCov	Best	MostTyp
255	Tanzania	Morocco	both	0.470	none
130	Pakistan	Morocco	both	0.509	none
155	Tanzania	Philippines	both	0.538	none
117	Pakistan	Philippines	both	0.577	none
138	Tanzania	Egypt	both	0.712	none
223	Pakistan	Egypt	both	0.751	none
240	Tanzania	Moldova	both	0.859	none
289	Pakistan	Moldova	both	0.898	none
164	Philippines	Morocco	both	0.936	none
14	Tanzania	Indonesia	both	1.027	none

---

[12] When confronting conjunctions, argument `cases` should be set to 1; see Chapter 4.

As output O 3.8 shows, for focal disjunct *LD*, the best-matching pair consists of Kazakhstan and Armenia, both of which are uniquely covered, but none of them is the most typical case for *LD*. Similarly, for disjunct *LH*, Tanzania and Morocco are identified as the best available pair of two typical cases, even though none of the two is the most typical case, but both are uniquely covered by *LH*. Case pairs are ordered by first checking if both typical cases are uniquely covered or just one or none, which pair scores lower in column "Best" (using Formula 2.8), and if both, one, or none of the cases qualifies as the most typical case, according to formula 2.4.

3.5 Conclusion

The presence of more than one sufficient term in a QCA solution formula triggers various consequences for SMMR. The classification of case types needs to be refined. There are four additional sub-types: uniquely covered typical, jointly covered typical, globally uncovered iir, and globally uncovered deviant coverage cases. We also need additional principles that guide the choice among the types of cases. There are three additional principles: uniquely covered, globally uncovered, and the focal disjunct principle. These new principles apply to single and comparative SMMR designs and to both crisp and fuzzy sets. All formulas for identifying the best available case or pair of cases continue to apply in the same form as explained in Chapter 2.

One practical consequence of equifinality is that it increases the number of within-case analyses. A disjunct doubles the number of possible within-case analysis compared to a non-equifinal QCA solution formula. In applied research, the number of within-case analyses needed for a complete SMMR design can quickly become practically unfeasible. Researchers then have two mutually nonexclusive options. They can reduce the number of disjuncts by moving up on the ladder of generality and subsuming two or more disjuncts under a single higher-order concept. They can also focus on just one or a few disjuncts and ignore the others and use theoretical and substantive arguments for this choice. SMMR can still guide the selection of the best available cases for the chosen disjunct, though. Plus, by laying out all required within-case analyses, the SMMR framework serves as a reminder to applied researchers how much is needed for determinate causal (and descriptive) inference and by how much a given applied research comes short of fulfilling the ideal standard. As we will see in Chapter 4, an increase in the complexity of QCA solution formulas in the form of conjunctions also triggers the need for additional principles and, with this, the number of both case selection criteria to take into account and within-case analyses to perform.

4
Conjunctions
$A * B \Rightarrow Y$

Conjunctions are another core feature of causal complexity in set-theoretic methods. In applied QCA, it is the rule rather than the exception that solution formulas indicate that the combination of two or more conditions is sufficient for an outcome, rather than a single condition on its own. Whenever there is a logical AND in the solution formula, such conjunctural claims are made. In the example that I am using in this chapter, $PD * RO$ is the conjunction that consists of the two conjuncts PD and RO. Following the flow of the argument in Chapter 3, I first introduce the empirical example and then turn to the analytic challenges that conjunctions create for SMMR. As will become clear, those challenges affect only causal inference SMMR designs. After that, I turn to the solutions. They consist of adhering to four plus two additional principles and introducing slightly reformulated formulas. In the final section, I empirically illustrate how SMMR is performed with the smmr() function in the presence of conjunctions.

4.1 Empirical Example

For illustration of the consequences for SMMR designs triggered by the presence of conjuncts, I use the study by Haesebrouck and Van Immerseel (2020). In their fuzzy-set QCA on 69 military employment decisions, the goal consists in identifying the factors that explain why some of those decisions lead to high political contestation while others do not. For didactical reasons, I simplify their analysis and focus only on the nonoccurrence of the outcome, that is, why deployment decisions do *not* lead to political contestation. Furthermore, I drop one of their seven conditions from the analysis and recalibrate the membership of some cases in some of the remaining conditions.

> **Learning Goals 4.1: Conjunctions**
>
> - Understand the challenges for causal inference SMMR designs triggered by conjunctions
> - Learn about how additional principles guide case selection in causal inference SMMR designs in the presence of conjunctions
> - Distinguish between focal and complementary conjuncts
> - Get acquainted with ranks for cases and case pairs in causal inference SMMR designs and how those ranks reflect which SMMR principles are fulfilled and which ones are violated
> - Learn about INUS conditions that qualify as necessary for the outcome, and the consequences this triggers for purposeful case selection in causal inference SMMR designs
> - Understand why increased complexity of QCA solution formulas in the form of conjunctions also increases the complexity of causal inference SMMR designs

> **Empirical Example 4.1: When does politics stop at the water's edge? A QCA of parliamentary consensus on military deployment decisions, (Haesebrouck and Van Immerseel, 2020)**
>
> - *Research question*: Which factors lead to lack of political contestation about military deployment decisions?
> - *Cases*: 69 military deployment decisions
> - *Set type:* Fuzzy
> - *Outcome*: No political contestation ($\sim PC$)
> - *Conditions:* Not potentially divisive operation (PD),[a] high-risk operation (HR), parliament involved (PI), parliament fractionalized (PF), right opposition (RO), government strong (GS),[b] government polarized (GP)[c]
>
> [a] For didactic reasons, this condition has been negated
> [b] For didactic reasons, condition GS is not used in the analysis
> [c] For didactic reasons, the scores of some cases in some sets have been altered

Table 4.1 displays the most parsimonious solution for outcome "no political contestation" ($\sim PC$). The QCA solution formula consists of one sufficient term, which, in turn, is a conjunction comprising two conjuncts: $PD * RO$. The combination of not being politically divisive (PD) and the presence of a right-of-center opposition in parliament (RO) is sufficient for the outcome of there not being political contestation to the government's decision to deploy military abroad.

4.1 Empirical Example

Table 4.1 *Most parsimonious solution, outcome "no political contestation"* $\sim PC$

	inclS	PRI	covS	covU
*PD*RO*	0.839	0.800	0.517	
Solution	0.839	0.800	0.517	

PD: not politically divisive operation; *RO*: right opposition

Because there is only one term, the parameters of fit for this term are, of course, identical to those for the solution formula. Consistency is at a commonly accepted high-enough level (0.839). Coverage at 0.517 is normal for a sufficient term. For a solution formula, however, this value is at the lower end of what is commonly observed in applied QCA. Barely more than half of the membership scores in the outcome are covered, or explained, by this solution formula.[1] Such low coverage is not surprising given the fact that only one sufficient term is identified and that term is a conjunction. Conjunctions tend to be smaller sets and thus cover less of the outcome. Low coverage means that there are good reasons to engage in model-specification SMMR designs that aim at adding an omitted disjunct. As explained in previous chapters, this is done by SMMR designs involving deviant coverage cases, either alone or in a comparison with iir cases.

The XY plot in Figure 4.1 visualizes the finding. The relatively high consistency is reflected by the low number of only three deviant consistency cases in kind (lower-right quadrant). The large majority of deviant consistency cases are deviant in degree only (lower triangle in the upper-right quadrant). The relatively low solution coverage is visualized by the many cases in the upper-left quadrant where the deviant coverage cases are located.

For the sake of illustration, let the mechanism be composed of two elements, each triggered by one of the two conjuncts at the cross-case level. As Figure 4.2 shows, conjunct "not politically divisive military operation" (*PD*) triggers the mechanism of the opposition not seeing any political gains in opposing the deployment decision by the government (M_{PD}) (Haesebrouck and Van Immerseel, 2020, p. 375). Here to "trigger" is a synonym of "is sufficient for". Conjunct "right opposition" (*RO*), in turn, triggers the mechanism of that opposition not wanting to send the wrong signals to international allies and enemies and thus abstaining from politically opposing the military deployment (M_{RO}) (Haesebrouck and Van Immerseel, 2020, p. 374). Each conjunct is expected to

---

[1] The original, equifinal, solution formula by Haesebrouck and Van Immerseel (2020) covers over 80%.

Figure 4.1 XY plot: sufficient term $PD * RO$, outcome PC

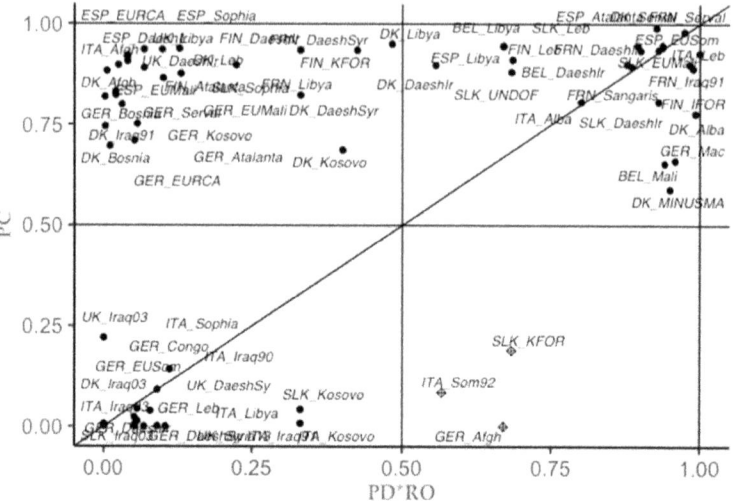

trigger its element of the mechanism. And it is only in the presence of the other conjunct, which triggers its element of the mechanism, that the conjunctive mechanism as a whole leads to the outcome. Each element of the mechanism requires the presence of the other element to jointly produce the outcome. In other words, we not only see a sufficient conjunction at the cross-case level, but also expect to find a conjunctive mechanism at the within-case level.

Figure 4.2 Cross-case and within-case levels for outcome "no political contestation"

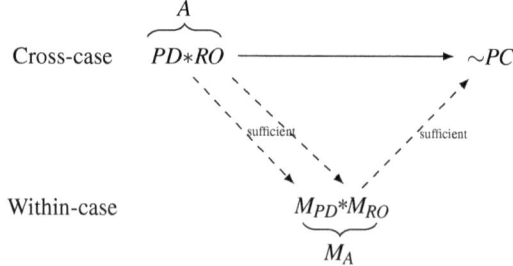

PD: not politically divisive; RO: right opposition; $\sim PC$: no political contestation; A: appeased opposition
M_{PD}: low anticipated chance of political gains; M_{RO}: avoidance of wrong signals to allies and enemies
M_A: opposition not deeming it opportune to object to deployment

It is important to point out that all SMMR principles and designs introduced so far, and those that I introduce now, remain unaffected by whether or not different conjuncts trigger the same or different elements of the mechanism. We could safely subsume all mechanismic elements under the label of one mechanism M_A. This more abstract mechanism M_A could be labeled as "opposition forces not deeming it opportune to oppose the military deployment". The only difference is in applied SMMR: the empirical sources of information must be adequate for capturing the mechanismic elements under investigation. When analyzing mechanism M_{PD}, researchers need to look at all opposition parties and find traces of their political calculations on what the potential gains of opposing the military deployment would be. When analyzing mechanism M_{RO}, instead, only opposition forces on the right of the political spectrum are relevant and the goal needs to be to find traces of their assessment of foreign policy consequences of them opposing the military deployment. And if M_A is deemed the analytically relevant mechanism, then both political and military-strategic considerations of all opposition parties need to be taken into consideration.

4.2 The Challenge

In previous chapters, I explained that, in SMMR, sufficient term S is deemed causal if it makes a difference not only to outcome Y but also to mechanisms M. In QCA, more often than not, a sufficient term consists of a conjunction. This means that it is the joint presence of two or more conjuncts that are sufficient for the outcome. In SMMR, we are interested in whether or not the conjunction triggers the mechanisms that then leads to the outcome. Showing that the mechanism and the outcome does not occur if the *entire* conjunction is absent is not enough for inferring causal properties of the conjunction, though. For a conjunction to be a difference maker to the mechanism and the outcome, and thus causal, each conjunct in the context of the conjunction needs to qualify as a difference maker.

At the cross-case level, QCA's minimization algorithm aims at identifying and eliminating causally redundant conjuncts, that is, conjuncts that do not make a difference to the outcome. The most parsimonious solution is defined as the solution for which it can be empirically shown that all conjuncts contained in it are difference makers for the outcome.[2] The within-case analysis in causal inference SMMR designs serves the purpose of testing whether each conjunct

---

[2] See the introductory Chapter 2 and Section 5.4 for arguments why, in SMMR, all solution types – conservative, intermediate, and most parsimonious – can be used in causal inference

is also a difference maker for the mechanism. Only if this hurdle is also passed is the causal analysis complete. The challenge for SMMR in the presence of conjunctions, therefore, consists in isolating the effect of single conjuncts, without, of course, neglecting the fact that it is the conjunction as a whole that triggers the mechanism.[3]

Applied to our empirical example, it is not enough to show that, in the presence of conjunct *PD*, the absence of *RO* leads to the absence of the outcome ∼*PC* and, vice versa, in the presence of *RO*, the absence of *PD* also leads to the absence of ∼*PC*. In addition, the same must hold for the causal mechanism: taking away one of the conjuncts while keeping the other present – either counterfactually or via a comparative SMMR design – must lead to the absence of the mechanism. Otherwise, the conjunct is not causal. In the current example by Haesebrouck and Van Immerseel (2020), in which the mechanism consists of two elements, that mechanism is expected to not trigger the outcome if one or both elements are not present.

4.3 The Solutions

The challenge posed by conjunctions affects only those SMMR designs that aim at causal inference. The requirement of making a difference does not apply to model-refining descriptive inference SMMR designs. The solution to this challenge consists in disentangling the conjunction and performing tests on each of its conjuncts. We need to test whether one conjunct makes a difference to the mechanism, "holding constant" the other conjuncts in the conjunction (see also Goertz 2017, chap. 5). In a sense, this amounts to investigating the "N" in INUS condition (Mackie, 1965). It tests whether the conjunct is necessary for triggering the mechanism, that is, whether without that conjunct the mechanism does not occur. Even if *RO* is present, in the absence of *PD* not only outcome ∼*PC* is absent (as shown by the QCA solution), but also M_{PD} and thus M_A are absent. If the within-case analysis reveals this pattern, then *PD* can be deemed a causal conjunct. For this task, four plus two new principles need to be formulated. In combination with the principles already introduced so far, they govern SMMR for causal inference in the presence of conjunctions.

SMMR designs, and why, in the case of contradictory evidence for causal inference at the cross-case and within-case levels, the latter takes precedence over the former.

[3] Or, as Goertz (2017, p. 12) puts it: "The causal mechanism analysis must focus on how X_1 and X_2 together produce Y. At the same time one needs to look at how the absence of X_1 or X_2 prevents Y from occurring."

4.3 The Solutions

4.3.1 Climbing the Ladder of Generality

Before turning to the new principles, I briefly mention the possibility to "turn off conjunctions" by theorizing them away. In Chapter 3, I have already discussed this strategy in the context of turning off equifinality, or disjunctions. The strategy for conjunctions is the same. Researchers can move up on the ladder of generality: define a higher-order concept A as the single-set sufficient condition for the outcome and each conjunct as definitorial necessary and a jointly sufficient component of A. For instance, conjuncts PD and RO could be theorized to be the necessary and jointly sufficient elements of the higher-order concept "appeased opposition" A. We define $A = PD * RO$. Then it is A that is stipulated as the sufficient cause for outcome noncontested deployment decision ($A \Rightarrow {\sim}PC$),[4] and A does so by triggering the mechanism M_A (see Figure 4.2). As with any form of aggregation, this merging of two (or more) conjuncts into a single set comes with loss of information. The difference in membership in PD and RO, respectively, is ignored and by this assumed to be irrelevant for which element of the mechanism is triggered. This price can be paid if one also moves up on the ladder of generality with regard to the mechanism; instead of there being various elements that jointly compose the mechanism, one would ignore this fine-grained distinction and only postulate a more abstract mechanism M_A (see Figure 4.2).

In Chapter 3, I discussed that the aggregation of a disjunction into one single set creates the problem of qualitative heterogeneity among cases in the new set: cases can hold qualitatively different membership scores in the underlying disjuncts. When aggregating conjuncts, as discussed here, such qualitative heterogeneity in the higher-order concept A cannot occur, though: members of A are all members of all underlying conjuncts. There is, however, heterogeneity among *non*members of the new set A. Some hold membership in PD but not RO, for others it is vice versa, and yet others hold membership in neither PD nor RO. It will be crucial to "control for" this heterogeneity of nonmembers when testing the causal properties of a conjunction, and also when that conjunction is not aggregated into a single set. I now discuss this strategy of handling conjunctions in causal inference SMMR designs.

---

[4] Schneider and Makszin (2014) (discussed in further detail in Chapter 5), for instance, subsume various institutional attributes under the label "coordinated welfare regime" and other conjuncts under the higher-order concept "protective welfare regime". Similarly, Schneider (2008) subsumes various conjuncts representing different political–institutional designs under the higher-order concept of "power-sharing political regimes" and other conjuncts under the label "power-dispersing regimes". And Schneider and Maerz (2017) summarize different conjunctions of autocratic regime attributes under the labels "adaptive" and "rigid" authoritarianism.

4.3.2 Additional Principles

Some new terms need to be introduced before discussing the additional principles. In a conjunction of two or more conjuncts, the conjunct that we put at the center of our analysis is called the *focal conjunct (FC)*. The other conjuncts in the conjunction are called *complementary conjuncts (CC)*.[5] A full causal analysis of a conjunction requires that each conjunct in turn is analyzed as the focal conjunct. In the following sections, I discuss each additional principle in further detail. Jointly, these principles, in combination with already existing ones, aim at distilling the effect of specific conjuncts on the mechanism via the purposeful choice of cases for within-case analysis.

Focal Conjunct Principle

In Chapter 3, we learned that the focus of our analysis should be the sufficient term (the disjunct) rather than the entire solution formula (the disjunction). We need to proceed along similar lines in the presence of a conjunction. The focus in causal analysis needs to be on a single condition (the conjunct), rather than the sufficient term as a whole (the conjunction). This can be formulated in the following principle.

Focal conjunct principle: For within-case analysis with the goal of causal inference, perform analyses for each conjunct separately.

As explained, the conjunct at the center of our analysis is the focal conjunct, whereas the remaining conjuncts in the conjunction are summarized under the label of complementary conjuncts. If a conjunction consists of two conjuncts, at least two within-case analyses would need to be performed. In our example, this means one analysis on conjunct *PD* and one on *RO*. I say "at least" because the focal conjunct principle applies to all three SMMR designs that aim at causal inference: the analysis of a single typical case, a comparison of two typical cases, and of a typical with an iir case. With n conjuncts, there are then $3*n$ more possible analyses to be performed, in theory. This increase in within-case analyses needed is logical: the more complex a causal claim is, the more it takes to establish its causal properties.[6]

Focusing on single conjuncts in a conjunction is rather novel in the SMMR literature. Pattyn et al. (2022) suggest a focus on conjunctions (as opposed to single conjuncts) and postulate it as an antidote to mechanismic

---

[5] If there is more than one complementary conjunct, they are summarized using the logical AND.

[6] In the concluding chapter of this book (see especially Section 7.2), I discuss strategies to reduce the number of within-case analyses in applied SMMR.

4.3 The Solutions

heterogeneity because all members of a conjunction must also be members of each conjunct. The latter is true and does, indeed, make the *assumption* of mechanismic homogeneity among cases of the same type (i.e. members of the same (conjunctural) sufficient term), the most plausible assumption. Empirically, however, it can still be that the same conjunction triggers different mechanisms. It therefore seems more appropriate to unpack conjunctions and test if each conjunct triggers the mechanism (or specific elements of it). This is because, as explained previously, in SMMR a cause is defined as a difference maker to the within-case mechanism and that needs to be empirically tested for each conjunct in a conjunction.[7]

iir Focal Conjunct Unique Nonmembership Principle

Once we have established that each conjunct in turn needs to be the focus of an SMMR analysis, the next question is as follows: which cases to choose for the within-case analysis on the causal properties of a conjunct? From the previous chapters, we know that SMMR designs for causal inference must involve at least one typical case (the causal inference selection principle). We have identified three such within-case designs: in a single typical case, in two typical cases, and in a typical–iir case pair. We now need to further differentiate cases within each of the three designs because within the group both of typical and of iir cases analytically relevant differences exist that need to be taken into account if the sufficient term consists of a conjunction.

Let us begin with iir cases. To be able to infer that it is the focal conjunct that makes a difference to the mechanism, we need to choose an iir case that is identical to the typical case except for its membership in the focal conjunct (and the outcome, of course). Ideally, both the iir and the typical case have full membership in the complementary conjuncts. Plus, ideally the iir case is a full nonmember of the focal conjunct, whereas the typical case is a full member of the focal conjunct. The principle can be stated as follows.

Principle of iir focal conjunct (FC) unique nonmembership: In a comparison with a typical case, an iir case should be a nonmember of the focal conjunct and a member of the complementary conjuncts.

Table 4.2 depicts the principle. The typical case, by definition, holds membership scores of >0.5 in the focal conjunct, the complementary conjuncts, and the outcome. This is what we know from our cross-case QCA. Following the test corridor principle (see Section 2.3), which we now need to apply to

---

[7] Pattyn et al. (2022) seem to follow a different definition of a cause that does not require the unpacking of a conjunction into its conjuncts.

the focal conjunct, in the within-case analysis we expect to find that the typical case's membership in the focal conjunct provides the floor and the outcome membership the ceiling for its membership in the mechanism: $FC \leq M \leq Y$.[8]

Table 4.2 *iir FC unique nonmember principle*

iir FC unique nonmember	type	Cross-case known FC	Cross-case known CC	Within-case expected **M**	Cross-case known Y
	Typical	>0.5	>0.5	$FC \leq \mathbf{M} \leq Y$	>0.5
✓	iir$_1$	<0.5	>0.5	$FC \leq \mathbf{M} \leq Y$	<0.5
	iir$_2$	<0.5	<0.5	$FC + CC \leq \mathbf{M} \leq Y$	<0.5

FC: focal conjunct; *CC*: complementary conjuncts; +: logical OR

The iir FC unique nonmembership principle dictates that we match the typical case with an iir case whose membership is <0.5 in the focal conjuncts and >0.5 in the complementary conjuncts. If the focal conjunct is a difference maker for the mechanism *M*, we expect its membership in *FC* to provide the floor for this case's membership in *M*. This scenario is depicted in the second row of Table 4.2 (iir$_1$). If, however, we choose an iir case with membership below 0.5 in both the focal and the complementary conjuncts, then we do not know whether the difference to *M* is caused by the focal or the complementary conjunct. This scenario is depicted in the last row of Table 4.2 (iir$_2$).

To isolate the effect of the focal conjunct, it must be the only qualitative difference between the typical and the iir cases. Neglect of the iir FC unique nonmembership principle leads to comparisons in which both the focal and complementary conjuncts differ between the typical and iir cases. This comparison could be called indeterminate (Rohlfing, 2012) because it is difficult, if not impossible, to tell if the mechanism is absent because the focal conjunct is absent, the complementary conjuncts are absent, or both. Our causal inferences would be unnecessarily uncertain because we cannot tell which of the three possible inferences is correct.

For illustration, take the example by Haesebrouck and Van Immerseel (2020). Imagine we choose the typical case of France's noncontested decision to deploy military to Mali (FRN_Serval), focus on the focal conjunct *RO*, and are given the choice between two iir cases: Germany's contested military deployment decision against Daesh in Iraq (GER_DaeshIr) or in Syria

---
[8] Based on only the information that the typical case's membership in both the focal (*FC*) and complementary (*CC*) conjuncts are above 0.5, one cannot know which of the two provides the minimum in the conjunction, and thus the floor for *M*. For this, we need to introduce the attribution principle (see below).

(GER_DaeshSy). As Table 4.3 shows, only GER_DaeshIr adheres to the iir FC unique nonmembership principle. Its membership in *RO* is below 0.5 (0.05) and in the complementary conjunct *PD* it is above 0.5 (1). GER_DaeshSy, instead, scores below 0.5 in both *RO* (0.05) and *PD* (0.33). The choice of the latter iir case would increase the indeterminacy of the within-case findings because it would be more difficult to establish that the iir case's nonmembership in the mechanism M_{RO} is due to its nonmembership in *RO* rather than *PD*.[9]

Table 4.3 *iir FC unique nonmember principle, example*

iir FC unique nonmember	case	Focal RO	Complementary PD	Outcome $\sim PC$
	FRN_Serval	0.98	1	0.98
✓	GER_DaeshIr	0.05	1	0.01
	GER_DaeshSy	0.05	0.33	0

In a sense, the iir FC unique nonmembership principle mimics Mill's method of difference (Mill, 1874), also often discussed under the label of the most-similar systems design (Przeworski and Teune, 1970). Unlike Mill's method of difference, though, in SMMR we neither have to assume that the focal conjunct is the only cause, nor that there could not be other pathways to the outcome than the conditions used for establishing similarity between the typical and the iir cases. In other words, in SMMR, we are far from assuming additivity and unifinality. From the QCA results that we use for selecting cases in SMMR, we already know if there is a conjunctural and an equifinal pattern. Equifinality is incorporated into SMMR designs via the focal disjunct principle, the unique membership principle, and the unique nonmembership principle (see Chapter 3). And conjunctural causation is accounted for by the four principles introduced in this chapter. SMMR, thus, overcomes well-known inferential shortcomings of Mill's methods.

Attribution Principle and Clean Corridor Principle

The previous principle exclusively applies to iir cases in a comparison with typical cases. It focuses only on the location of the focal and complementary conjuncts above or below the 0.5 qualitative anchor. That is, the principle is

---

[9] I postpone to the next section a discussion of the fact that, in both iir cases, the focal conjunct membership exceeds their membership in the outcome, albeit by only a small margin. In other words, the floor of the test corridor for the mechanism is higher than the ceiling, thus constituting what I call a "broken corridor" scenario (see the excursuses in Sections 2.3 and 4.4).

about differences in kind. The two principles that I present now, in contrast, address differences in degree, and also apply to typical cases. They concern the location of the focal conjunct vis-à-vis the complementary conjuncts and the outcome. These principles work only with fuzzy sets.

In a nutshell, the point will be as follows: if membership in the focal conjunct is smaller than in the complementary conjuncts, then the membership in the mechanism can be attributed to that focal conjunct.

In addition to the focal conjunct FC providing the minimum and thus the floor of the corridor, we also want that corridor to be clean. The test corridor is clean if none of the complementary conjuncts CC is located between the focal conjunct FC and the outcome Y. A clean corridor, thus, looks as follows: $FC \leq Y < CC$. A contaminated corridor, instead, looks as follows: $FC < CC \leq Y$.[10] As a rule, the choice of those iir and typical cases is preferred in which the test corridor is clean.

Clean corridor principle: For causal inference SMMR designs, choose cases with a clean corridor.

With clean corridors, it is more straightforward to attribute the membership in the mechanism M to the focal conjunct FC, an argument I spell out in detail now.

Attribution in iir Cases

In Table 4.2, we have seen that the iir_1 case fulfills the unique FC nonmembership principle whereas case iir_2 does not. However, it could be that while in case iir_2 both the focal and the complementary conjuncts are smaller than 0.5, the focal conjunct still provides the minimum. If so, we could still *attribute* the floor for the mechanism M to the focal conjunct, rather than to any of the complementary conjuncts.

Table 4.4 displays the four different variants of iir cases that can occur with regard to their membership in the focal and the complementary conjuncts. Case iir_1 provides the ideal scenario for causal inference in a comparison with a typical case: it fulfills the iir FC unique nonmember principle and, as a consequence, its membership in the focal conjunct is smaller than in the complementary conjuncts. Therefore, its membership in the mechanism can be attributed to the focal conjunct. Let us condense the notion of attribution into a principle.

---

[10] For a corridor to be contaminated, it is enough that one of the complementary conjuncts falls within the corridor ($FC < CC_1 \leq Y < CC_2$).

4.3 The Solutions

Attribution principle: The typical and iir cases should have their minimum in the focal conjunct.

The attribution principle applies to both typical and iir cases. It requires fuzzy sets because it operates on differences in degrees of membership in the focal and the complementary conjuncts. The attribution principle is fulfilled by design for iir cases whenever the iir FC unique nonmembership principle is fulfilled, as is the case for the iir_1 case in Table 4.4. But the attribution principle can also be fulfilled when the iir FC unique nonmember principle is violated. Case iir_2 in Table 4.4 illustrates this. Even though it scores below 0.5 in the focal *and* the complementary conjuncts, the membership in M can still be attributed to the focal conjunct because it is smaller than in the complementary conjuncts. Stronger inference can be drawn by choosing case iir_1 rather than iir_2, but both are superior to iir_3 and iir_4. The latter two violate the principles that govern SMMR case selection in the presence of conjunctions. Case iir_3, at least, scores below 0.5 in the focal conjunct, but it does not provide the minimum. Case iir_4 is the worst choice for causal inference on the focal conjunct because it scores above 0.5 in the focal conjunct.

Table 4.4 *iir Case: Unique FC nonmember and attribution principles*

			Principles		
	FC	CC	iir FC unique nonmember	Attribution	FC nonmember
iir_1	<0.5	>0.5	✓	✓	✓
iir_2	min	<0.5		✓	✓
iir_3	<0.5	min			✓
iir_4	>0.5				

min: minimum value across conjuncts; FC: focal conjunct; CC: complementary conjuncts

Because the various possible constellations between the focal and the complementary conjuncts are crucial for understanding the iir FC unique nonmember principle, the attribution principle, and the clean corridor principle, it is worth visualizing the information depicted in Table 4.4. Figure 4.3 shows such a visualization. The solid circle represents the focal conjunct. The complementary conjuncts are represented by the gray-shaded circles. Some single complementary conjuncts are represented by hollow small circles. For case iir_1, the focal conjunct sits alone in the upper triangle in the lower-left quadrant, thus fulfilling all three principles: attribution, iir FC unique nonmembership, and clean corridor. For case iir_2, all conjuncts are below the

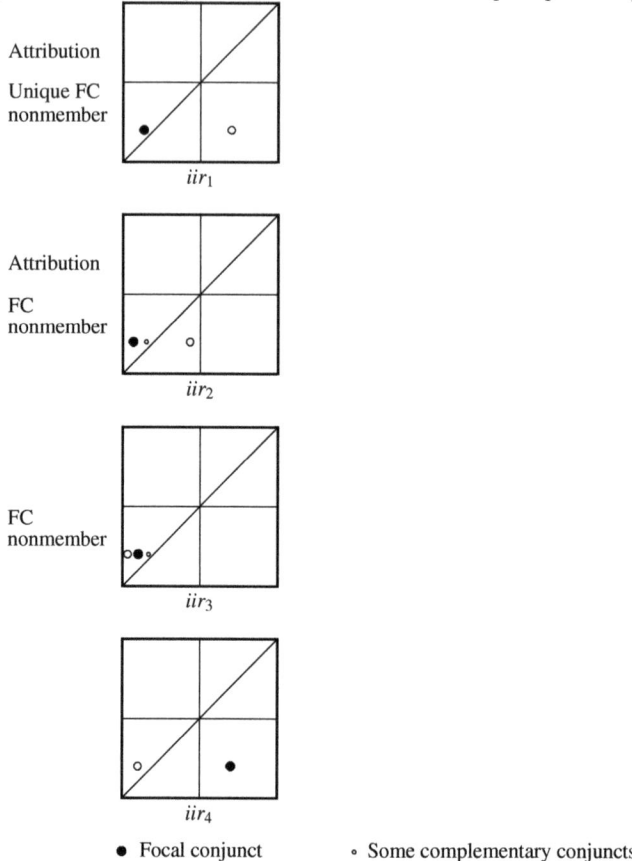

Figure 4.3 iir case: unique FC nonmember and attribution principle – XY plots

• Focal conjunct ∘ Some complementary conjuncts
o Conjunction of complementary conjuncts

0.5 anchor, but at least the focal conjunct provides the minimum, thus fulfilling the attribution principle. For case iir_2, we can distinguish two scenarios: a clean corridor in which membership in all complementary conjuncts is higher than in the outcome and a contaminated corridor in which membership in one or more complementary conjuncts is smaller than in the outcome. In SMMR, clean corridors are preferred.

For case iir_3, the complementary conjuncts provide the minimum, but at least the focal conjunct is below the 0.5 anchor, thus fulfilling the weak principle of FC nonmembership (see Section 4.4). Also for case iir_3, we can distinguish between clean and contaminated corridors and prefer the selection of cases with clean corridors. Case iir_4 represents the worst choice, as none

4.3 The Solutions

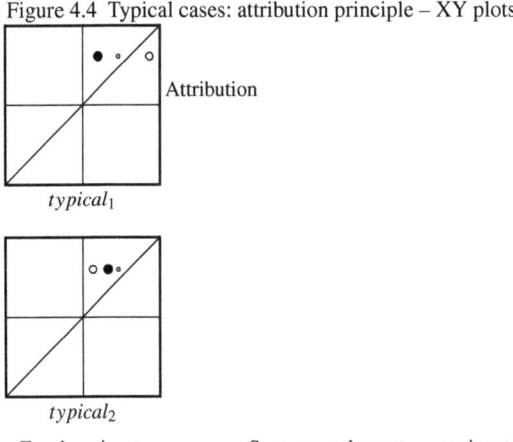

Figure 4.4 Typical cases: attribution principle – XY plots

● Focal conjunct   ○ Some complementary conjuncts
○ Conjunction of complementary conjuncts

of the principles is fulfilled and the focal conjunct is inconsistent with the statement of sufficiency.[11]

As mentioned, the clean corridor and the attribution principles require the use of fuzzy sets. With crisp sets, the four scenarios depicted in Figure 4.3 collapse into three: either the focal conjunct provides the minimum (iir_1), it jointly provides the minimum together with the complementary conjuncts (iir_2 and iir_3), or it does not provide the minimum (iir_4).

Clean Corridor and Attribution in Typical Cases

As mentioned, the clean corridor and attribution principles apply to both iir and typical cases. In a typical case, the membership score in the mechanism can be attributed to the focal conjunct, if a typical case is chosen whose membership in the focal conjunct is smaller than in the complementary conjuncts. And a corridor is clean if no complementary conjunct falls between the case's membership scores in the focal conjunct and the outcome. Table 4.5 and Figure 4.4 show the two scenarios: either the focal conjunct provides the minimum ($typical_1$) or it does not ($typical_2$). In both scenarios the corridor can be clean or contaminated, as illustrated by the small marker for more complementary conjuncts in Figure 4.4. For typical cases, there can, thus, be only two constellations between focal and complementary conjuncts instead of four for iir cases. This is because, for typical cases, no conjunct, by definition, can be below 0.5.

---

[11] In the excursus in Section 4.4 and Chapter 6, I discuss scenarios in which a condition exceeds the outcome membership under the label of necessary conjuncts.

When identifying the best available typical case in a data set, scenario 1 is classified as "rank 1" and scenario 2 as "rank 2". For causal inference, typical cases from rank 1 are preferred over cases from rank 2. For both ranks, a clean corridor is preferred. For rank 1, this implies that membership in the complementary conjuncts exceeds that in the outcome ($FC < Y < CC$). For rank 2, this only means that no complementary conjunct falls between the focal conjunct and the outcome ($CC < FC \leq Y$).[12] By necessity, one and the same typical case can only be of rank 1 with regard to one focal conjunct. For the other focal conjuncts, it will have to be rank 2. This is why a *single* typical case study on a conjunction will have to fail the attribution principle by design. Strictly speaking, then, the causal properties of a conjunction cannot be empirically tested in one single case. It is necessary to analyze more than one case or pair of cases.

Table 4.5 *Rank order of possible membership constellations between the focal conjunct and complementary conjuncts in a single typical case*

Rank	Attribution principle Typical $FC < CC$
1	✓
2	

Table 4.6 shows the four possible scenarios in which two typical cases can be matched, and ranks them from highest to lowest in terms of usefulness for causal inference on the focal conjunct. Case pairs in rank 1 consist of two typical cases, both of which fulfill the attribution principle. Rank 2 matches two typical cases in which the more typical case (according to Formula 2.4) fulfills the attribution principle and the less typical case does not. For rank 3, it is vice versa: the more typical case does not and the less typical does fulfill the attribution principle,[13] whereas case pairs in rank 4 consist of two typical cases of which none displays a lower membership in the focal conjunct than in the complementary conjuncts. Within each rank, cases with a clean corridor are preferred.

---

[12] In rank 1 the focal conjunct and in rank 2 the complementary conjuncts are consistent by definition, otherwise the case in question would not qualify as a typical case but would be a deviant consistency case in degree. In both ranks, however, it can happen that either the focal or the complementary conjunct is located above the diagonal. In rank 1, we prefer cases with $FC < Y$ & $CC > Y$. In rank 2, we prefer cases with $FC < Y$ & $CC < Y$.

[13] The difference between ranks 2 and 3 is therefore minimal and they could be treated as de facto the same.

Table 4.6 *Rank order of possible membership constellations between the focal conjunct and complementary conjuncts in a comparison of two typical cases*

Rank	Attribution principle	
	Typical 1 $FC < CC$	Typical 2 $FC < CC$
1	✓	✓
2	✓	
3		✓
4		

Why would one ever want to choose cases or case pairs of ranks lower than 1? The question is not whether one would want to choose lower rank cases, but rather whether one is constrained to do so due to the lack of alternatives. In a given data set, there simply might not be (pairs of) cases in rank 1 for each focal conjunct. In such a situation, one should choose cases from the highest rank available in the data at hand. The rank provides information on the constellation of membership scores in the focal and complementary conjuncts (and the outcome) and thus helps to identify in which ways causal inference is limited when choosing cases from lower ranks.

The clean corridor and attribution principles do not apply when only crisp sets are used in the QCA. When choosing a single typical case or two typical cases, there are, therefore, no ranks.[14]

Clean Corridor and Attribution in a Comparison of Typical and iir Cases

If we combine the ranking based on the attribution principle in Table 4.5 with the iir FC unique nonmember principle shown in Table 4.4, we arrive at a ranking of all possible scenarios for matching a typical and an iir case. This ranking system is displayed in Table 4.7 and visualized in Figure 4.5. The left column in Figure 4.5 shows the four possible constellations in an iir case and the right column the two scenarios in a typical case. The eight ranks from Table 4.7 are displayed on the lines that link an iir case on the left side of Figure 4.5 with a typical case constellation on the right side of the same figure. In addition, the clean corridor principle is visualized by distinguishing two scenarios for complementary conjuncts within four of the six XY plots in Figure 4.5. The small hollow markers represent complementary conjuncts that contaminate the corridor.

---

[14] The smmr() function will return value rank = 2 (single typical case) and 4 (pair of two typical cases), reflecting the fact that membership in M cannot be attributed to the focal conjunct.

Table 4.7 *Rank order of possible membership constellations between the focal and complementary conjuncts in a comparison of typical and iir cases in a sufficient conjunction*

Rank	iir FC unique nonmember principle		Attribution principle	
	Yes $FC < 0.5 < CC$	No $FC < 0.5$	Typical $FC < CC$	iir $FC < 0.5$ & $FC < CC$
1	✓	✓	✓	✓
2	✓	✓		✓
3		✓	✓	✓
4		✓	✓	
5		✓		✓
6		✓		
7			✓	
8				

FC: focal conjunct; CC: complementary conjuncts
Source: adapted from Schneider and Rohlfing (2019).

Case pairs in rank 1 fulfill both the iir FC unique nonmember principle and the attribution principle for both cases.[15] In addition, the clean corridor principle is fulfilled by design in the iir case. Case pairs in rank 8 do not fulfill any principle, plus the focal conjunct in the iir case is above the 0.5 anchor. For case pairs in rank 2, the iir case is in line with all three principles, but the typical case fails the attribution principle. In rank 3, both case types fulfill the attribution principle, but the iir case fails the FC unique nonmember principle while the focal conjunct is at least below the 0.5 anchor. In both cases the corridor can be clean or contaminated. For case pairs in both ranks 4 and 5, the iir case violates the FC unique nonmember principle, but at least either the typical case (rank 4) or the iir case (rank 5) fulfill the attribution principle. If both of them violate the attribution principle, then a case pair is in rank 6. If, on top of this, the iir case does not score below 0.5 in the focal conjunct, case pairs are in rank 7 if at least the typical case fulfills the attribution principle. In general, within each rank, clean corridors are preferred.[16]

The adequacy for causal inference differs enormously between case pairs in ranks that are far apart. Choosing cases from rank 1, 2, or 3 really is a big difference to case pairs from the ranks at the bottom. The differences between ranks in the middle of the scale are less drastic; in applied SMMR, there can be good nonmethodological reasons – such as familiarity with the case or ease

---

[15] Case pairs in rank 1, thus, adhere to the recommendation of Lijphart (1971, p. 687) to choose cases that score differently on the variable of interest and similarly on other variables.

[16] Contaminated corridors can occur in both cases in any of the eight ranks, except for the iir case in ranks 1 and 2, in which, by definition, the complementary conjuncts are located above 0.5.

Figure 4.5 Rank order of typical and iir case pairs for focal conjuncts in sufficient conjunctions

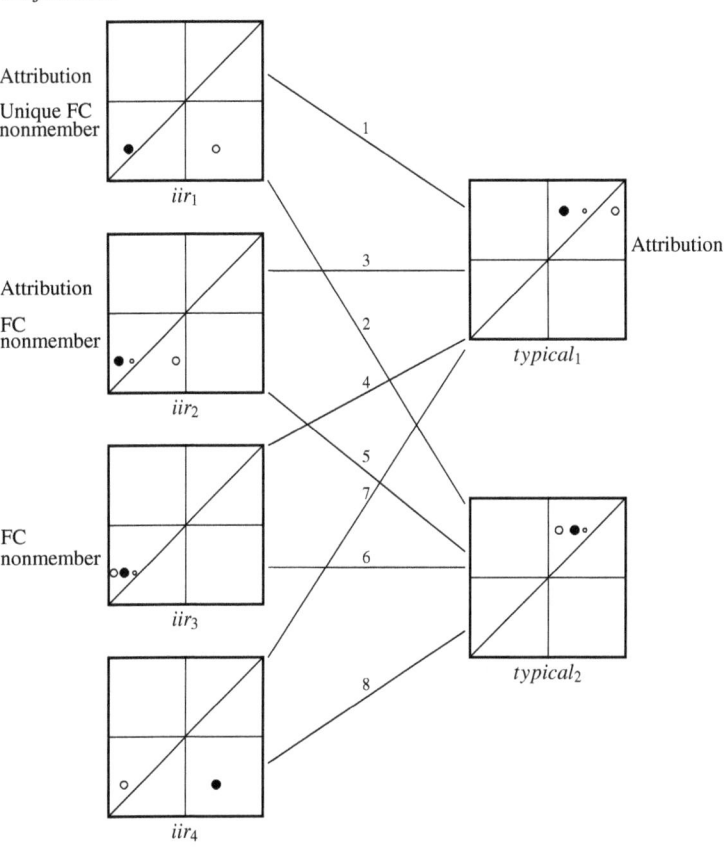

- ● Focal conjunct   ◦ Some complementary conjuncts
- o Conjunction of complementary conjuncts

of data access – to choose cases from somewhat lower ranks.[17] Even then, information on ranks still plays an important role: for any given choice of cases, it expresses which principles for a more determinate causal inference are violated. Luckily, most of the time, in applied SMMR pairs from high ranks are available, often also from the highest rank and for most of the focal conjuncts.

In a crisp-set QCA, because the attribution principle does not work, the number of ranks is limited to three (ranks 2, 6, and 8): ranks 1–2 in Figure

---

[17] In Section 7.2, I provide further reflections on applied SMMR.

4.5 are collapsed into rank 2, ranks 3–6 into rank 6, and ranks 7 and 8 into rank 8.

4.3.3 Additional Formulas

With the additional principles in place that govern the choice of cases in the presence of conjunctions, I can now present the remaining formulas for identifying the best available (pairs of) cases in any given data set. Because the implications of conjunctions affect only SMMR designs that aim at causal inference, the three remaining formulas to be presented are for the within-case analysis of a single typical case (Formula 4.1), the matching of a typical and an iir case (Formula 4.2), and the comparative analysis of two typical cases (Formula 4.3). They refine Formulas 2.4. 2.7, and 2.8 and make them fit for handling conjunctions.

As for all other SMMR formulas, also for the new ones, lower values indicate better choices for within-case analysis. All relevant principles are integrated either in the formulas themselves, the ranking system, or the information if the corridor is clean or not. The formula values are used to distinguish between (pairs of) cases in the same rank. This means that better ranks trump better formula values, but within the same rank, lower (i.e. better) formula values trump higher values. Applying the formulas makes sense only if fuzzy sets are used.

The best available typical case is the one whose values in the focal conjunct (FC) and the outcome (Y) are as similar as possible (test corridor principle) and whose membership in the sufficient term (S) is high. This formula is very similar to the one introduced previously (Formula 2.4). The only difference is that the corridor is now established with regard to the focal conjunct rather than the entire term.[18]

$$TYP = \underbrace{(2 * |Y - FC|)}_{\text{small corridor focal conjunct}} + \underbrace{(1 - S)}_{\text{large membership in term}} \quad (4.1)$$

The formula for identifying the best-matching pair of a typical and an iir case applies the test corridor principle to both cases. Furthermore, the greater the difference between both cases in terms of membership in the focal conjunct

---

[18] Note that in this and the other two formulas for causal inference SMMR designs, we take the absolute difference, rather than the difference, between a case's membership in the outcome and the focal conjunct. This makes the formulas applicable also in scenarios in which membership in the necessary focal conjunct is higher than in the outcome (see the excursuses in Sections 2.4 and 4.4).

and the outcome, the better. Likewise, the greater the similarity between them in terms of membership in the complementary conjuncts (*CC*), the better.

$$\begin{aligned}
TYP - IIR = &\; [1 - (FC_{TYP} - FC_{IIR})] && \text{\small large difference in focal conjunct} \\
&+ [1 - (Y_{TYP} - Y_{IIR})] && \text{\small large difference in outcome} \\
&+ |CC_{TYP} - CC_{IIR}| && \text{\small small difference in complementary conjuncts} \\
&+ 2 * |Y_{TYP} - FC_{TYP}| && \text{\small small corridor for typical case} \\
&+ |Y_{IIR} - FC_{IIR}| && \text{\small small corridor for iir case}
\end{aligned} \quad (4.2)$$

The formula for identifying the best-matching pair of two typical cases is identical, except for the mathematical adjustment to the fact that the differences in focal conjunct and outcome memberships between two typical cases can, by design, be only half as big as between a typical and an iir case.

$$\begin{aligned}
TYP_1 - TYP_2 = &\; [0.5 - (FC_{TYP_1} - FC_{TYP_2})] && \text{\small large difference in focal conjunct} \\
&+ [0.5 - (Y_{TYP_1} - Y_{TYP_2})] && \text{\small large difference in outcome} \\
&+ |(CC_{TYP_1} - CC_{TYP_2})| && \text{\small small difference in complementary conjuncts} \\
&+ 2 * |Y_{TYP_1} - FC_{TYP_1}| && \text{\small small corridor for typical case 1} \\
&+ 2 * |Y_{TYP_2} - FC_{TYP_2}| && \text{\small small corridor for typical case 2}
\end{aligned} \quad (4.3)$$

All formulas equally apply to necessary INUS conditions, a topic I turn to in the next section.

4.4 Excursus: Focal Conjuncts Inconsistent with Sufficiency Claims, or How to Handle *Necessary* INUS Conditions

So far, I have largely disregarded whether or not a case's membership in the focal conjunct is smaller than in the outcome, that is, whether or not the focal conjunct is in line with a statement of sufficiency. However, in a sufficient conjunction, one or more, but not all, conjuncts *can* be bigger than the outcome – as long as at least one conjunct is smaller than the outcome. This is because a case's membership in a conjunction is determined by the conjunct with the smallest value, and as long as there is at least one conjunct with a value smaller than a case's membership in the outcome, the conjunction fulfills the criterion of sufficiency – regardless of how high the membership scores in the other conjuncts are.

Focal conjuncts that exceed a case's membership in the outcome are candidates for being *necessary* conjuncts. For this, the conjunct in question needs to pass all relevant tests of necessity (Schneider, 2018). It is perhaps even more adequate to put it the other way around. Whenever a researcher identifies a necessary condition, that condition must be part of all sufficient conjunctions. In fact, procedures such as the updated two-step QCA approaches (Schneider, 2019) even produce, by default, such necessary INUS conjuncts and SMMR needs to be equipped for handling them.

For empirical illustration, take the study by Schneider et al. (2010) on the conditions of export success in the high-tech industry sector (*EXPORT*). Based on their data, condition "large stock market size" (*STOCK*) does (barely) pass the empirical criteria for being a necessary condition (consistency 0.891, relevance of necessity 0.628, coverage 0.719). The sufficiency analysis yields the three sufficient terms shown in Table 4.8. This is the enhanced[19] most parsimonious solution in which the necessary condition *STOCK* is an INUS condition in all three sufficient terms. I return to this example in the applied SMMR Section 4.5.

Table 4.8 *Sufficient conditions, outcome "high-tech export success" EXPORT*

	inclS	PRI	covS	covU
~EMP*OCCUP*STOCK	0.863	0.668	0.319	0.008
BARGAIN*UNI*STOCK	0.796	0.665	0.497	0.183
~OCCUP*STOCK*~MA	0.890	0.788	0.374	0.149
Solution	0.798	0.696	0.708	

STOCK: big stock market size; *EMP*: high employment protection; *OCCUP*: a lot of occupational training; *BARGAIN*: high collective bargaining; *MA*: a lot of mergers and acquisitions

For the moment, let us talk about necessary INUS conditions in abstract terms. Figure 4.6 displays the possible constellations of focal and complementary conjuncts in iir and typical cases if and when membership in the focal conjunct exceeds membership in the outcome. The solid marker represents the focal conjunct and the other markers the complementary conjuncts, subdivided into the conjunction of complementary conjuncts (gray-shaded) and a single complementary conjunct in that conjunction (small hollow circle). Based on this graphical visualization it is easier to explain how and why some of the SMMR principles and the rank order need to be adapted if and when

---

[19] For the enhanced standard analysis (ESA), see Schneider and Wagemann (2012), and for the use of the esa() function, see Oana and Schneider (2018). There is model ambiguity. I report here the first of the two models.

4.4 Excursus: Necessary INUS Conditions

researchers focus on a necessary conjunct in a sufficient conjunction. Later on, I dedicate all of Chapter 6 to SMMR based on necessity claims.

When investigating necessary conjuncts it is required that the FC provides the *maximum* within the conjunction rather than the minimum as in the attribution principle for sufficient conjuncts introduced above.

Attribution principle for necessity: The typical and iir cases should have their maximum in the focal conjunct.

By pure logic, if the focal conjunct provides the maximum, as required by the attribution principle for necessity, then the principle of iir FC *unique* nonmembership cannot be fulfilled. This principle – required in the comparative causal inference SMMR design matching a typical and an iir case – therefore needs to be slightly modified when dealing with necessary (INUS) conditions.

Principle of iir focal conjunct (FC) nonmembership for necessity: In a comparison with a typical case, an iir case should be a nonmember of the focal conjunct.

The principle requires the choice of iir cases that are nonmembers of the focal conjunct because the test of necessity consists in checking whether, in the absence of the necessary focal conjunct, the mechanism is absent, too. This is a weaker requirement than the original iir FC *unique* nonmember principle because it cannot any longer be required that the iir case has membership below 0.5 in *only* the focal conjunct. The left column in Figure 4.6 visualizes the trade-off between the focal conjunct providing the maximum and it being the only conjunct below 0.5.

How does the *test corridors principle* work for a sufficient conjunction if and when $FC > Y$? The short answer is that the test corridor remains in place: a case's membership in FC and Y should be as similar as possible. The only adaptation to necessary conjuncts is that the floor and ceiling are inverted. A case's membership in Y constitutes the floor and in the FC the ceiling.

Likewise, the *clean corridor* principle also still applies. This means, a case's membership in the complementary conjuncts should not fall in between its memberships in the focal conjunct and the outcome. In Figure 4.6 the difference between clean and contaminated corridors is visualized by the possible presence of one or more complementary conjunct(s), represented by the small circled markers. Scenarios with clean corridors are preferred over contaminated corridor scenarios.

114   Conjunctions $A * B \Rightarrow Y$

Figure 4.6 Rank order of typical and iir case pairs for necessary conjunct in sufficient conjunction

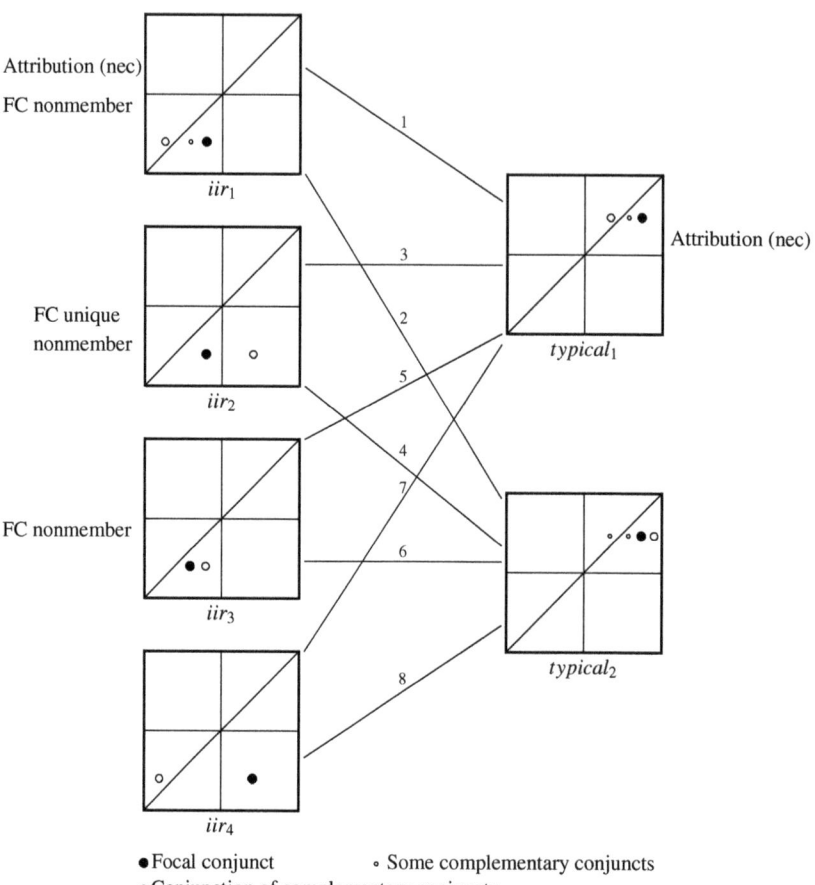

- Focal conjunct   ∘ Some complementary conjuncts
- Conjunction of complementary conjuncts

What do these adapted principles mean for the rank order of best available pairs of typical and iir cases? As Figure 4.6 shows, there are eight ranks. In a typical case, two constellations are possible, in which the focal conjunct exceeds membership in the outcome. In one, the focal conjunct presents the maximum ($typical_1$), thus fulfilling the attribution principle for necessity. In the second scenario, a complementary conjunct provides the maximum ($typical_2$).[20]

---

[20] For scenario 2 to occur, the sufficient conjunction must consist of at least three conjuncts because at least one conjunct must be smaller than the case's membership in the outcome. If *all* complementary conjuncts of the sufficient conjunction X exceeded the outcome membership, the case would cease to be a typical case and turn into a deviant consistency case in degree for the sufficiency statement $X \Rightarrow Y$.

4.4 Excursus: Necessary INUS Conditions

For the iir case, four different scenarios are possible: the focal conjunct either provides the maximum or it does not. In case of the former, it can either be below 0.5 membership (iir_1 in Figure 4.6), thus fulfilling the attribution for necessity principle, or above 0.5 (iir_4). In the case of the former, the focal conjunct can be the only conjunct below 0.5 (iir_2), thus fulfilling the FC unique membership principle, or not (iir_3). The small circle markers represent contaminated corridors. Within each rank, clean corridors are preferred over contaminated corridors.

Rank 1 matches the typical case with an iir case in which the focal conjunct provides the maximum in both cases. The attribution principle for necessity and the iir FC nonmembership principle for necessity are fulfilled.[21] In rank 2, the attribution principle for necessity is fulfilled only in the iir case. In rank 3, the iir FC unique nonmember principle and the attribution principle in the typical case are fulfilled. In rank 4, the latter principle is not fulfilled. In ranks 5 and 6, the weaker iir FC nonmember principle is fulfilled (with attribution in the typical case for rank 5), whereas ranks 7 and 8 provide weak grounds for causal inference because, even though the focal conjunct provides the maximum, it does so by exceeding the 0.5 qualitative membership threshold.

The updated rank system for single typical cases and for pairs of two typical cases are now easier to explain and understand. Let us focus on only the right-hand side of Figure 4.6. We see that in typical cases only two possible scenarios exist: either the attribution principle for necessity is fulfilled or it is not. In both scenarios the corridor can be clean or not, but this information is provided separately rather than being incorporated into the rank system. For the single-typical case SMMR design on necessary INUS conditions, rank 1 denotes that the attribution principle for necessity is fulfilled, rank 2 that it is not fulfilled. In the SMMR design matching two typical cases, the rank system is as follows: attribution principle for necessity is fulfilled in both typical cases (rank 1), only in the more typical case (rank 2), only in the less typical case (rank 3), and in none of the two cases (rank 4).

***

In the excursus in Section 2.4, I discussed the various empirical scenarios in which a case's membership in mechanism M can be located vis-à-vis its membership scores in the sufficient condition and the outcome. I explained that, next to a sufficiency chain, also the two broken corridor scenarios – a nec-suf chain and a suf-nec chain – can be causally interpreted. Only one scenario rules out that the sufficient condition is causal for the mechanism.

---

[21] Preferably, in this constellation, the focal conjunct is the only conjunct that exceeds the case's membership in the outcome (that is, only the *FC* is located above the diagonal), and therefore keeps the corridor clean.

How does this work when the INUS condition is necessary for the outcome? Applied researchers can also be confronted with four scenarios here vis-à-vis the location of mechanism M in the context of a necessary conjunct ($FC \Leftarrow Y$). Figure 4.7 shows the three causally interpretable scenarios ($M_1 - M_3$) and a fourth one (M_4) that indicates that the mechanism is not causal.

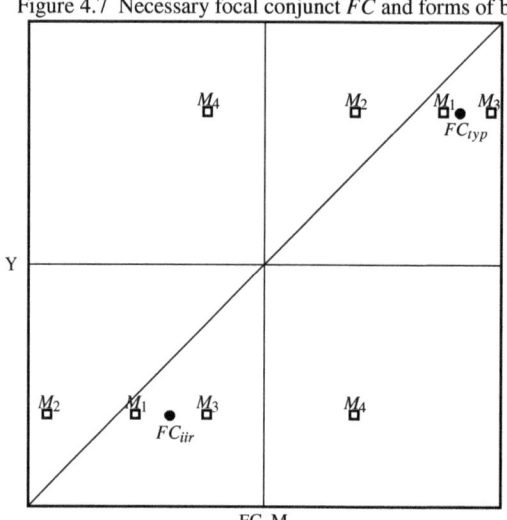

Figure 4.7 Necessary focal conjunct FC and forms of broken corridors M

- Cross-case condition
- Within-case mechanism: M_1 necessity chain; M_2 "broken floor (Y)" ("nec-suf chain"); M_3 "broken ceiling (FC)" ("suf-nec chain"); M_4 noncausal

First, the researcher might find arguments for a necessity chain: $FC \Leftarrow M_1 \Leftarrow Y$. If a necessity chain is postulated, the within-case test consists of verifying whether the case's membership in M falls inside the corridor formed by FC and Y. Mechanisms M_1 in Figure 4.7 is in line with such a necessity chain.

A second possibility is that the researcher, based on theory, postulates a "nec-suf chain" as discussed in Section 2.4. With a focal conjunct deemed necessary for Y ($FC \Leftarrow Y$), such a broken floor corridor[22] has the form of $FC \Leftarrow M_2 \Rightarrow Y$. Mechanism M_2 depicts such a scenario. Or, third, the researcher has theoretical reasons to expect a "suf-nec chain". In the context of a necessary FC, such a broken ceiling corridor[23] looks as follows: $FC \Rightarrow M_3 \Leftarrow Y$. In Figure 4.7, M_3 represents such a scenario.[24]

---

[22] If $FC > Y$ and $M_2 < Y$, then $FC > M_2$, hence no floor for M_2.
[23] If $FC > Y$ and $FC < M_3$, then $M_3 > Y$, hence no ceiling for M_3.
[24] Mahoney et al. (2009) provide interpretations of all logically possible sequences between three sets, including the three scenarios with $FC > Y$ described here. Even though not framed

4.4 Excursus: Necessary INUS Conditions

Each of the three locations of M (M_1, M_2, M_3) is in line with one of the possible scenarios that are causally interpretable. Only if M is located on the wrong side of the qualitative anchor, as represented by M_4, can this particular mechanism be discarded as the causal mechanism that underpins the cross-case relation of necessity $FC \Leftarrow Y$. Wrong side means below 0.5 for the typical case and above 0.5 for the iir case. In Chapter 5, I provide empirical illustrations of the different scenarios for the location of M vis-à-vis FC and Y.

***

What follows from this for applied researchers? I suggest as a hard rule that if there are cases with consistent focal conjuncts and others with inconsistent focal conjuncts, the latter should be chosen only if this focal conjunct has passed the test of necessity (Schneider, 2018). The test corridor and the clean corridor principles still fully apply if a necessity chain is tested. And even for the two broken corridor scenarios, choosing cases with similar memberships in FC and Y is recommended because it increases the expected importance of M for both cross-case level sets (see Mahoney et al., 2009 and the excursus in Section 2.4 on this point).[25] Whichever relation is hypothesized – necessity chain (inverted corridor), broken ceiling, or broken floor – it must be hypothesized to be in place in all cases in a specific comparative SMMR design, that is, in both the typical and the iir cases or in both typical cases. If, for instance, a hypothesized necessity chain is verified in the typical case but not the iir case, then empirical support for the hypothesis is weakened.

In conclusion, note that the phenomenon of sufficient conjunctions that contain conjuncts that are inconsistent with the statement of sufficiency can occur only with fuzzy sets. With crisp (or multi-value) sets, in a typical case all conjuncts in a sufficient conjunction are in line with the statement of sufficiency. In fact, researchers with too little faith in the fine-grained differences of the fuzzy-set membership scores in FC and Y could simply forgo this information and treat both membership scores as identical,[26] or even treat both as crisp sets. The task of the within-case analysis would then simply be

---

in terms of cross-case conditions and within-case mechanisms, their discussion helps further illuminating scenarios that researchers can encounter in SMMR.

[25] Mahoney et al. (2009) also argue that both the suf-nec and the nec-suf chain contextualize the $FC \Leftarrow Y$ relation.

[26] Very small inconsistencies can often be interpreted as being in the realm of measurement error or simply too small to reflect any meaningful conceptual difference. In both scenarios such very small inconsistencies could be ignored and the membership scores in FC and Y be treated as identical. In Section 7.2.6, I further dwell on the consequences of different set types and levels of coarseness of fuzzy sets for SMMR.

118 Conjunctions $A * B \Rightarrow Y$

to find out whether or not M is present as well.[27] Such a strategy would make the formulas superfluous that I have introduced in Section 4.3.3.

Core Points 4.1: Conjunctions

- Conjunctions require refinements for causal inference SMMR designs and leave model-refining SMMR designs unaffected
- A distinction between focal and complementary conjuncts is needed
- Case selection in the presence of conjunctions requires four additional principles: focal conjunct principle, iir focal conjunct unique nonmembership principle, attribution principle, and clean corridor principle
- More conjuncts, and thus more complex solution formulas, require more within-case analyses
- The new principles are incorporated in formulas and rank orders for identifying the best available (pairs of) cases for those SMMR designs that aim at causal inference: the within-case analysis of one typical case, a comparison of two typical cases, and a comparison of a typical and an iir case
- Ranks denote which principles are fulfilled by a given (pair of) case(s)
- The more principles are fulfilled, the more determinate is the causal inference
- If convincing theoretical and conceptual arguments exist, conjunctions can be theorized away by moving up the ladder of generality, thus subsuming multiple conjuncts under a single set
- To handle necessary INUS conditions, two slightly altered versions of existing principles are needed: the attribution principle for necessity and the principle of iir focal conjunct nonmembership
- Only minor adjustments to some principles and the rank system are needed to properly handle INUS conditions that are necessary for the outcome

---

4.5 Applying SMMR

I demonstrate the use of SMMR in the presence of conjunctions using as an example the modified version of the study by Haesebrouck and Van Immerseel

[27] It would collapse the three scenarios M_1–M_3 in Figure 4.7 and contrast them with scenario M_4.

4.5 Applying SMMR

(2020) introduced above. Later, I use the example by Schneider et al. (2010) to illustrate the handling of necessary INUS conditions.

With code C 4.1, we obtain the truth table and most parsimonious solution for outcome "no political contestation" ($\sim PC$), shown in output O 4.1. We learn that the conjunction of not being a potentially divisive operation (PD) and the presence of a right-leaning opposition (RO) is sufficient for the lack of political contestation of a military deployment decision. None of the two conjuncts qualifies as a necessary condition on its own. As discussed above, consistency is at acceptable levels, whereas coverage is modest: barely 50% of the membership scores in the outcome are explained.[28]

Even though conjunctions affect only the causal inference designs of SMMR, I also show the implementation of model-refining, descriptive inference SMMR designs. This not only helps in getting accustomed to the R code and the output it produces, but is particularly warranted in situations in which solution coverage is relatively low.

C 4.1

```
TT_yn <- truthTable(data = HAES.d, outcome = "~PC",
                    conditions = c("PD", "HR", "PI","PF", "RO", "GP"),
                    incl.cut = 0.75,
                    show.cases = TRUE,
                    complete = FALSE,
                    sort.by = c("OUT", "incl"))
TT_yn

sol_nyp <- minimize(TT_yn,
                    include = "?",
                    details = TRUE)
sol_nyp
```

O 4.1

```
M1: PD*RO -> ~PC
```

		inclS	PRI	covS	covU
1	PD*RO	0.839	0.800	0.517	–
	M1	0.839	0.800	0.517	

4.5.1 Descriptive Inference SMMR

As already learned, a QCA model can be refined by identifying a disjunct missing from the solution formula or a conjunct missing from a term. The

---
[28] Because there is just one sufficient term, the raw coverage of this term is also the solution coverage.

lower the solution coverage, the more arguments there are for searching for one or more disjuncts that are missing from the solution formula. Likewise, the lower the consistency of a term, the more arguments there are for searching for a conjunct missing from that term.

Identifying Omitted Disjuncts

In our example, solution coverage is rather low (0.517), visualized by the many cases in the upper-left quadrant in the XY plot in Figure 4.1. We therefore start with SMMR designs aiming at identifying omitted disjuncts. There are two such designs. We can either opt for a single within-case study of a deviant coverage case or compare this case with an appropriate iir case. Code C 4.2 implements the single-case SMMR design. Because there are many deviant coverage cases, output O 4.2 displays a long list. Following the truth table row principle (see Chapter 2), cases are sorted into the truth table row to which they belong. Within each truth table row, the best available deviant coverage case is identified using Formula 2.1. We see that the set of deviant coverage cases is quite heterogeneous. They populate twelve different truth table rows. Several rows contain just one deviant coverage case, such as, for instance, SLK_Sophia in row 001111 or FRN_DaeshSyr in row 010010. Other rows contain several cases, for instance, row 101100, for which DK_Leb is listed as the best available deviant coverage case for within-case analysis. It is not the most deviant coverage case – according to Formula 2.1 this is FIN_Atalanta – but its row membership is consistent (column TT<=Y), namely, smaller than its outcome membership, whereas for FIN_Atalanta it is not.

C 4.2

```
dcov <- smmr(results = sol_nyp,
             outcome = "~PC",
             match = FALSE,
             cases = 4)
dcov
```

O 4.2

Deviant Coverage Cases :

	Case	Sol	TT_PD	TT_HR	TT_PI	TT_PF	TT_RO	TT_GP	TT_row	Outcome	TT<=Y	Best	MostDCOV
24	SLK_Sophia	0.130	0	0	1	1	1	1	0.570	0.876	TRUE	0.430	TRUE
15	FRN_DaeshSyr	0.330	0	1	0	0	1	0	0.670	0.935	TRUE	0.330	TRUE
21	GER_Kosovo	0.002	0	1	1	1	0	0	0.569	0.819	TRUE	0.431	TRUE
3	DK_DaeshSyr	0.330	0	1	0	0	1	0	0.670	0.824	TRUE	0.330	TRUE
5	DK_Kosovo	0.400	0	1	1	1	0	0	0.600	0.687	TRUE	0.400	FALSE
11	ESP_Sophia	0.041	1	0	1	0	0	0	0.707	0.921	TRUE	0.293	TRUE
8	ESP_DaeshIr	0.041	1	0	0	0	0	0	0.670	0.921	TRUE	0.330	FALSE
9	ESP_EUMali	0.041	1	0	1	0	0	0	0.670	0.907	TRUE	0.330	FALSE
20	GER_EURCA	0.052	1	0	1	0	0	1	0.641	0.710	TRUE	0.359	TRUE
6	DK_Leb	0.099	1	0	1	1	0	0	0.830	0.936	TRUE	0.170	FALSE
22	GER_Serval	0.020	1	0	1	0	0	0	0.806	0.824	TRUE	0.194	FALSE
19	GER_EUMali	0.020	1	0	1	0	0	0	0.670	0.832	TRUE	0.330	FALSE
12	FIN_Atalanta	0.100	1	0	1	1	0	0	0.887	0.866	FALSE	0.113	TRUE
4	DK_Iraq91	0.002	1	0	1	1	0	1	0.683	0.746	TRUE	0.317	TRUE
13	FIN_DaeshIr	0.128	1	0	1	0	0	0	0.670	0.938	TRUE	0.330	FALSE
17	GER_Atalanta	0.057	1	0	1	1	0	0	0.656	0.751	TRUE	0.344	FALSE
14	FIN_KFOR	0.424	1	0	0	0	0	1	0.576	0.935	TRUE	0.424	FALSE
16	FRN_Libya	0.223	1	1	0	1	0	0	0.670	0.898	TRUE	0.330	TRUE
26	UK_Libya	0.069	1	1	0	1	0	0	0.670	0.936	TRUE	0.330	TRUE
23	ITA_Afgh	0.025	1	1	0	1	0	0	0.670	0.898	TRUE	0.330	TRUE
10	ESP_EURCA	0.041	1	1	1	0	0	0	0.767	0.920	TRUE	0.233	TRUE
18	GER_Bosnia	0.031	1	1	1	0	0	0	0.670	0.800	TRUE	0.330	FALSE
25	UK_DaeshIr	0.069	1	1	1	0	0	0	0.670	0.891	TRUE	0.330	FALSE
1	DK_Afgh	0.005	1	1	1	1	0	0	0.670	0.884	TRUE	0.330	FALSE
7	DK_Libya	0.483	1	1	1	1	0	0	0.517	0.950	TRUE	0.483	FALSE
2	DK_Bosnia	0.011	1	1	1	1	0	0	0.909	0.696	FALSE	0.091	TRUE

Rather than counterfactually arguing that adding a conjunct to a given truth table row would make a difference to the occurrence of the outcome and the mechanism, this argument can be subjected to empirical investigation by matching a deviant coverage case with the appropriate iir case. As explained, appropriate means that the iir case must be in the same truth table row as the deviant coverage case. Code C 4.3 identifies, for each relevant truth table row, the best available pair of a deviant coverage and an irr case. The list of such pairs is shown in output O 4.3. Note that there are much fewer deviant coverage–iir case pairs than deviant coverage cases. This is because, out of the 12 truth table rows with deviant coverage cases, only five also contain at least one iir case. In other words, there is more diversity among deviant coverage cases than iir cases.

C 4.3

```
dcoviir <- smmr(results = sol_nyp,
                outcome = "~PC",
                match = TRUE,
                cases = 4)
dcoviir
```

O 4.3

Matching Deviant Coverage–IIR Cases :

	DCOV	IIR	TT_PD	TT_HR	TT_PI	TT_PF	TT_RO	TT_GP	TT_DCV<=Y	Best
1	FRN_DaeshSyr	UK_Iraq03	0	1	0	0	1	0	TRUE	0.946
2	GER_Kosovo	UK_DaeshSy	0	1	1	0	0	0	TRUE	1.081
3	GER_EURCA	GER_DaeshIr	1	0	1	0	0	1	TRUE	1.013
4	GER_EURCA	GER_EUSom	1	0	1	0	0	1	TRUE	1.032
5	FIN_DaeshIr	GER_Leb	1	0	1	1	0	1	TRUE	0.762
6	FIN_KFOR	GER_Leb	1	0	1	1	0	1	TRUE	0.928
7	GER_Atalanta	GER_Leb	1	0	1	1	0	1	TRUE	0.949
8	DK_Iraq91	GER_Leb	1	0	0	1	0	1	TRUE	0.955
9	ITA_Afgh	ITA_Libya	1	1	1	1	0	0	TRUE	0.762
10	ITA_Afgh	ITA_Iraq91	1	1	0	1	0	0	TRUE	0.763

Identifying Omitted Conjuncts

Because the consistency of the sufficient term $PD * RO$ is already quite high and there are only very few deviant consistency cases in kind, it would probably not be of the highest importance for an applied researcher to perform an SMMR design aimed at discovering a missing conjunct. We already saw in the XY plot in Figure 4.1 that there are only three deviant consistency cases in kind.

Code C 4.4 reveals which of them can be considered the best available deviant consistency case, using Formula 2.2 introduced in Chapter 2. Output O 4.4 identifies the contested German decision to deploy military to Afghanistan. It scores lowest on column "Best", the only criteria for this SMMR design. This case is most puzzling because, despite this decision being not potentially divisive and despite there being a right-leaning opposition, it represents an ideal case of political contestation against the decision. Within-case analysis of this case would need to reveal which conjunct from conjunction $PD * RO$ is missing that can explain why the mechanism leading to outcome $\sim PC$ was not triggered. Because in this example the mechanism M consists of the two components M_{PD} and M_{RO}, each is expected to be triggered by one of the conjuncts; therefore, the absence of M could be the result of the absence of M_{PD}, of M_{RO}, or both. Depending on which scenario is supported by within-case evidence determines which and how many conjuncts are missing from $PD * RO$.

C 4.4

```
dcons <- smmr(results = sol_nyp,
              outcome = "~PC",
              match = FALSE,
              cases = 3)
dcons
```

O 4.4

Deviant Consistency Cases :

	Cases	Term	TermMemb	Outcome	Best	MostDCONS
1	GER_Afgh	PD*RO	0.670	0.000	0.660	TRUE
3	SLK_KFOR	PD*RO	0.683	0.189	0.823	FALSE
2	ITA_Som92	PD*RO	0.566	0.084	0.952	FALSE

This within-case analysis could be done by using counterfactual reasoning. Alternatively, a deviant consistency case can be compared to a typical case. Code C 4.5 reveals the best available pair of a typical and a deviant consistency case. Output O 4.5 shows that the deviant consistency case of political contestation of Germany's decision to deploy military to Afghanistan should be matched with the typical case of Denmark's politically noncontested decision to deploy military in the French-led Operation Serval in Mali. This pair shows a slightly better value (column "Best", using Formula 2.5) than matching the

4.5 Applying SMMR   125

contested German decision with that of the typical case of France's politically noncontested military deployment to Mali in the context of Operation Serval, despite the fact that the latter is actually the most typical case for the term $PD * RO$ (using Formula 2.4).

C 4.5

```
typdcons <- smmr( results = sol_nyp,
                  outcome = "~PC",
                  match = TRUE,
                  cases = 3)
typdcons
```

O 4.5

Term PD*RO :

	TYP	DCONS	Best	MostTypTerm	MostDCONS
1	DK_Serval	GER_Afgh	0.670	FALSE	TRUE
2	FRN_Serval	GER_Afgh	0.680	TRUE	TRUE
3	ESP_Atalanta	GER_Afgh	0.713	FALSE	TRUE
4	BEL_Libya	GER_Afgh	0.714	FALSE	TRUE
5	SLK_Leb	GER_Afgh	0.714	FALSE	TRUE

Note that, with a conjunction, deviance consistency could also be the consequence not of a missing conjunct, but of the *temporal sequence* in which the two conjuncts *PD* and *RO* occurred in a case. For the sake of illustration, assume that, in all typical cases, there already is a right-of-center opposition (*RO*) in place before opposition forces start to evaluate a deployment as potentially not divisive (*PD*). For deviant consistency cases, in contrast, the sequence is the opposite: opposition forces already deem a deployment as not potentially divisive and then a right-wing opposition emerges – for instance through elections – that deems opposition to deployment inappropriate. This difference in sequence among known conjuncts remains invisible and is deemed analytically irrelevant by the Boolean expression $PD * RO$ but might explain the puzzle of deviant consistency cases. In addition to focusing on missing conjuncts, within-case analysis of deviant consistency cases can also try to evaluate if the sequence of conjuncts matters for the presence of mechanisms M.

For instance, it could be that newly emerged right-wing opposition parties do not consider it a problem, or probable, that their opposition to military deployment would send the wrong signal to enemies, either because they consider themselves too irrelevant for being noticed in the international political sphere and/or because other opposition parties have already signaled their approval (i.e. mechanism M_{PD} has already been triggered). Mechanism M_{RO} would therefore not be triggered because *RO* occurred after *PD*. The puzzle of deviant consistency cases would then be solved by finding within-case evidence that the sequence matters for the mechanism. In Section 7.3.4, I discuss in more detail the different ways in which time-infused QCA solution formulas – via two-step QCA (Schneider, 2019), temporal QCA (Caren and Panofsky, 2005), or coincidence analysis (Baumgartner, 2009) – can be useful for SMMR designs.[29]

4.5.2 Causal Inference SMMR

The within-case analysis of a single typical case aims at probing the difference-making properties of conjuncts in a conjunction. Code C 4.6 produces output O 4.6. For each of the two conjuncts *PD* and *RO*, a ranking of the best available typical cases is shown. The criteria based on which the list of typical cases is ordered from best to worst follows the ordering in which these criteria appear in the output: low to high values in "Rank", then whether the corridor is clean, followed by whether membership in the focal conjunct is consistent ("FC<=Y"), then whether the case is uniquely covered ("UniqCov"), then the values in column "Best",[30] followed by whether it is the most typical case vis-à-vis the focal conjunct ("MostTypFC") and then vis-à-vis the entire sufficient conjunction ("MostTypTerm", using Formula 2.4).

C 4.6

```
typ_foc <- smmr(results = sol_nyp,
                outcome = "~PC",
                match = FALSE,
                cases = 2)
typ_foc
```

---

[29] On further forms of sequences and their relevance for SMMR, see also Beach and Rohlfing (2018).
[30] Calculated based on Formula 4.1.

Typical Cases — Focal Conjunct PD :

	FC	Outcome	CC_Min	Term	Rank	CleanCorr	FC<=Y	UniqCov	Best	MostTypFC	MostTypTerm
ESP_Libya	0.67	0.944	0.937	0.670	1	FALSE	TRUE	TRUE	0.878	FALSE	FALSE
BEL_Libya	0.67	0.946	0.940	0.670	1	FALSE	TRUE	TRUE	0.882	FALSE	FALSE
FRN_Serval	1.00	0.980	0.975	0.975	2	TRUE	FALSE	TRUE	0.065	TRUE	FALSE
DK_Serval	1.00	0.990	0.927	0.927	2	TRUE	FALSE	TRUE	0.093	FALSE	FALSE
ESP_Atalanta	1.00	0.947	0.937	0.937	2	TRUE	FALSE	TRUE	0.169	FALSE	FALSE

Typical Cases — Focal Conjunct RO :

	FC	Outcome	CC_Min	Term	Rank	CleanCorr	FC<=Y	UniqCov	Best	MostTypFC	MostTypTerm
FRN_Serval	0.975	0.980	0.975	0.975	1	TRUE	TRUE	TRUE	0.035	TRUE	FALSE
ESP_EUSom	0.937	0.942	0.937	0.937	1	TRUE	TRUE	TRUE	0.072	FALSE	FALSE
SLK_EUMali	0.930	0.935	0.930	0.930	1	TRUE	TRUE	TRUE	0.080	FALSE	FALSE
ESP_Atalanta	0.937	0.947	0.937	0.937	1	TRUE	TRUE	TRUE	0.082	FALSE	FALSE
FRN_Sangaris	0.885	0.894	0.885	0.885	1	TRUE	TRUE	TRUE	0.133	FALSE	FALSE

For focal conjunct *PD*, SMMR identifies the politically noncontested Spanish decision to deploy military to Libya as the best available typical case. It is in rank 1 and uniquely covered, as is Belgium's noncontested decision to deploy military to Libya. In both these cases with rank = 1, the corridor is not clean (column "CleanCorr"), which means that their membership value in the complementary conjunct *RO* falls between their membership in focal conjunct *PD* and outcome ~*PC*. But for both cases, the membership in focal conjunct *PD* is smaller than the outcome (column "FC<=Y"). Belgium is ranked second with only a negligibly smaller formula value.[31] Both Spain's and Belgium's scores in column "Best" (Formula 4.1) are much higher (i.e. worse) than that of the case of France's noncontested decision to deploy military to Mali in Operation Serval. The latter, however, is in rank 2 and therefore an inferior choice for within-case analysis on focal conjunct *PD*. Recall (see Table 4.7 and Figure 4.5) that rank 2 means that, for the typical case, membership in the focal conjunct *PD* exceeds that in the complementary conjuncts *RO* and therefore the attribution principle is not fulfilled in the typical case of FRN_Serval.

Not surprisingly, therefore, for focal conjunct *RO*, FRN_Serval is in rank 1 and constitutes the best available typical case for within-case analysis on this focal conjunct. As output O 4.6 shows, for focal conjunct *RO*, there are several further typical cases that provide close to ideal conditions for within-case analysis on the mechanism M_{RO}. They are all in rank 1, have a clean corridor, their focal conjunct membership is consistent with a claim of sufficiency, they are uniquely covered, and hold very small values in column "Best".

When performing a single within-case analysis, the claim of difference-making properties of a focal conjunct must rest on counterfactual reasoning. Wherever empirical information is available, such counterfactuals should be substituted with a comparison of a typical and an iir case. Code C 4.7 implements such an SMMR design and produces output O 4.7. The best available pairs are reported for each of the two focal conjuncts.

Similar to the ordering for single typical cases, the best available pair of a typical and an iir case is based on the following sequence of criteria: first, the value in "Rank"; second, whether the corridor is clean ("CleanCorr"); third, whether the typical and iir cases' membership in *FC* is is smaller than its outcome membership ("FC<=Y"); fourth, whether the typical case is uniquely covered ("UniqCov"); fifth, whether the iir case is globally uncovered ("GlobUncov"); sixth, the value in column "Best" (calculated using Formula 4.2); seventh, whether the typical case is the most typical vis-à-vis the focal conjunct ("MostTypFC"); and, finally, eighth, whether the typical case is the

---

[31] Since in this example the solution formula consists of a single term, all typical cases are uniquely covered by design.

most typical vis-à-vis the entire sufficient conjunction ("MostTypTerm", using Formula 2.4).

C 4.7

```
typiir_foc <- smmr(results = sol_nyp,
                   outcome = "~PC",
                   match = TRUE,
                   cases = 2,
                   max_pairs = 10)
typiir_foc
```

O 4.7

Focal Conjunct PD :

	TYP	IIR	PairRank	CleanCorr	FC<=Y	UniqCov	GlobUncov	Best	MostTypFC	MostTypTerm
232	ESP_Libya	UK_Iraq03	1	iir	both	TRUE	TRUE	1.532	FALSE	FALSE
227	BEL_Libya	UK_Iraq03	1	iir	both	TRUE	TRUE	1.536	FALSE	FALSE
142	ESP_Libya	ITA_Kosovo	1	iir	typ	TRUE	TRUE	1.642	FALSE	FALSE
137	BEL_Libya	ITA_Kosovo	1	iir	typ	TRUE	TRUE	1.646	FALSE	FALSE
202	ESP_Libya	SLK_Kosovo	1	iir	typ	TRUE	TRUE	1.848	FALSE	FALSE
197	BEL_Libya	SLK_Kosovo	1	iir	typ	TRUE	TRUE	1.853	FALSE	FALSE
229	DK_Serval	UK_Iraq03	2	both	iir	TRUE	TRUE	0.617	FALSE	FALSE
236	FRN_Serval	UK_Iraq03	2	both	iir	TRUE	TRUE	0.695	TRUE	TRUE
239	SLK_Leb	UK_Iraq03	2	both	iir	TRUE	TRUE	0.718	FALSE	TRUE
230	ESP_Atalanta	UK_Iraq03	2	both	iir	TRUE	TRUE	0.757	FALSE	FALSE

Focal Conjunct RO :

	TYP	IIR	PairRank	CleanCorr	FC<=Y	UniqCov	GlobUncov	Best	MostTypFC	MostTypTerm
116	FRN_Serval	ITA_Iraq90	1	both	both	TRUE	TRUE	0.238	TRUE	TRUE
111	ESP_EUSom	ITA_Iraq90	1	both	both	TRUE	TRUE	0.313	FALSE	FALSE
110	ESP_Atalanta	ITA_Iraq90	1	both	both	TRUE	TRUE	0.318	FALSE	FALSE
118	SLK_EUMali	ITA_Iraq90	1	both	both	TRUE	TRUE	0.328	FALSE	FALSE
176	FRN_Serval	ITA_Sophia	1	both	both	TRUE	TRUE	0.340	TRUE	TRUE
109	DK_Serval	ITA_Iraq90	1	both	both	TRUE	TRUE	0.392	FALSE	FALSE
171	ESP_EUSom	ITA_Sophia	1	both	both	TRUE	TRUE	0.415	FALSE	FALSE
114	FRN_Daeshlr	ITA_Iraq90	1	both	both	TRUE	TRUE	0.416	FALSE	FALSE
170	ESP_Atalanta	ITA_Sophia	1	both	both	TRUE	TRUE	0.420	FALSE	FALSE
115	FRN_Sangaris	ITA_Iraq90	1	both	both	TRUE	TRUE	0.422	FALSE	FALSE

4.5 Applying SMMR

For focal conjunct *PD*, the best pair consists of Spain's noncontested deployment decisions to Libya (typical case) and the politically contested UK decision to send troops into Iraq in 2003 (iir case). The pair is in rank 1. In both cases the corridor is clean and both cases' scores in focal conjunct *PD* are smaller than their outcome membership, and thus consistent with the claim of sufficiency. Spain is uniquely covered and the UK globally uncovered.[32] The pair's value in column "Best" is small (0.238). Spain, however, is neither the most typical case for the focal conjunct *PD*, nor for the entire sufficient term $PD * RO$.[33] As output O 4.7 shows, there are several case pairs that fulfill the same criteria and display only slightly lower scores on the formula for the best available case pair (Formula 4.2).

The same holds for focal conjunct *RO*: there are several case pairs that are in rank 1 and match a uniquely covered typical case with a globally uncovered iir case with clean corridors and consistent membership scores in *RO*. The pair of France's noncontested decision on sending troops to Mali (Operation Serval) and Italy's contested decision to send troops to Iraq in 1990 qualifies as the best available pair. The case of France even qualifies as the most typical with regard to both the sufficient term $PD * RO$ and the focal conjunct *RO*. Several other pairs tick similar criteria and score similarly low in column "Best".

The comparison between two typical cases aims at probing whether the mechanism linking a conjunct to the outcome is regular. Code C 4.8 identifies the best available pair of two typical cases. The results are shown in output O 4.8. The ordering from better to worse case pairs is similar to the one for typical-iir pairs: first on values in "Rank", then whether the corridor is clean, then whether the typical cases' membership in the focal conjunct is smaller than in the outcome, then whether they are uniquely covered ("UniqCov1" and "UniqCov2"), then whether the value in column "Best" (using Formula 4.3) is the smallest, and, finally, whether one of the cases is the most typical with regard to the focal conjunct (Formula 4.1) and then the sufficient term (Formula 2.4).

C 4.8

```
typtyp_foc <- smmr(results = sol_nyp,
                   outcome = "~PC",
                   match = TRUE,
                   cases = 1)
typtyp_foc
```

[32] With a solution formula that consists of only one term, not only are all typical cases uniquely covered, but also all iir cases globally uncovered by design.

[33] Note that most of the ten best-matching pairs involve neither the most typical case vis-à-vis the entire term, nor for the focal conjunct. And the pair that does – FRN_Serval-UK_Iraq03 - is in rank 2 only and the typical case's membership in *FC* is inconsistent.

O 4.8

Focal Conjunct PD :

	TYP1	TYP2	PairRank	CleanCorr	FC<=Y	UniqCov	Best	MostTypFC	MostTypTerm
22	ESP_Libya	BEL_Libya	1	none	both	both	2.105	none	none
37	ESP_Libya	DK_Daeshlr	2	typ2	typ1	both	2.418	none	none
32	BEL_Libya	DK_Daeshlr	2	typ1	typ1	both	2.422	none	none
94	DK_Serval	ESP_Libya	3	typ1	typ2	both	1.203	none	none
19	DK_Serval	BEL_Libya	3	typ1	typ2	both	1.211	none	none

Focal Conjunct RO :

	TYP1	TYP2	PairRank	CleanCorr	FC<=Y	UniqCov	Best	MostTypFC	MostTypTerm
176	FRN_Serval	ITA_Alba	1	both	both	both	0.673	typ1	typ1
171	ESP_EUSom	ITA_Alba	1	both	both	both	0.747	none	none
170	ESP_Atalanta	ITA_Alba	1	both	both	both	0.752	none	none
178	SLK_EUMali	ITA_Alba	1	both	both	both	0.762	none	none
169	DK_Serval	ITA_Alba	1	both	both	both	0.827	none	none

4.5 Applying SMMR

For focal conjunct *PD*, Belgium's and Spain's noncontested decisions to send troops to Libya form the best available pair of two typical cases. It is the only pair in rank 1 and therefore clearly qualifies as the best choice for this SMMR design on focal conjunct *PD*. Sharing the same target country for deployment increases comparability, on the one hand, and raises questions of generalizability, on the other. For this or other reasons, a researcher might want to choose the next best pair – ESP_Libya–DK_DaeshIr – with rank = 2. The downside of this choice would be that for the less typical case DK_DaeshIr, membership in the mechanism M_{PD} could not unequivocally be attributed to the membership in *PD* because it exceeds that in the complementary conjunct *RO*.

For focal conjunct *RO*, Spain_Atalanta and Italy_Alba are the best among several case pairs that are all in rank 1. All these pairs also display clean corridors, display consistent membership scores in *RO*, are uniquely covered, and have much smaller scores in column "Best" than the best available pairs for focal conjunct *PD*. This means that the empirical information at hand is such that causal inference on focal conjunct *RO* is more facilitated than that on focal conjunct *PD*.

***

As discussed in Section 4.4, researchers sometimes encounter *INUS conditions that qualify as necessary conditions*. Only the three causal inference SMMR designs are affected by this because only they rest on the distinction between focal and complementary conjuncts. The rankings of best available cases and pairs of cases need to be adapted, as outlined in Section 4.4. For empirical illustration, I return to the study by Schneider et al. (2010) in which the presence of a big stock market (*STOCK*) is identified as being necessary for success in the export of high-tech products (*EXPORT*). For the sake of brevity, I focus on sufficient term $\sim OCCUP * STOCK * \sim MA$: next to the necessary presence of a big stock market, the absence of both strong occupational training ($\sim OCCUP$) and many mergers and acquisitions ($\sim MA$) form a sufficient conjunction for the success in exporting high-tech products (see Table 4.8 for the entire solution formula).

Code C 4.9 identifies the best available typical case. The syntax is almost identical to the ones without necessary INUS conditions. The one extra argument that is needed is nec.cond, with which we specify the necessary INUS condition *STOCK*. In output O 4.9, the crucial piece that changes is the information provided for the necessary INUS condition *STOCK*. The information in column "Rank" is based on the logic explained in Section 4.4. Likewise, the information in column "CleanCorr" now takes into account that membership in *STOCK* should exceed that in the outcome *EXPORT*. Finally, for *STOCK*, the column is called $FC >= Y$ instead of $FC <= Y$ as it is for all the other, nonnecessary, INUS conditions.

We learn that, for the necessary INUS condition *STOCK*, the best available typical case is the USA in 1990, but also the USA in 2003 or Japan in 1999 appear almost equally adequate choices, with only slightly worse values in column "Best" (using Formula 4.1). Japan 2003 or the USA in 1995 are somewhat worse choices because, while still from rank 1, their corridors are not clean.

C 4.9

```
typ_foc <- smmr(results = sol_yp,
                outcome = "EXPORT",
                match=FALSE,
                cases=2,
                term = 3,
                nec.cond = "STOCK")
typ_foc
```

O 4.9

Typical Cases -- Focal Conjunct ~OCCUP :

	FC	Outcome	CC_Min	Term	Rank	CleanCorr	FC<=Y	UniqCov	Best	MostTypFC	MostTypTerm
Japan_95	0.85	0.85	0.95	0.85	1	TRUE	TRUE	TRUE	0.15	TRUE	FALSE
Japan_03	0.87	0.94	0.94	0.87	1	FALSE	TRUE	TRUE	0.27	FALSE	FALSE
Japan_99	0.84	0.96	0.92	0.84	1	FALSE	TRUE	TRUE	0.40	FALSE	FALSE
USA_03	0.97	0.98	0.83	0.83	2	TRUE	TRUE	TRUE	0.19	FALSE	FALSE
Ireland_90	0.84	0.98	0.51	0.51	2	TRUE	TRUE	TRUE	0.77	FALSE	FALSE

Typical Cases -- Necessary Focal Conjunct STOCK :

	FC	Outcome	CC_Min	Term	Rank	CleanCorr	FC>=Y	UniqCov	Best	MostTypFC	MostTypTerm
USA_90	0.95	0.93	0.85	0.85	1	TRUE	TRUE	TRUE	0.19	TRUE	FALSE
USA_03	1.00	0.98	0.83	0.83	1	TRUE	TRUE	TRUE	0.21	FALSE	FALSE
Japan_99	1.00	0.96	0.84	0.84	1	TRUE	TRUE	TRUE	0.24	FALSE	FALSE
Japan_03	1.00	0.94	0.87	0.87	1	FALSE	TRUE	TRUE	0.25	FALSE	FALSE
USA_95	1.00	0.91	0.85	0.85	1	FALSE	TRUE	TRUE	0.33	FALSE	FALSE

Typical Cases -- Focal Conjunct ~MA :

	FC	Outcome	CC_Min	Term	Rank	CleanCorr	FC<=Y	UniqCov	Best	MostTypFC	MostTypTerm
USA_95	0.85	0.91	0.97	0.85	1	TRUE	TRUE	TRUE	0.27	FALSE	FALSE
USA_90	0.85	0.93	0.95	0.85	1	TRUE	TRUE	TRUE	0.31	FALSE	FALSE
USA_03	0.83	0.98	0.97	0.83	1	FALSE	TRUE	TRUE	0.47	FALSE	FALSE
Ireland_90	0.51	0.98	0.53	0.51	1	FALSE	TRUE	TRUE	1.43	FALSE	FALSE
Japan_03	0.94	0.94	0.87	0.87	2	TRUE	TRUE	TRUE	0.13	TRUE	FALSE

The identification of the best available pairs of typical and iir cases follows the same logic. In code C 4.10, we again use argument nec.cond to specify the necessary INUS condition *STOCK*. And from output O 4.10 we learn that for the focal conjunct *STOCK*, the best available pair of cases consists of the typical case USA in 2003 with the iir case Norway in 1999. This pair is from rank 1, both have a clean corridor, in both membership in *STOCK* exceeds that in the outcome *EXPORT*, the typical case is uniquely covered and the iir case is globally uncovered, and the formula value in "Best" (using Formula 4.2) is low. The fact that the USA in 2003 is the most typical for neither the focal conjunct nor the entire term is not of much relevance, as these are the two least important criteria for identifying the best matching pair of typical and iir cases. There are several other pairs of cases that are all in rank 1 and involve Norway 1999. For all but one, however, the typical case fails to display a clean corridor (Japan in 1999 is the exception).

C 4.10

```
typiir_foc <- smmr(results = sol_yp,
                   outcome = "EXPORT",
                   match=TRUE,
                   cases=2,
                   term = 3,
                   nec.cond = "STOCK",
                   max_pairs = 10)
typiir_foc
```

O 4.10

Focal Conjunct -OCCUP :

	TYP	IIR	PairRank	CleanCorr	FC<=Y	UniqCov	GlobUncov	Best	MostTypFC	MostTypTerm
192	Japan_95	Italy_99	1	both	both	TRUE	TRUE	1.10	TRUE	TRUE
122	Japan_95	Finland_95	1	both	both	TRUE	FALSE	1.50	TRUE	TRUE
24	Japan_95	Denmark_90	1	both	typ	TRUE	TRUE	1.62	TRUE	TRUE
195	Japan_03	Italy_99	1	both	both	TRUE	TRUE	1.12	FALSE	FALSE
194	Japan_99	Italy_99	1	iir	both	TRUE	TRUE	1.21	FALSE	FALSE
125	Japan_03	Finland_95	1	iir	both	TRUE	FALSE	1.52	FALSE	FALSE
124	Japan_99	Finland_95	1	iir	both	TRUE	FALSE	1.61	FALSE	FALSE
27	Japan_03	Denmark_90	1	iir	typ	TRUE	TRUE	1.64	FALSE	FALSE
26	Japan_99	Denmark_90	1	iir	typ	TRUE	TRUE	1.73	FALSE	FALSE
196	USA_03	Italy_99	2	both	both	TRUE	TRUE	0.75	FALSE	FALSE

Necessary Focal Conjunct STOCK :

	TYP	IIR	PairRank	CleanCorr	FC>=Y	UniqCov	GlobUncov	Best	MostTypFC	MostTypTerm
210	USA_03	Norway_99	1	both	both	TRUE	TRUE	1.77	FALSE	FALSE
208	Japan_99	Norway_99	1	both	both	TRUE	TRUE	1.84	FALSE	FALSE
205	USA_90	Norway_99	1	iir	both	TRUE	TRUE	1.89	TRUE	FALSE
209	Japan_03	Norway_99	1	iir	both	TRUE	TRUE	1.93	FALSE	FALSE
207	USA_95	Norway_99	1	iir	both	TRUE	TRUE	2.00	FALSE	FALSE
206	Japan_95	Norway_99	1	iir	iir	TRUE	TRUE	2.18	FALSE	TRUE
204	Ireland_90	Norway_99	2	iir	iir	TRUE	TRUE	2.78	FALSE	FALSE
21	USA_03	Belgium_90	3	both	both	TRUE	TRUE	0.78	FALSE	FALSE
19	Japan_99	Belgium_90	3	both	both	TRUE	TRUE	0.85	FALSE	FALSE
203	USA_03	New Zealand_99	3	both	both	TRUE	TRUE	1.06	FALSE	FALSE

Focal Conjunct -MA :

	TYP	IIR	PairRank	CleanCorr	FC<=Y	UniqCov	GlobUncov	Best	MostTypFC	MostTypTerm
184	USA_90	Canada_99	1	both	both	TRUE	TRUE	1.24	FALSE	FALSE
186	USA_95	Canada_99	1	both	both	TRUE	TRUE	1.24	FALSE	FALSE
212	USA_90	Spain_99	1	both	both	TRUE	FALSE	1.05	FALSE	FALSE
214	USA_95	Spain_99	1	both	both	TRUE	FALSE	1.05	FALSE	FALSE
247	USA_90	Norway_03	1	both	both	TRUE	FALSE	1.38	FALSE	FALSE
249	USA_95	Norway_03	1	both	both	TRUE	FALSE	1.38	FALSE	FALSE
219	USA_90	Australia_03	1	both	both	TRUE	FALSE	1.51	FALSE	FALSE
221	USA_95	Australia_03	1	both	both	TRUE	FALSE	1.51	FALSE	FALSE
142	USA_90	New Zealand_95	1	both	typ	TRUE	TRUE	0.93	FALSE	FALSE
144	USA_95	New Zealand_95	1	both	typ	TRUE	TRUE	0.93	FALSE	FALSE

To obtain the list of best-matching pairs of two typical cases, code C 4.11 is used to produce output O 4.11. Focusing again on necessary INUS condition *STOCK*, it is revealed that, while there are several pairs in rank 1, only one such pair fulfills the clean corridor principle in both typical cases: Japan in 1999 and the USA in 2003. The same holds true for focal conjunct $\sim$*MA*, for which the pair of the USA in 1995 and 1990 is identified as the best choice for a within-case analysis on the mechanism triggered by the INUS condition $\sim$*MA*. For INUS condition $\sim$*OCCUP*, in turn, there is no pair in rank 1 with both cases displaying a clean corridor. To obtain a clean corridor, one would need to choose a pair from rank 2 – Japan in 1995 and the USA in 2003. As explained previously, rank 2 means that the attribution principle is not fulfilled in the less typical case.

C 4.11

```
typtyp_foc <- smmr(results = sol_yp,
            outcome = "EXPORT",
            match=TRUE,
            cases=1,
            term = 3,
            nec.cond = "STOCK")
typtyp_foc
```

O 4.11

Focal Conjunct ~OCCUP :

	TYP1	TYP2	PairRank	CleanCorr	FC<=Y	UniqCov	Best	MostTypFC	MostTypTerm
38	Japan_95	Japan_03	1	typ1	both	both	1.26	typ1	typ1
31	Japan_95	Japan_99	1	typ1	both	both	1.37	typ1	typ1
34	Japan_03	Japan_99	1	none	both	both	1.39	none	none
45	Japan_95	USA_03	2	both	both	both	1.39	typ1	typ1
3	Japan_95	Ireland_90	2	both	both	both	1.84	typ1	typ1

Necessary Focal Conjunct STOCK :

	TYP1	TYP2	PairRank	CleanCorr	FC>=Y	UniqCov	Best	MostTypFC	MostTypTerm
47	Japan_99	USA_03	1	both	both	both	1.15	none	none
44	USA_90	USA_03	1	typ2	both	both	1.20	typ1	none
30	USA_90	Japan_99	1	typ2	both	both	1.21	typ1	none
48	Japan_03	USA_03	1	typ2	both	both	1.24	none	none
34	Japan_03	Japan_99	1	typ2	both	both	1.25	none	none

Focal Conjunct ~MA :

	TYP1	TYP2	PairRank	CleanCorr	FC<=Y	UniqCov	Best	MostTypFC	MostTypTerm
11	USA_95	USA_90	1	both	both	both	1.32	none	none
46	USA_95	USA_03	1	typ1	both	both	1.47	none	none
44	USA_90	USA_03	1	typ1	both	both	1.51	none	none
2	USA_90	Ireland_90	1	typ1	both	both	2.23	none	none
4	USA_95	Ireland_90	1	typ1	both	both	2.23	none	none

4.6 Conclusion

Conjunctions create challenges for causal claims. The conjunction must be unpacked and the causal role of each conjunct be probed to infer that the conjunction as a whole is causal. The remedy against the analytic challenges for causal inference posed by conjunctions consists of using additional principles when selecting cases for within-case analysis: the focal conjunct principle, the principle of iir FC unique nonmembership, the attribution principle, and the clean corridor principle. Together with the already introduced principles, they jointly help to isolate single conjuncts and allow for the analysis of their difference-making properties for the causal mechanism at the within-case level. They govern all three SMMR designs whose goal is causal inference: single typical case, two typical cases, and a typical–iir comparison.

Sometimes, one or more INUS conditions in a sufficient conjunction qualify as stand-alone necessary conditions. Causal inference SMMR designs are taking this on board via two further principles and a concomitant adjustment of the rank system for each of the three causal inference designs: the attribution principle for necessity and the principle of iir focal conjunct nonmembership for necessity.

The more conjuncts there are in a conjunction, the more within-case analyses are required. This is a direct consequence of the complex causal claims entailed in conjunctions: each conjunct must be deemed causal for the conjunction to be causal. The requirement to probe each conjunct's effect on the within-case mechanism(s) can become very taxing. Due to limited resources or lack of diversity in the data at hand, applied researchers will often have to limit their within-case analysis to some conjuncts. Even in such a scenario, it is beneficial to know how much and in which ways one has come short of implementing the ideal SMMR design. This information is crucial when assessing the level of certainty one should have about one's causal inferences.

One strategy to reduce the requirements for SMMR triggered by conjunctions consists in conceptualizing them away. By moving up the ladder of abstraction, a conjunction is summarized in a single set. As is often the case in social science research, there are benefits and costs for such design decisions. This form of aggregation assumes away potentially relevant differences between conjuncts, but reduces demands for the within-case analysis that otherwise would potentially be impossible to meet. In Section 7.2.5, I spell out further strategies of reducing the number of designs implemented in applied SMMR.

5
INUS Conditions
$A * B + C * D \Rightarrow Y$

We now have all tools in place for performing SMMR based on a typical QCA result that features both disjunctions (equifinality) and conjunctions (conjunctural causation) and, as a consequence of this, INUS conditions. The goal of this chapter is to demonstrate SMMR in a typical research setting to highlight some common issues and indicate trade-offs. No new principles, formulas, or types of cases are introduced. What is new in this chapter is that the empirical example showcases cases' membership scores in the within-case level causal mechanism. This will help in further illustrating the issue of broken corridor scenarios and the analytic consequences for causal inference that it triggers. In addition, I explain how to interpret situations in which the cross-case and within-case levels provide contradicting evidence on the causal status of a QCA solution. Because in SMMR token-level evidence beats type-level evidence, it follows that any QCA solution type can be used in causal inference SMMR designs (not just the most parsimonious solution) and, vice versa, any solution might turn out to be noncausal upon within-case evidence (including the most parsimonious solution).

Learning Goals 5.1: Full Complexity

- Practice all SMMR designs on a typical QCA solution formula showing full complexity (disjuncts and conjuncts)
- Get acquainted with the conclusions drawn from evidence on a case's membership in the within-case mechanisms
- Understand that all QCA solution types – conservative, intermediate, most parsimonious – can be the basis for descriptive and causal inference SMMR designs

---

5.1 Empirical Example

> **Empirical Example 5.1: Forms of welfare capitalism and education-based participatory inequality (Schneider and Makszin, 2014)**
> - *Research question*: Which factors and mechanisms explain low participatory inequality in politics?
> - *Cases*: 77 welfare regimes
> - *Set type*: Fuzzy
> - *Outcome*: Low participatory inequality (LPI)
> - *Conditions*: High employment protection (EP), high union density (UN), high labor market expenditure (LM), high wage coordination (WC)
> - *Mechanisms*: Material and cognitive resources, social engagement

For the empirical example, I return to the study by Schneider and Makszin (2014), already briefly introduced in Chapter 1, on the role of welfare regime characteristics in mitigating education-based inequalities in political participation across capitalist democracies. Empirical Example 5.1 contains the basic features of the analysis. In a nutshell, their argument is that specific types of welfare regimes mitigate unequal participation in politics. They identify three such welfare regime types: coordinated, protective, and unorganized. The first two are further subsumed under the label "supportive" welfare regimes.

Table 5.1 *Sufficient welfare regime conditions, outcome "low participatory inequality" LPI, most parsimonious solution*

Welfare regime		Conditions	inclS	PRI	covS	covU
Supportive {	Coordinated	$LM*WC$	0.813	0.760	0.257	0.044
	Protective	$LM*EP$	0.868	0.835	0.346	0.056
	Unorganized	$\sim UN*EP$	0.859	0.828	0.414	0.208
		Solution	0.839	0.804	0.598	

WC: high wage coordination; LM: high labor market expenditure; UN: high union density; EP: high employment protection

Table 5.1 shows the most parsimonious QCA solution formula and indicates the combination of conditions that constitute the three types of welfare regimes. For instance, their "coordinated" version of the supportive welfare regime is composed of the attributes of high wage coordination (*WC*) and

5.1 Empirical Example

high labor market protection (*LM*). Around 26% (covS = 0.257) of low participatory inequality is covered, or explained, by this welfare regime. The "protective" version of the supportive welfare regime covers 35% (covS = 0.346) and the uncoordinated regime even more (covS = 0.414). These regimes are not mutually exclusive. This means some cases are members of more than one regime.[1] This overlap is expressed in Table 5.1 by column unique coverage (covU). It indicates how much of the outcome "low participatory inequality" is covered only by a given welfare regime. The coordinated and protective regimes overlap (both contain high labor market expenditure among their attributes), which results in lower unique coverage. As explained (in particular in Chapter 3), for various forms of within-case analyses it is crucial to select cases that are uniquely covered by one sufficient term. Because of the conceptual and empirical overlap, Schneider and Makszin (2014) subsume coordinated and protective welfare regimes under the higher-order concept of supportive regimes.

As within-case mechanisms that underpin these cross-case patterns, they identify material and cognitive resources and social engagement. Supportive welfare regimes trigger these mechanisms, which, in turn, produce the outcome low participatory inequality. Figure 1.1 visualizes the cross-case–within-case argument. The solution formula in Table 5.1 is derived based on the truth table displayed in Table 5.2. The XY plot in Figure 5.1 graphically displays each case's membership in the QCA solution and the outcome low participatory inequality.

There are several reasons why I chose this empirical example for further detailing issues in applied SMMR. First, it is an applied QCA that contains an explicit theory and empirical test of the underlying within-case mechanisms. Second, in the interpretation of the QCA findings, Schneider and Makszin (2014) move up the ladder of generality twice: first they "give names" to each of the three sufficient terms (coordinated, protective, uncoordinated), and then subsume the first two under the label "supportive" welfare regime. The aggregation of a conjunction (e.g. $LM * WC$) into a single set ("coordinated" welfare regime) assumes that all conjuncts trigger the same mechanism. Likewise, the aggregation of disjuncts assumes that each disjunct (e.g. "coordinated" or "protective") triggers the same mechanism. With the SMMR tools at hand, and adequate data on the mechanisms available, we can subject these assumption to empirical tests. Third, the number of cases is in the range in which the use of the SMMR machinery is most fruitful. For analyses with a (much) smaller

---

[1] For instance, Germany's welfare regime in 2000 and 2005 is classified as both coordinated and protective.

144   INUS Conditions $A*B+C*D \Rightarrow Y$

Table 5.2 *Truth table, outcome "low participatory inequality" LPI*

WC	UN	EP	LM	OUT	n	incl	PRI
0	0	1	1	1	4	0.911	0.871
0	1	1	1	1	5	0.900	0.833
1	0	1	1	1	7	0.873	0.839
0	0	1	0	1	9	0.825	0.744
1	1	0	1	1	2	0.825	0.698
1	0	1	0	1	2	0.818	0.730
1	1	1	1	1	6	0.800	0.663
1	1	1	0	0	5	0.781	0.683
1	1	0	0	0	4	0.769	0.666
0	1	0	1	0	5	0.759	0.618
0	1	1	0	0	5	0.754	0.576
0	1	0	0	0	6	0.726	0.578
0	0	0	1	0	1	0.686	0.476
1	0	0	0	0	3	0.642	0.486
0	0	0	0	0	12	0.537	0.399
1	0	0	1	?	0		

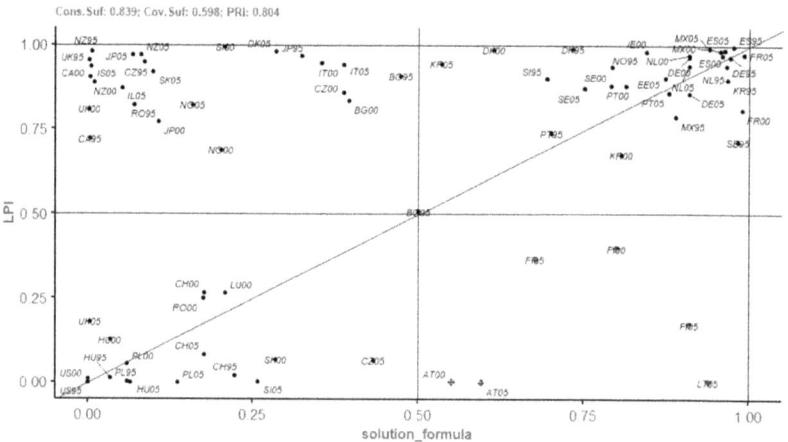

Figure 5.1 XY plot: solution formula, outcome "low participatory inequality" *LPI*

N, many of the SMMR principles can be applied "by hand", that is, it might often be possible to identify the best available cases and pairs of cases without the help of the smmr() functions. And, fourth, data is available to illustrate the set membership of cases in various within-case mechanisms.

5.2 Descriptive Inference SMMR

We start with model-refining SMMR. The parameters of fit in Table 5.1 show that the consistency scores of the three terms are in a standard range. Solution coverage, however, is relatively low (0.598). This means that only about 60% of the outcome is covered by the three sufficient terms. This makes the use of SMMR designs geared toward identifying missing disjuncts a plausible endeavor.

Missing Disjuncts

SMMR designs with the goal of increasing solution coverage must contain deviant coverage cases. We have learned that there are two such designs: the within-case analysis of a single deviant coverage case and a comparison of this case with an iir case.

The XY plot of the solution formula (Figure 5.1) shows the numerous deviant coverage cases in the upper-left quadrant. What this graph does not show is the following crucial information: to which truth table row each case belongs and, related to that, whether there is a lot of heterogeneity among deviant coverage cases or whether they all stem from the same, or a few, truth table rows. This matters: the more heterogeneity, the more diverse the reason for the cases' deviance, and the more likely it is that various disjuncts need to be discovered to explain those cases.

Code C 5.1 produces the list of deviant coverage cases and the truth table they belong to (output not shown). It reveals that deviant coverage cases are distributed over eight different truth table rows. This is a lot. Consider that the truth table consists of only 16 rows. Seven of them are included in the minimization and one is a logical remainder, and therefore cannot, by definition, contain a deviant coverage case.[2] All of the remaining rows – the ones coded $OUT = 0$ – contain at least one deviant coverage case.[3]

C 5.1

```
dcov <- smmr(results = sol_yp,
             outcome = "LPI",
             match = FALSE,
             cases = 4)
dcov
```

---

[2] Only if the frequency cut for truth table rows is set to a value higher than 1 could there be cases in remainder rows.
[3] It is worth remembering that a truth table row with $OUT = 0$ means that this specific row is not considered sufficient for the outcome of interest *LPI*. It does not mean, however, that none of the cases that are members of such rows can be members of outcome *LPI*. Deviant coverage cases are precisely this: members of the outcome in truth table rows that are deemed insufficient for the outcome.

In their study, Schneider and Makszin (2014) exclusively focus on welfare regime traits for explaining participatory inequality, rather than also other known factors, such as social inequality or electoral rules. Deviant coverage cases exist either because not all relevant welfare regime dimensions are included in the truth table or because factors unrelated to welfare regimes cause low participatory inequality in some or all of the deviant coverage cases. The SMMR approach to answering this question is to engage in within-case analyses. Ideally, this analysis is performed for each qualitatively different deviant coverage case type, that is, for at least one case in each truth table row.

Identifying the conjunct that is missing from a particular truth table row is facilitated if the deviant coverage case is compared to an iir case. Code C 5.2 produces the list of best-matching pairs of deviant coverage and iir cases shown in output O 5.1.

C 5.2

```
dcov_iir <- smmr(results = sol_yp,
                 outcome = "LPI",
                 match = TRUE,
                 cases = 4)
dcov_iir
```

O 5.1

Matching Deviant Coverage–IIR Cases :

	DCOV	IIR	TT_WC	TT_UN	TT_EP	TT_LM	TT_DCV<=Y	Best
1	NZ05	US95	0	0	0	0	TRUE	0.278
2	NZ05	HU05	0	0	0	0	TRUE	0.278
3	NZ05	US00	0	0	0	0	TRUE	0.287
4	JP05	US95	0	0	0	0	TRUE	0.384
5	JP05	HU05	0	0	0	0	TRUE	0.384
6	UK95	HU00	0	1	0	0	TRUE	1.157
7	CA00	HU00	0	1	0	0	TRUE	1.205
8	IL05	HU00	0	1	0	0	TRUE	1.242
9	CZ00	HU00	0	1	0	0	TRUE	1.252
10	UK00	HU00	0	1	0	0	TRUE	1.303
11	DK05	HU95	0	1	0	1	TRUE	0.652
12	NZ95	HU95	0	1	0	1	TRUE	0.835
13	NZ95	PL95	0	1	0	1	TRUE	0.934
14	DK05	PL95	0	1	0	1	TRUE	0.935
15	CA95	HU95	0	1	0	1	TRUE	1.042
16	BG00	RO00	0	1	1	0	TRUE	1.203
17	BG00	LU00	0	1	1	0	TRUE	1.220
18	BG95	RO00	0	1	1	0	TRUE	1.285
19	BG95	LU00	0	1	1	0	TRUE	1.303
20	RO95	RO00	0	1	1	0	FALSE	0.779
21	JP95	CH95	1	0	0	0	TRUE	0.702
22	JP00	CH95	1	0	0	0	TRUE	1.022
23	CZ95	SK00	1	1	0	0	TRUE	0.908
24	IS05	SK00	1	1	0	0	TRUE	0.920
25	IT05	SK00	1	1	0	0	TRUE	0.929
26	SI00	SI05	1	1	1	0	TRUE	0.526
27	IT00	SI05	1	1	1	0	TRUE	0.764
28	NO05	SI05	1	1	1	0	FALSE	0.698
29	NO00	SI05	1	1	1	0	FALSE	0.831

For each row, the best available pairs are NZ05–US95 (row 0000), UK95–HU00 (0100), DK05–HU95 (0101), BG00–RO00 (0110), JP95–CH95 (1000), CZ95–SK00 (1100), and SI00–SI05 (1110).[4]

By design, the within-case analysis of deviant coverage cases is exploratory. These cases show the outcome "low participatory inequality" for unknown reasons. There exists, therefore, no hunch about the possible mechanism linking the truth table conjunction to the outcome.

For example, how come New Zealand in the year 2005 shows low levels of participatory inequality despite the fact that it displays none of the four welfare characteristics deemed supportive for this outcome?[5] A comparison with the USA in 1995 serves the purpose of identifying the analytically relevant difference between these two cases that can explain why the USA does not and New Zealand does show low participatory inequality of the underprivileged. Researchers might, for instance, identify "ethnic homogeneity" as an analytically relevant difference: in ethnically much more homogeneous New Zealand, the mechanisms triggering equal turnout across social groups (resources and engagement) are feasible even in the absence of welfare regimes promoting these mechanisms. The fact that ethnically homogeneous Japan (JP95) is the other deviant coverage case in truth table row 0000 lends further plausibility to this claim. And so does iir case HU95: Hungary has a sizable ethnic minority Roma population, which is known to be discriminated against in the political arena. Whether ethnic homogeneity only enables low participatory inequality in the *absence* of supportive welfare regimes, or whether it triggers low participatory inequality no matter what, is the subject of the within-case analysis. In the latter scenario, ethnic homogeneity would be sufficient for triggering the mechanism, and in the former it would be an INUS condition. Some further condition(s) would need to be identified that, together with ethnic homogeneity, produce the outcome low participatory inequality. To answer these questions, the condition "ethnic homogeneity" should be added to the truth table and a new QCA solution formula obtained.

Findings from the within-case analysis of some cases of a truth table row are assumed to travel to all cases in the same truth table row. In contrast, cases in other rows are qualitatively different and require a separate within-

---

[4] These are pairs from only seven truth table rows. The eights row that contains a deviant coverage case (row 0001 with NZ00) does not contain any iir case.

[5] New Zealand's outcome membership becomes even more puzzling if we consider that, according to the data by Schneider and Makszin (2014), in previous years New Zealand did show some of the welfare traits (NZ95: 0101 and NZ00: 0001). In other words, over time, New Zealand seems to have dismantled aspects of its welfare state, yet participatory inequality remained low. This could suggest a time lag in the effect of welfare regime changes on participatory inequality. To test this hunch, cases would need to be traced over a longer time period, something not feasible with the data at hand.

case analysis on the missing conjunct from the truth table row. Whether or not cases from all truth table rows are subjected to within-case analysis depends on the resources (time, money, skills) of a researcher. As mentioned, the need for the study of deviant coverage cases increases the lower the solution coverage is. Furthermore, in principle, researchers need to add the newly discovered condition(s) to their truth table and rerun their analysis. This will change the solution formula and the classification of cases as typical, deviant, and individually irrelevant. This is why SMMR designs on deviant coverage cases should be performed first. For the example at hand, I will not alter the truth table and stick to the results displayed in Table 5.1.

Missing Conjuncts

The consistency of all three sufficient terms is reasonably high (above 0.8). The identification of missing conjuncts is therefore not very pressing. It nevertheless is always worth looking at the deviant consistency cases to see if there are any analytically relevant patterns.

Code C 5.3 produces the list of all deviant consistency cases for each sufficient term, shown in output O 5.2. We note that Austria 2005 (AT05) is a deviant consistency case with regard to all three terms (and AT10 for two out of three). This might suggest a model-unrelated reason for the deviance of Austria: the membership in the outcome of the Austrian case is probably miscalibrated. Instead of a nonmember of *LPI*, Austria in 2005 (and 2010) perhaps is a member of *LPI* and it was miscalibrated due to idiosyncratic reasons (flawed raw data, transcription error, etc.). A closer look at these matters might solve the puzzle of the deviant consistency case of Austria 2005. This example goes to show that, although SMMR is geared toward model-related issues of descriptive and causal inference, the SMMR framework can also be helpful in detecting model-unrelated reasons for deviance.

Another noteworthy observation is that, for term $LM*EP$, the only deviant consistency case next to Austria is Finland over one decade (1995–2005). Assuming that this is not due to idiosyncratic reasons, the goal of within-case analysis of one or all three of these Finnish cases is to find out what is blocking the mechanisms – resources and engagement – from linking $LM*EP$ with outcome *LPI*.

C 5.3

```
dcons <- smmr(results = sol_yp,
              outcome = "LPI",
              match = FALSE,
              cases = 3)
dcons
```

5.2 Descriptive Inference SMMR

O 5.2

Deviant Consistency Cases :

	Cases	Term	TermMemb	Outcome	Best	MostDCONS
21	LT05	~UN*EP	0.939	0.003	0.125	TRUE
11	AT05	~UN*EP	0.546	0.000	0.908	FALSE
12	AT00	EP*LM	0.550	0.003	0.903	TRUE
22	AT05	EP*LM	0.546	0.000	0.908	FALSE
31	FI95	EP*LM	0.676	0.366	1.014	FALSE
5	FI05	EP*LM	0.523	0.173	1.127	FALSE
41	FI00	EP*LM	0.602	0.398	1.194	FALSE
4	FI05	WC*LM	0.909	0.173	0.356	TRUE
3	FI00	WC*LM	0.799	0.398	0.801	FALSE
2	AT05	WC*LM	0.595	0.000	0.810	FALSE
1	AT00	WC*LM	0.550	0.003	0.903	FALSE

As already mentioned on various occasions, the analytic goal pursued in the study of deviant consistency cases is better achieved in a comparison with a typical case. Code C 5.4 produces the list of best-matching pairs of typical and deviant consistency cases for each sufficient term in output O 5.3.

C 5.4

```
typdcons <- smmr(results = sol_yp,
                 outcome = "LPI",
                 match = TRUE,
                 cases = 3)
typdcons
```

For example, for the coordinated welfare regime (*LM* ∗ *WC*), several typical cases (the Netherlands and Germany at different points in time) could be matched with deviant consistency case Finland 2005. Their scores in column "Best" are very similar. The within-case analysis should ask what the analytically relevant difference is that could resolve the puzzle as to why term *LM* ∗ *WC* triggers the engagement and resource mechanisms in a typical case such as NL00, but fails to do so in a deviant consistency case such as FI05. As explained, this difference cannot consist in any of the features captured in the truth table. Instead, a hitherto overlooked factor specific to *LM* ∗ *WC* needs to be discovered. This factor could either be another welfare regime trait or a feature of the sociopolitical system, or both.

O 5.3

Term WC*LM :

	TYP	DCONS	Best	MostTypTerm	MostDCONS
1	NL00	FI05	0.385	FALSE	TRUE
2	DE95	FI05	0.390	FALSE	TRUE
3	DE00	FI05	0.391	FALSE	TRUE
4	NL95	FI05	0.417	TRUE	TRUE
5	NL05	FI05	0.417	TRUE	TRUE

Term ~UN*EP :

	TYP	DCONS	Best	MostTypTerm	MostDCONS
1	ES95	LT05	0.130	FALSE	TRUE

```
  2 MX05 LT05 0.136       FALSE    TRUE
  3 ES05 LT05 0.139       FALSE    TRUE
  4 MX00 LT05 0.142       FALSE    TRUE
  5 ES00 LT05 0.154       TRUE     TRUE

Term EP*LM :
_____
    TYP DCONS  Best MostTypTerm MostDCONS
  1 ES95 AT00 0.907       TRUE     TRUE
  2 ES95 AT05 0.913       TRUE     FALSE
  3 DK95 AT00 0.914       FALSE    TRUE
  4 ES05 AT00 0.917       FALSE    TRUE
  5 DK95 AT05 0.920       FALSE    FALSE
```

5.3 Causal Inference SMMR

We have learned that there are three SMMR designs that focus on the difference-making, causal properties of cross-case conditions on the mechanism: single typical case studies and a comparison of a typical case with either an iir case or another typical case. For reasons of space, I limit the discussion to the comparison between a typical and an iir case. Furthermore, the focal disjunct and focal conjunct principles require separate within-case analyses of each sufficient term and, within those, on each focal conjunct. The solution formula of Schneider and Makszin (2014) consists of three disjuncts, and each of them of two conjuncts, thus creating the need for six comparisons between typical and iir cases. I present only four of them, on the two "supportive" welfare regime types $LM * WC$ and $LM * EP$.[6]

As mentioned earlier, Schneider and Makszin (2014) stipulate two mechanisms that link their two welfare regimes to the outcome "low participatory inequality": a more equal distribution of resources and engagement across privileged and less privileged social groups (see Figure 1.1). For illustration, I operationalize the mechanisms as follows.[7] The resource mechanism is captured by the feeling of political efficacy (both internal and external) and how big the difference between this efficacy feeling is between rich (top 20%) and poor (bottom 20%)[8] citizens in a welfare regime. The set capturing this

---
[6] Since Schneider and Makszin (2014) move up the ladder of generality and label term $LM * WC$ as the "coordinated" and $LM * EP$ as the "protective" welfare regime, one could also forgo the focal conjunct principle and analyze the conjunction as a whole. Moreover, because Schneider and Makszin (2014) further subsume the "coordinated" and the "protectice" regime under the label of "supportive" welfare regime, one could forgo the focal disjunct principle and analyze those two terms jointly. As discussed earlier (see Section 4.3), such aggregation assumes that all conjuncts (and disjuncts) trigger the same mechanism(s).

[7] All data is from the Comparative Study of Electoral Systems, waves 1–4. My thanks go to Manuel Bosancianu for preparing the raw data.

[8] Schneider and Makszin (2014) focus on educated vs. noneducated citizens, which here I replace with rich vs. poor citizens due to data availability. The years in which data on the

mechanism is called "low difference in political efficacy feelings between rich and poor citizens" ($lodif\_poleff$). The engagement mechanism I capture with an indicator on whether or not citizens feel represented by a political party. If this feeling is equally present among rich and poor citizens in a welfare regime, then this case has a high membership in the set of "low difference between rich and poor citizens in feeling politically represented by a party" ($lodif\_repres$).

For both sufficient terms and each conjunct in them, I hypothesize a sufficiency chain ($FC \Rightarrow M \Rightarrow Y$). As outlined earlier, alternative scenarios could be a "broken floor" or a "broken ceiling" corridor (see Section 2.4 for a detailed discussion).

Focal Conjuncts in Sufficient Term *LM*WC*

Let us start with the coordinated welfare regime $LM * WC$. Code C 5.5 identifies the best available pairs of typical and iir cases, separate for each of the two focal conjuncts. These first pairs are listed in output O 5.4. For focal conjunct WC, the best-matching pair consists of Germany 1995 (DE95) as the typical case and Poland 1995 (PL95) as the iir case. This pair ticks almost all boxes for the perfect pair: rank 1, uniquely covered typical, globally uncovered iir, consistent membership in the focal conjunct of both cases, and a clean corridor. Just Germany 1995 is neither the most typical case for the entire term, nor for the focal conjunct – but these two criteria are the least important for ordering the typical–iir case pairs from best to worst.

C 5.5

```
typ_iir_LMWC <- smmr(results = sol_yp,
                     outcome = "LPI",
                     match = TRUE,
                     cases = 2,
                     term = 1,
                     max_pairs = 100)
typ_iir_LMWC
```

cross-case and within-case levels are collected differ by up to three years (and for Germany 1995, seven years).

O 5.4

Focal Conjunct WC :

	TYP	IIR	PairRank	CleanCorr	FC<=Y	UniqCov	GlobUncov	Best	MostTypFC	MostTypTerm
65	DE95	PL95	1	both	both	TRUE	TRUE	0.505	FALSE	FALSE
20	DE95	HU95	1	both	both	TRUE	TRUE	0.546	FALSE	FALSE
64	DK00	PL95	1	both	both	TRUE	TRUE	1.440	FALSE	FALSE
19	DK00	HU95	1	both	both	TRUE	TRUE	1.481	FALSE	FALSE
11	DE95	FI95	1	both	typ	TRUE	FALSE	1.116	FALSE	FALSE

....

Focal Conjunct LM :

	TYP	IIR	PairRank	CleanCorr	FC<=Y	UniqCov	GlobUncov	Best	MostTypFC	MostTypTerm
112	IE00	SI05	1	both	typ	TRUE	TRUE	0.577	FALSE	FALSE
121	IE00	CH95	1	both	typ	TRUE	TRUE	0.986	FALSE	FALSE
103	IE00	SK00	1	both	typ	TRUE	TRUE	1.119	FALSE	FALSE
116	NO95	SI05	1	both	typ	FALSE	TRUE	0.685	FALSE	FALSE
125	NO95	CH95	1	both	typ	FALSE	TRUE	1.094	FALSE	FALSE

....

| 31 | IE00 | HU00 | 4 | both | both | TRUE | TRUE | 1.690 | FALSE | FALSE |

Figure 5.2 XY plot: term $LM * WC$, focal conjunct WC, and membership in mechanisms of typical and iir cases, outcome "low participatory inequality" LPI

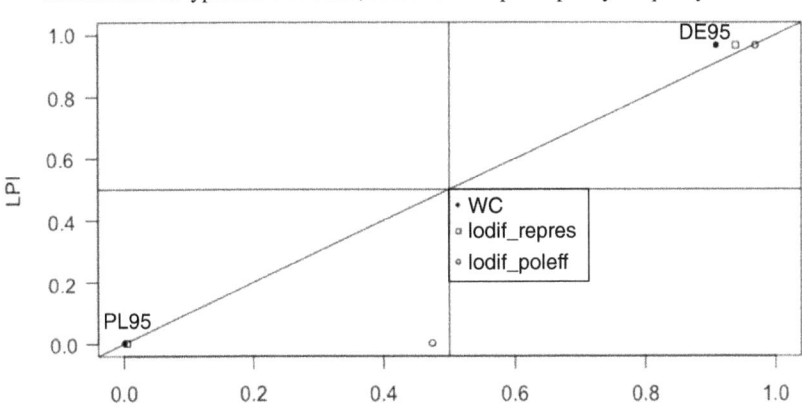

Cross-case focal conjunct WC and within-case mechanisms

The XY plot in Figure 5.2 shows the two cases' membership scores in the outcome LPI on the y-axis. On the x-axis, it shows each case's score in the focal conjunct (here WC, solid marker) and the two mechanisms (hollow markers).[9] It is important to remember that information on each case's membership in the mechanism(s) plays *no* role during the QCA. Instead, information on mechanism membership derives from the within-case analysis and becomes known and relevant only after the QCA has been performed.

The fact that membership in the focal conjunct WC is consistent with the statement of sufficiency is visualized by its location above the main diagonal for both the typical and the iir cases. The hypothesis of a sufficiency chain $(WC \Rightarrow M \Rightarrow LPI)$ requires that the mechanism is located in between each case's focal conjunct and the main diagonal (that is, its membership in the outcome).

In the typical case Germany 1995, membership in both mechanisms falls inside the sufficiency corridor and thus confirms our expectations that there is a sufficiency chain in which focal conjunct WC is sufficient for the mechanisms, which, in turn, are sufficient for the outcome LPI. The evidence from the iir case Poland 1995 only partially corroborates this: its membership in the "political representation mechanism" is in line with a sufficiency chain argument, whereas membership in feeling politically efficacious is not. The latter is in line, instead, with a broken ceiling, or suf-nec chain, in which focal

---

[9] For better visualization, I leave out markers for the complementary conjunct LM. From output O 5.4, we know for which case pairs the corridor is clean.

conjunct *WC* is sufficient for this mechanism (*WC* ⇒ *lodif_poleff*), which, in turn, is necessary for the outcome *LPI* (*lodif_poleff* ⇐ *LPI*). Based on the evidence at hand, the inference remains indeterminate which form of cross-case–within-case chain is operative. But the evidence in Figure 5.2 seems to clearly support the general claim that *WC* is causally linked to *LPI* via these two mechanisms because both cases' memberships in the mechanisms are on the side of the qualitative 0.5 anchor where we would expect them: above 0.5 in the typical case and below 0.5 in the iir case. We could say that the deviation from a sufficiency chain in the iir case is a deviance only in degree, not in kind.

The selection of a case pair for focal conjunct *LM* is more difficult. There are several pairs in ranks 1, 2, and 3 (not displayed in output O 5.4), but for none of them is data available on both cases in the mechanism. These practical constraints are typical in applied social science research. Here they force us to choose the pair of Ireland 2000 (IE00, typical case) and Hungary 2000 (HU00, iir case). This case pair is from rank 4. As explained in Chapter 4 (see, in particular, Figure 4.5), this means that, for the typical case, the attribution principle is fulfilled; for the irr case, however, neither the attribution nor the iir FC unique nonmembership principle hold. More specifically, in HU00 membership in the focal conjunct is bigger than in the complementary conjuncts, but at least both memberships are smaller than 0.5 membership in the focal conjunct, which is consistent with the statement of sufficiency, that is, it is smaller than HU00's membership in the outcome (see Figure 5.3). Furthermore, IE00 is uniquely covered, HU00 is globally uncovered, and the value of the "Best" indicator is not too high.

Figure 5.3 XY plot: term *LM* ∗ *WC*, focal conjunct *LM*, and membership in mechanisms, outcome "low participatory inequality" *LPI*

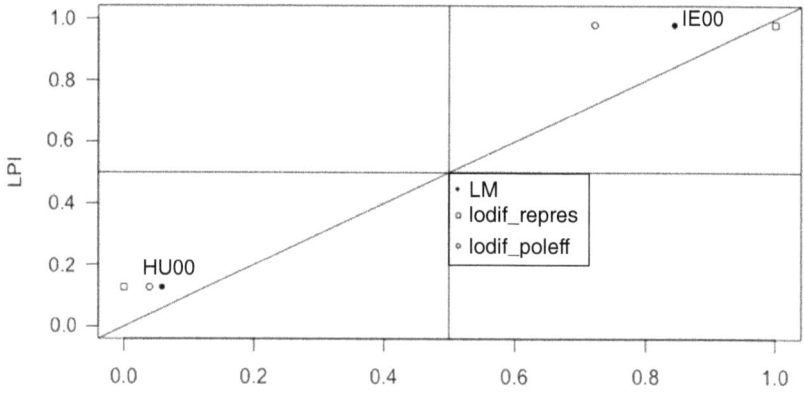

As Figure 5.3 shows, in both cases none of the two mechanisms is located in the sufficiency chain corridor. Based on this evidence, the sufficiency chain hypothesis finds no support for focal conjunct WC in the sufficient term $LM*WC$. At the same time, Figure 5.3 also does not provide strong evidence *against* a causal role of focal conjunct WC on the two within-case mechanisms underpinning the cross-case sufficiency relation $LM*WC \Rightarrow Y$: both mechanisms in both cases are located on the "correct" side of the qualitative anchor 0.5. The typical case Ireland 2000 is a member of both "low difference in feeling represented" and "low difference in feeling politically efficacious", whereas the iir case Hungary 2000 is not a member of any of the two mechanisms, that is, the difference between the feelings of the rich and those of the poor of being represented by a party and of being politically efficacious is *not* small in Hungary. The empirical evidence on the mechanism capturing feelings of political efficacy is in line with a broken floor, or nec-suf chain ($WC \Leftarrow lodif\_poleff \Rightarrow LPI$). For the mechanism on feelings of political representation, instead, the evidence in the two cases is not congruent. In the typical case, it suggests a broken ceiling, or suf-nec chain, whereas in the iir case, it is in line with the "opposite", a nec-suf chain, or broken floor. Remember that, for the iir case, the choice of Hungary 2000 was sub-optimal from a methodological point of view because neither the attribution principle nor the iir FC unique nonmembership principles are fulfilled. This makes the inferences drawn based on this case less determinate – both in favor of and against the sufficiency chain hypothesis.

Overall, there is relatively strong evidence that both conjuncts in the conjunction $LM*WC$ make a difference to both mechanisms. Information on the precise form – sufficiency chain, broken floor, or broken ceiling – is ambiguous, though. This indeterminacy could be reduced only by including more cases, preferably from higher ranks, to the within-case analysis.

Focal Conjuncts in Sufficient Term *LM*EP*

The second sufficient term discussed here is the combination of high labor market expenditure and high employment protection ($LM*EP$). As explained, according to Schneider and Makszin (2014), together with the "coordinated" welfare regime, this "protective" welfare arrangement represents the "supportive" welfare regime type. This implies that the same within-case mechanisms underpin the effect of these regime configurations on the outcome of low participatory inequality between rich and poor citizens (see Chapter 1, in particular Figure 1.1). I therefore test if, for focal conjunction $LM*EP$, all typical and iir cases display their membership in the two mechanisms (feeling of political representation and of efficacy) within the sufficiency chain test corridor.

Code C 5.6 produces the list of the best available pairs of typical and iir cases for each of the two focal conjuncts *LM* and *EP*, shown in output O 5.5.[10]

C 5.6

```
typ_iir_LMEP <- smmr(results = sol_yp,
                    outcome = "LPI",
                    match = TRUE,
                    cases = 2,
                    term = 3,
                    max_pairs = 100)
typ_iir_LMEP
```

---

[10] Due to space constraints, for each focal conjunct only five pairs are displayed, not 100, as requested by argument max_pairs = 100.

O 5.5

Focal Conjunct EP :

	TYP	IIR	PairRank	CleanCorr	FC<=Y	UniqCov	GlobUncov	Best	MostTypFC	MostTypTerm
25	SE00	HU95	1	both	typ	TRUE	TRUE	0.872	FALSE	FALSE
90	SE00	PL95	1	both	typ	TRUE	TRUE	0.905	FALSE	FALSE
14	DK95	HU95	1	both	typ	TRUE	TRUE	1.166	FALSE	FALSE
79	DK95	PL95	1	both	typ	TRUE	TRUE	1.199	FALSE	FALSE
...										
39	SE05	HU00	3	none	both	TRUE	TRUE	1.639	FALSE	FALSE

Focal Conjunct LM :

	TYP	IIR	PairRank	CleanCorr	FC<=Y	UniqCov	GlobUncov	Best	MostTypFC	MostTypTerm
119	FR05	RO00	1	both	both	TRUE	TRUE	0.904	FALSE	FALSE
67	FR05	LU00	1	both	both	TRUE	TRUE	0.927	FALSE	FALSE
125	SI95	RO00	1	both	both	TRUE	TRUE	1.341	FALSE	FALSE
73	SI95	LU00	1	both	both	TRUE	TRUE	1.354	FALSE	FALSE
145	FR05	SI05	1	both	typ	TRUE	TRUE	0.506	FALSE	FALSE

The XY plot in Figure 5.4 shows the membership in focal conjunct EP and in the two mechanisms of the typical case Sweden 2005 (SE05) and the iir case Hungary 2000 (HU00). This is the best available pair in the data at hand. There are many pairs that would be better choices, but data on the within-case mechanisms is not available for any of them. Hungary 2000 has already been the iir case in our previous analysis of focal conjunct LM in conjunction $LM * WC$, so its membership scores in the two mechanism are the same as before. What has changed is the location of these mechanism scores vis-à-vis focal conjunct EP. The mechanism on political efficacy falls inside the sufficiency test corridor, whereas the mechanism on political representation does not, and, instead, suggests a broken floor, or nec-suf chain. Such a causal interpretation of the effect of EP on the political representation mechanism, however, is contrasted by the fact that the typical case Sweden 2005 is also a *non*member of this mechanism. In fact, HU00 and SE05 have almost identically low membership scores in this mechanism. In light of this, it is unconvincing to argue that focal conjunct EP in conjunction $LM * EP$ makes a difference to the presence of mechanism "low difference between rich and poor in the feeling of being politically represented by a political party".

For the other mechanism (political efficacy), the evidence is less condemning. The typical case SE05 is, and the iir case HU00 is not, a member of this mechanism, thus suggesting that focal conjunct EP does make a difference to the occurrence of this mechanism and, via that, to the outcome LPI. What remains unresolved, though, is whether it is a sufficiency or a suf-nec chain, because for SE05, membership in the mechanism exceeds that in both the outcome and the focal conjunct. Again, this indeterminacy can be mitigated only by further within-case analyses of additional pairs of typical and iir cases, preferably from higher ranks.

In contrast to this, the within-case evidence on the causal nature of focal conjunct LM in conjunction $LM * EP$ seems unequivocal: LM does *not* make a difference to any of the two mechanisms. As Figure 5.5 shows, the typical case Ireland 2000 and the iir case Romania 2000 hold almost identical non-membership scores in both mechanisms. There can hardly be any stronger counter-evidence to our hypothesis that there is a sufficiency chain linking LM via these two mechanisms to outcome LPI.[11]

---

[11] The only evidence even stronger would be if the iir case held membership in both mechanisms *above* the 0.5 anchor.

Figure 5.4 XY plot: term *LM* ∗ *EP*, focal conjunct *EP*, and membership in mechanisms, outcome "low participatory inequality" *LPI*

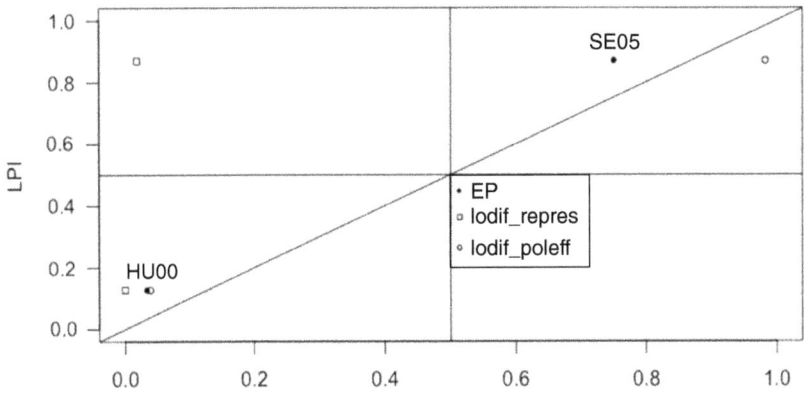

Cross-case focal conjunct EP and within-case mechanisms

Figure 5.5 XY plot: term *LM* ∗ *EP*, focal conjunct *LM*, and membership in mechanisms, outcome "low participatory inequality" *LPI*

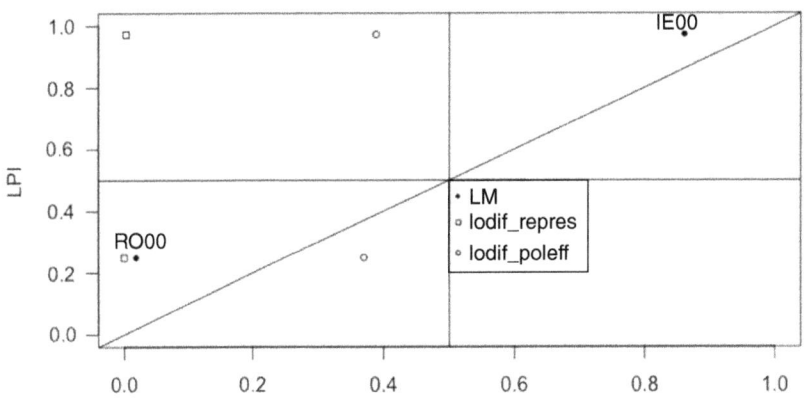

Cross-case focal conjunct LM and within-case mechanisms

5.4 Conclusion

Overall, the within-case evidence on the causal properties of the cross-case QCA solution are mixed. For sufficient term *LM* ∗ *WC*, evidence is stronger that it is a difference maker for the within-case mechanisms. For sufficient term *LM* ∗ *EP* that evidence is weaker. Comparing the two hypothesized

> **Core Points 5.1: Full Complexity**
>
> - Irrespective of the level of complexity of the QCA solution formula, the set of (sub-)types of cases, of SMMR principles, ranks, and formulas suffice to distinguish better from worse available (types of) cases for descriptive and causal inference SMMR designs
> - Within-case evidence of typical and iir cases' memberships in mechanism M vis-à-vis their memberships in the condition and the outcome gives room to various scenarios. Provided there is sound theoretical and conceptual support, three out of four scenarios can be interpreted causally: sufficiency chains, broken-floor chains, and broken-ceiling chains
> - All QCA solution types can be used in descriptive and in causal SMMR designs. The causal status of a QCA solution is determined by evidence found on the mechanisms at the within-case level

mechanisms, the evidence for political efficacy being a causal mechanism is more coherent than for political representation.

How far do these findings travel? The general take in SMMR is that these findings apply to all cases of the same kind. This means that findings are assumed to travel to all typical and iir cases for the same conjunct in the same conjunction. This assumption, and thus the inference, can, of course, be wrong. This risk goes up as sub-optimal cases (from worse ranks, with inconsistent scores, etc.) are chosen. As SMMR reports on these qualities of the cases chosen, this information can, and should, be factored in when expressing the degree of confidence in one's inferences. For the example at hand, note that the "risk" of being wrong in inferring to unstudied cases works both ways: when a hypothesis is found to be confirmed in the cases chosen *and* when it is not confirmed. For instance, our inference that focal conjunct LM in conjunction $LM * EP$ is noncausal could be an artifact of the cases we have selected. There might be idiosyncratic reasons why the typical case Ireland 2000 is a nonmember in both mechanisms (see Figure 5.5) and that with (any) other typical case the within-case evidence would look more in line with the expectation of a sufficiency chain. The purpose of the SMMR design comparing two typical cases is precisely to shed light on the question of how regular a mechanism is.

For space reasons, I have forgone the presentation of the SMMR designs studying a single typical case and comparing two typical cases. Applied researchers should perform the latter design, though, in particular if and when evidence from the typical–iir design is as heterogeneous as in our example in this chapter. Another, probably quite radical, simplification is that I reduced the mechanism to two sets and determined each case's membership in these sets based on readily available mass survey data. Most likely, in applied SMMR more mechanism elements are stipulated, and determining a case's membership in them will require more time-consuming and fine-grained data collection efforts. Any such more realistic and detailed approaches will not, however, change the basic logic of SMMR. In other words, having used simplified examples should not distract from the fact SMMR can be used in applied research for descriptive and causal inference. Such inferences, especially on complex statements as they are typically formulated in QCA, do require a lot of additional information. SMMR is a tool for directing researchers to the kind of information needed for scrutinizing their causal and descriptive claims.

5.5 Excursus: QCA Solution Types and Causal Inference SMMR Designs

Before moving to the next chapter on SMMR based on necessity claims, I explain why any QCA solution type can be used for causal inference in SMMR. In QCA, different solution formulas can be obtained (Ragin, 2008). They vary in their degree of complexity, ranging from the conservative solution over the (enhanced) intermediate to the (enhanced) most parsimonious solution (Schneider and Wagemann, 2012). The latter represents the shortest possible way in which the empirical data at hand can be summarized. This solution type contains INUS conditions that are difference makers for the outcome only at the cross-case level. From the perspective of a causal interpretation at the cross-case level, there are strong arguments in favor of the most parsimonious solution (Baumgartner, 2009).

In the framework of SMMR, the choice of solution type should not be restricted to the most parsimonious solution, though. This is not only because in applied QCA there are still unresolved practical hurdles for obtaining and causally interpreting this solution (Schneider, 2018). Even more important is the fact that, in SMMR, to count as a cause, a condition needs to make a difference to the outcome at the cross-case level *and* a difference to the mechanism at the within-case level. The most parsimonious solution, just as all other QCA solution types, is mute on this within-case level aspect of causal analysis.

It is true that only the most parsimonious solution reveals constant conjunctions because it is redundancy free: all conjuncts are difference makers *at the cross-case level*. However, in SMMR, causal inference requires that each conjunct is also a difference maker for the mechanisms *at the within-case level*. It therefore is possible that conjuncts that look like causes at the cross-case level are not causal when within-case evidence is taken on board. Even more so, it is possible that within-case evidence identifies causes that are not included in the most parsimonious solution. In other words, within-case evidence might reveal that the most parsimonious solution is either incomplete or (partially) wrong or both (Arel-Bundock, 2022). SMMR is based on a regularity theory of causality in which within-case evidence (token causality) trumps cross-case patterns (type causality). This position is in line with the work of other multi-method scholars, such as Beach and Rohlfing (2018, p. 13), Mahoney (2021), Ragin (2023: p.8), or Runhardt (2022).[12]

From this position it follows that solution types other than the most parsimonious solution – such as the intermediate and the conservative solutions – can, in principle and practice, fare better in terms of completeness and correctness, and thus be more adequate for performing SMMR. This is an empirical question and researchers using SMMR designs should therefore be open to using any of the available QCA solution types.

In their overview article introducing the special issue on solution types and causal inference in QCA, Haesebrouck and Thomann (2022) juxtapose the "substantive importance" (SI) or realist approach and the "redundancy-free" (RF) or idealist approach.[13] Causal interpretation in the latter requires a minimally necessary disjunction of a minimally sufficient conjunction, whereas in the former empirical consistency, relevance, and substantive importance matter. Clearly, SMMR is located in the SI camp, but it adds an important point to the debate. For causal inference in SMMR, it is required that a cause makes a difference to the within-case mechanism. Without evidence that the cause makes a difference to the causal mechanism, the causal analysis and inference is incomplete. Several other contributions to the same special issue take a de facto identical stance (see Álamos-Concha et al., 2022; Mahoney and Acosta, 2022).

As has become clear, the empirical evidence at the cross-case and within-case levels does not always point in the same direction. Because, in SMMR,

---

[12] Giving precedence to within-case evidence over cross-case evidence does not tie SMMR to counterfactual or mechanismic theories of causation. Instead, as explained, I suggest that SMMR is firmly rooted in a regularity theory of causation in the version outlined by Mahoney (2021) and Mahoney and Acosta (2022).

[13] On realists and idealists in QCA, see Schneider (2018).

5.5 Excursus: QCA Solution Types and SMMR

evidence at the within-case level trumps that at the cross-case level, what should researchers do when discovering such contradictory evidence?

To answer this question and to spell out the different possible scenarios of cross-case and within-case evidence on the causal status of a conjunct, let us briefly recall the logic of causal inference SMMR designs. The causal inference designs in SMMR use within-case evidence to test whether each INUS conjunct really is a necessary (the "N" in INUS) element of the sufficient conjunction. The most parsimonious solution postulates precisely this. All conjuncts are so-called core conditions (Fiss, 2011). Any other solution type contains additional, so-called peripheral conditions next to the core conditions.[14] Now, if within-case analysis reveals that a given conjunct does not trigger a mechanism, then the consequences for the causal interpretation of the QCA solution formula depend on whether the condition in question is a core or a peripheral conjunct. Table 5.3 depicts the different scenarios and their interpretation.[15]

Table 5.3 *Causal status of QCA solution types in light of within-case evidence*

		Within-case evidence on difference-making status of conjunct is:	
		Confirming	Disconfirming
Cross-case status of conjunct is:	Core	MPS causal	no solution causal ("wrong")
	Peripheral	MPS "incomplete" IS/CS "complete"	IC/CS not causal ("wrong")

MPS: most parsimonious solution; IS: intermediate solution; CS: conservative solution

If within-case evidence reveals that all core conditions are also difference makers for the causal mechanism, then, and only then, can we interpret the most parsimonious solution as being causal for the outcome of interest. As a matter of fact, for any other solution type to also count as causal, all core conjuncts must be shown to be difference makers for the mechanism. If within-case evidence shows that one or more core conjuncts do not trigger a causal mechanism, then the most parsimonious solution should not be causally

---

[14] In applied QCA, often times only the enhanced most parsimonious solution is feasible if researchers want to avoid untenable assumptions on logical remainders (Schneider and Wagemann, 2012, chap. 8.2). By definition, the enhanced most parsimonious solution contains not only the core conjunct, but also at least one peripheral conjunct.

[15] For a slightly different angle on the possible scenarios of incongruent findings at the cross-case and within-case levels, see Beach and Rohlfing (2018, p. 13).

interpreted. It includes "wrong", that is, nondifference maker, conjuncts. From a within-case perspective, the solution is not redundancy free. One way forward could be to investigate which analytic decisions at the cross-case level made the conjunct appear as a difference maker. For all solution types it applies: if a core condition does not trigger a mechanism, then the causal status of that solution is hampered. In short, one can say that for all solution types to count as causal, it is necessary but not sufficient, that all core conjuncts pass the within-case level test.

If peripheral conditions in the conservative or intermediate solution turn out to be difference makers for the causal mechanism, then one has to conclude that the most parsimonious solution is incomplete: it does not contain all difference makers for the causal mechanism. The conservative or intermediate solution would then express the true causal structure more adequately because it fares better in terms of completeness and correctness. This is in line with the argument by Álamos-Concha et al. (2022) who favor the conservative solution because it guards against the risk of omitted conjuncts. If, however, no confirming evidence is found that peripheral conditions trigger a mechanism, then the intermediate or conservative solution cannot be the base for causal claims. For descriptive inference, such intermediate or conservative solutions could still be more useful, an argument made by, among others, Álamos-Concha et al. (2022).[16]

---

[16] Álamos-Concha et al. (2022) also argue that the conservative solution is the best antidote against mechanismic heterogeneity.

6
Necessary Conditions

Applied QCA is predominantly about the analysis of sufficient conditions. The most plausible source for this sufficiency bias (Schneider and Wagemann, 2012, chap. 9) is probably the fact that at the core of QCA's analytic moment is the truth table, and each row in that table constitutes a statement of sufficiency. Despite this, in the social sciences there is considerable interest in necessary conditions (Goertz and Starr, 2003) and scholars in the field of set-theoretic methods respond with methodological innovations on how to analyze them (Mahoney et al., 2009; Schneider, 2018, 2019; Vis and Dul, 2018). So far, the SMMR literature has paid little attention to SMMR designs on necessity claims (for exeptions, see Goertz, 2017; Rohlfing and Schneider, 2013; Schneider and Rohlfing, 2013). This chapter expands, modifies, specifies, and completes this literature.

In this chapter, I discuss which adaptations, if any, need to be made to the types of cases, principles, and formulas in SMMR if the focus of the analysis is statements of necessity rather than sufficiency. In a nutshell, almost all case types, principles, and formulas travel to the analysis of necessity without any, or only minor, adaptations. This might come as a surprise, given that claims of necessity are, in a sense, the opposite of claims of sufficiency: necessary conditions "constrain" (Goertz, 2017) the occurrence of the outcome, whereas sufficient conditions produce the outcome; the former are supersets and the latter are subsets of the outcome. As I explain in this chapter, in SMMR the goal is to select cases such that no difference is expected in the effect on the mechanism between necessary and sufficient conditions *in the cases selected*: both types of conditions are expected to produce – and in their absence to prevent – the mechanism in the selected cases. In other words, SMMR principles are designed such that both necessary and sufficient conditions are expected to make a difference to the within-case level mechanism.

Just as before, I structure the discussion based on an increasing level of complexity of the necessity claims. We start with the basics, based on a necessity claim of a single condition $A \Leftarrow Y$. Unlike for sufficiency claims, such single-condition necessity statements are the norm rather than the exception. This is followed by SUIN[1] conditions in the disjunction $A + B \Leftarrow Y$ and then conjunctive ININ[2] causes in claims such as $A * B \Leftarrow Y$. While the latter are very rare in applied QCA, the maximum level of complexity that combines both conjuncts and disjuncts in one necessity claim is virtually nonexistent in applied social science research. In the concluding section, I therefore dedicate some reflections to the more realistic and common scenario of a disjunction of conjunctions that is both necessary and sufficient, as expressed by the bidirectional arrow: $A * B + C * D \Leftrightarrow Y$. In fact, such formulas are the result of analyses of sufficiency if and when the truth tables that are logically minimized contain only rows with very high consistency and, as a result, the sufficiency solutions then also display very high solution coverage.

As said, only minor adaptations are needed for case types, forms of single-case and comparative SMMR designs, principles, formulas, and ranks. This, together with the aforementioned greater focus on sufficient conditions in applied QCA, explains why I dedicate only one (admittedly long) chapter to the topic of SMMR on necessary conditions. While I assume that readers are familiar with the material presented in all preceding chapters, this chapter also serves the function of repeating and rehearsing the core elements of SMMR.

6.1 Basics, $A \Leftarrow Y$

This section spells out the basics of SMMR designs on necessity claims. As we will see, most of what has been introduced in the previous chapters on SMMR, based on sufficiency claims, continues to apply: the basic principles, main case types, logic of formulas, types of single-case and comparative SMMR designs and their associated descriptive and causal inference goals remain virtually unaltered. Only minor adaptations are needed to these building blocks to make SMMR work with necessity claims.

6.1.1 Empirical Example

For illustration, I use the study by Bretthauer (2015). Her goal is to identify the conditions under which there is conflict or not between groups in resource-

---

[1] A sufficient (S) but unnecessary (U) part of a factor that is insufficient (I) but necessary (N) for an outcome (Mahoney et al., 2009, p. 126).

[2] A conjunct that is an insufficient (I) but necessary (N) element of a cause that is itself insufficient (I) but necessary (N) for an outcome.

6.1 Basics, $A \Leftarrow Y$

Learning Goals 6.1: Necessary Conditions

- Understand that only minor adjustments to SMMR types of cases, forms of single-case and comparative designs, principles, formulas, and ranks are needed when the cross-case solution postulates a necessary condition
- Consolidate the knowledge of SMMR principles, types of cases, and formulas

Empirical Example 6.1: Conditions for peace and conflict: applying a fuzzy-set qualitative comparative analysis to cases of resource scarcity (Bretthauer, 2015)

- *Research question*: Under which social, economic, and political conditions do conflicts occur in resource-scarce countries?
- *Cases*: 31 resource-scarce countries
- *Set type*: Fuzzy
- *Outcome*: Conflict (BDT) and nonconflict ($\sim BDT$)
- *Conditions*: Low-quality political institutions (PIN), political corruption (COR), ethnic exclusion (EEX), poverty (POV), dependence on agriculture (DEP), high levels of tertiary education (EDU), high economic development ($ECOD$)

scarce countries. The 31 cases are analyzed using six fuzzy sets. While the author also engages in analyses of sufficiency for both conflict and nonconflict, I focus on the analysis of necessity only.

For outcome nonconflict ($\sim BDT$), the analysis of necessity reveals that the absence of dependence on agriculture ($\sim DEP$) passes the empirical criteria for being a necessary condition. As shown in Table 6.1, consistency is virtually 0.9 and both the RoN[3] and coverage parameters indicate that the condition is not trivial. According to Bretthauer, this also makes substantive sense when she points to a mechanism according to which a lack of dependence on agriculture mitigates the conflict potential that arises through climate change and the concomitant reduction of arable land (Bretthauer, 2015, pp. 606ff.).

The XY plot in Figure 6.1 graphically displays the necessity relation $\sim DEP \Leftarrow \sim BDT$. In the remainder of the section, I provide answers to questions such as the following: Where in this plot are typical and deviant cases located? Which case, or pair of cases, should be chosen for within-case analysis for which analytic purpose? And which SMMR principles and formulas should guide this case selection?

---
[3] The parameter relevance of necessity (RoN) expresses the degree to which a superset of Y can be interpreted as a non-trivial necessary condition (Schneider and Wagemann, 2012, chap. 9).

Table 6.1 *Necessary condition, outcome "nonconflict"* ~BDT

	inclN	RoN	covN
~DEP	0.89	0.730	0.789

Condition ~DEP: no dependence on agriculture; outcome ~BTD: nonconflict

Figure 6.1 XY plot: necessary condition ~DEP for outcome "nonconflict" ~BDT

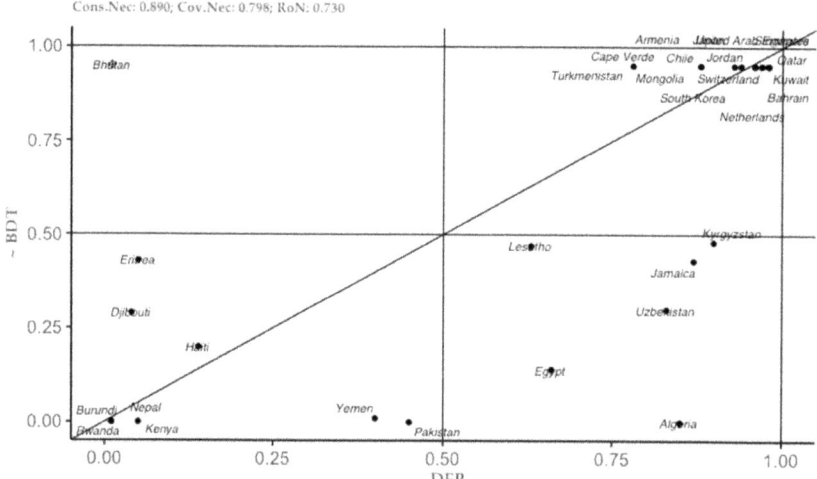

6.1.2 Single-Case SMMR

Virtually the same four basic types of cases as in SMMR on sufficiency also exist in SMMR on necessity. Figure 6.2 shows their location in a 2×2 table. As before, typical cases are located in the upper-right and individually irrelevant (iir) cases in the lower-left quadrant. Only the location of the two deviant case types have swapped places. Deviant consistency cases are located in the upper-left quadrant because they display the outcome ~BDT without being members of the necessary condition ~DEP, thus contradicting the claim that in order to observe outcome ~BDT, it is necessary to also observe condition ~DEP. The other deviant case is located in the lower-right corner and is labeled deviant relevance case. The reason why it is not called a deviant coverage case is because, by definition, a necessary condition covers all members of the outcome. This is also why the parameter of fit assessing the empirical importance, or relevance, of a necessary condition is called Relevance of Necessity (RoN) (Schneider and Wagemann, 2012, chap. 9).

6.1 Basics, A ⇐ Y

Figure 6.2 Types of cases, crisp-set SMMR on necessity

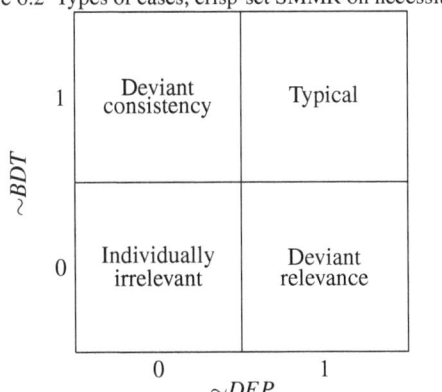

With fuzzy sets, several sub-types of cases exist. Deviant consistency cases are divided into deviant in kind and in degree. As Figure 6.3 shows, the former are located in the upper-left quadrant, whereas the latter are located in the triangle above the main diagonal in the upper-right quadrant. In Bretthauer's study on nonconflict, an example, or better, the only example, of a deviant consistency case in kind is Bhutan (see Figure 6.1). Bhutan is almost a full member of the outcome "nonconflict" but holds a very low membership in the necessary condition "no dependence on agriculture". In contrast, there are several deviant consistency cases in degree (e.g. Cape Verde or Mongolia). They are members of both the necessary condition $\sim DEP$ and the outcome $\sim BDT$, but their fuzzy set membership score in the condition is smaller than in the outcome ($\sim DEP_i < \sim BDT_i$), thus deviating from the necessity claim $\sim DEP \Leftarrow \sim BDT$, which requires $\sim DEP_i \geq \sim BDT_i$.

Within the group of typical cases, with fuzzy sets we can further identify the most typical and the just-so typical case. The *principle of maximum set membership*, introduced in Chapter 2, applies: The most typical case displays maximum set membership scores in the condition and the outcome. The former is located at the upper-right and the latter on the lower-left tip of the triangle denoting the area for typical cases. As the XY plot in Figure 6.1 shows, there is not really any good example for the latter sub-type. And for the most typical case, visual inspection reaches its limits. This is why below we will solicit the help of the dedicated R function smmr() for identifying this and all the other best available types of cases. Finally, among the group of deviant relevance cases, the most deviant is located in the lower-right corner of the quadrant in the bottom-right corner. Note that the distinction into sub-types based on fuzzy sets follows the *principle of differences in kind and degree*, introduced in Chapter 2: Differences in degree should be established only among cases that are similar in kind and located on the same side of the secondary diagonal.

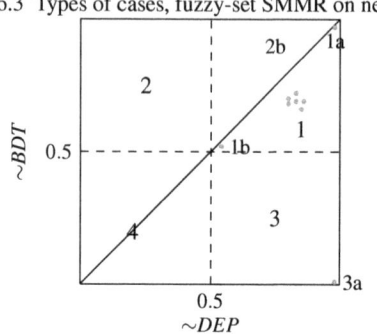

Figure 6.3 Types of cases, fuzzy-set SMMR on necessity

1: Typical; 1a: ideal typical; 1b: just-so typical; 2: deviant consistency in kind; 2b: deviant consistency in degree; 3: deviant relevance; 3a: ideal deviant relevance; 4: individually irrelevant

What are the goals of within-case analyses of these types of cases? Table 6.2 provides an answer to this question. Just as with sufficiency, there can be two broad goals: causal inference and descriptive inference/model specification. And just as before, causal inference requires involving at least one typical case, whereas model specification requires involving deviant cases. This follows from the *causal and the descriptive inference selection principles*, introduced in Chapter 2, which also apply to SMMR designs on necessity claims.

Table 6.2 *Types of cases and analytic goals of within-case analysis* $(X \Leftarrow Y)$

Type of case	Condition X	Outcome Y	Goal of single within-case analysis
			Causal inference
(1) Typical	>0.5	>0.5	$X \geq Y$ Test mechanism M
(4) iir	<0.5	<0.5	None
			Descriptive inference/model specification
(2) Dev consistency (kind)	<0.5	>0.5	Identify omitted disjunct
(2b) Dev consistency (degree)	>0.5	>0.5	$X \leq Y$ Not recommended
(3) Dev relevance	<0.5	<0.5	Identify omitted conjunct

6.1 Basics, $A \Leftarrow Y$

Typical Cases

As shown in Table 6.2, when performing within-case analysis in a case that is typical for a claim of necessity, the goal consists in identifying or testing the within-case mechanism M that links the cross-case condition $\sim DEP$ to the outcome $\sim BDT$. Why is it that the absence of dependence on agriculture is necessary for the absence of conflict? To answer this question, it is useful to engage in the counterfactual and ask: What would happen if the typical case *were* dependent on agriculture? If $\sim DEP$ really is necessary for $\sim BDT$, the answer must be: In the absence of $\sim DEP$, the outcome nonconflict ($\sim BDT$) would also be absent.

The presence of the necessary condition enables the presence of the mechanism and the absence of the necessary condition prevents the existence of this mechanism. As mechanism Bretthauer (2015, p. 609) hints at increased conflict over shrinking amounts of arable land due to climate change, which links being dependent on agriculture (*DEP*) to conflict (*BDT*). Let us label this mechanism as M_C. Bretthauer's counterfactual claim can be written as shown in Expression 6.1. Note that this counterfactual describes an iir case, that is, a case in which both the proclaimed cause ($\sim DEP$) and the outcome ($\sim BDT$) are absent.

$$DEP \Rightarrow M_C \Rightarrow BDT \qquad (6.1)$$

Using DeMorgan's laws, this sufficiency chain can be rewritten as a claim of necessity. Mirroring the sufficiency chain discussed for claims of sufficiency in Chapter 2, for claims of necessity, the most common and plausible chain is one of necessity: the necessary condition is necessary for the mechanism, which, in turn, is necessary for the outcome.[4]

$$\sim DEP \Leftarrow \sim M_C \Leftarrow \sim BDT \qquad (6.2)$$

According to Bretthauer, the absence of dependence on agriculture $\sim DEP$ is necessary not only for the absence of the outcome nonconflict $\sim BDT$ (cross-case), but also for the absence of the mechanism $\sim M_C$ (within-case). The first claim of necessity has been established via a cross-case QCA. The second necessity claim is the focus of the within-case analysis of typical (and irr) cases.

Goertz (2017) links necessary conditions to constraint causal mechanisms, that is, mechanisms that prevent the outcome from occurring. This is not much

---

[4] Alternatives to a necessity chain would be a nec-suf ($\sim DEP \Leftarrow M_C \Rightarrow \sim BDT$) or a suf-nec ($\sim DEP \Rightarrow M_C \Leftarrow \sim BDT$) chain. For more details, see the excursus in Sections 4.4 and 6.1.3.

different from the position I take here. Rather than starting with the question why outcome $\sim BDT$ does not occur, I focus on why its opposite, BDT, occurs in a counterfactual or iir case.[5] With both approaches – Goertz and mine – the iir cases, or the cases in the 0, 0 cell in Goertz' terminology, play a crucial role in investigating the causal properties of necessary conditions such as $\sim DEP$ in the current example. I therefore fully agree Goertz when he writes that "to see the causal mechanism in action is to choose cases from the (0, 0) cell" (Goertz, 2017, p. 101). In SMMR, the study of iir cases alone remains not recommended, though. Instead, the comparative SMMR design matching an iir case with a typical case is proposed (see Section 6.1.4).

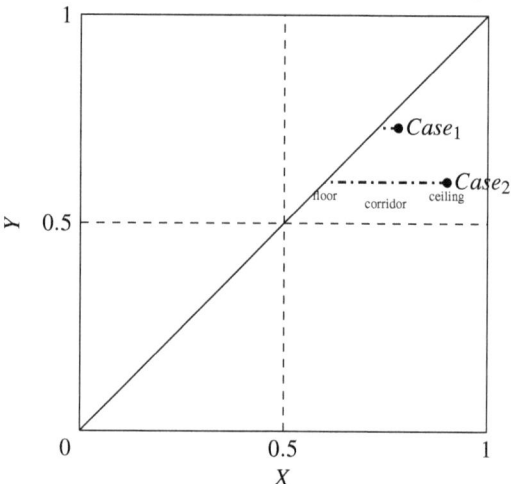

Figure 6.4 Visualizations of test corridor, necessity

The *test corridor principle*, introduced in Chapter 2, also holds for necessity chains. Its logic is visualized in Figure 6.4 and implies that, also for claims of necessity, the choice of cases with similar memberships in both the condition and the outcome are superior for within-case analysis. They provide for harder tests. The only difference in the test corridor for sufficient conditions is that floor and ceiling are inverted. With necessity claims, the floor is provided

---

[5] As Goertz (2017, chap. 4) rightly points out, this approach works best when the negation of the outcome of interest is well defined. In the present example, this seems to be the case: In a country there either is (M_C) or is not ($\sim M_C$) conflict over arable land due to climate change. Often times, though, the negation of a concept is not the same as its conceptual opposite. For instance, the logical negation of "war" is "not-war", which is not the same as the conceptual opposite "peace". Countries can be not at war without living in peace (think, for instance, of the USA and Iran). Likewise, the negation of "tall person" is "not-tall person", which is not the same as "small person" as there can also be "mid-sized persons" who are not tall.

6.1 Basics, $A \Leftarrow Y$

by a case's membership in outcome Y and the ceiling by its membership in necessary condition X. I have already introduced the notion of inverted corridors in Section 4.4 and it is nicely visualized in Figure 6.4.

As the brief discussion has already shown, necessity claims, more than sufficiency claims, draw attention to the individually irrelevant cases. This is because it is the *absence* of a necessary condition that creates precisely defined expectations for both the outcome and the within-case mechanism: they must be absent, too. The presence of the necessary condition, instead, does not predetermine the values of the mechanism or the outcome: they can both be present or absent without contradicting the claim of necessity. In typical cases, however, which, by definition, are members of the outcome, the mechanism is expected to be present. Within-case analysis of a single (or multiple) typical case(s) is therefore useful for probing the existence of the hypothesized mechanism. Nevertheless, ultimately it requires comparative within-case analysis to test the causal status of the necessary condition. This is why below I am turning to comparative SMMR designs.

With crisp sets, all typical cases are equally well suited for within-case analysis, or at least, their set membership scores in the condition and outcome cannot provide any guidance on which case to prefer over others. With fuzzy sets, such guidance exists. Formula 6.3 captures the test corridor principle and the requirement that high membership in the condition of interest is to be preferred.[6]

$$TYPnec = (2*|Y-N|) \quad \text{\small small corridor}$$
$$+ (1-N) \quad \text{\small large membership in necessary term} \tag{6.3}$$

TYPnec: typical case; N: necessary term of interest; Y: outcome

Just like for sufficiency, for necessity it also holds for all formulas that smaller values indicate better cases or pairs of cases. As most principles hold for both sufficiency and necessity, the formulas look very similar. They often need to adjust only for the fact that, with necessity, membership in the condition of interest is bigger than in the outcome, rather than the inverse, as is the case for sufficiency claims.

---

[6] This formula is similar to the corresponding formula for the best available typical case for statements of sufficiency (see Formula 2.4), except for the inversion of the subtrahend and minuend. In the necessity formula, we subtract the case's membership in the outcome Y from the necessary condition N because by definition, $N \geq Y$ in typical cases.

6.1.3 Excursus: Forms of Broken Necessity Corridors

In the excursus in Section 2.4, I spelled out different forms of broken corridors for sufficient conditions. The same holds for necessary conditions. A corridor is broken when a case's membership in the mechanism falls outside the corridor created by the case's membership in the condition and the outcome. Figure 6.5 visualizes the four possible scenarios in which membership in the mechanism can be located vis-à-vis necessary condition X and outcome Y. As with sufficiency, three locations can be causally interpreted if supported by theoretical arguments, whereas one location clearly rules out the necessary condition as causal for mechanism M and outcome Y.

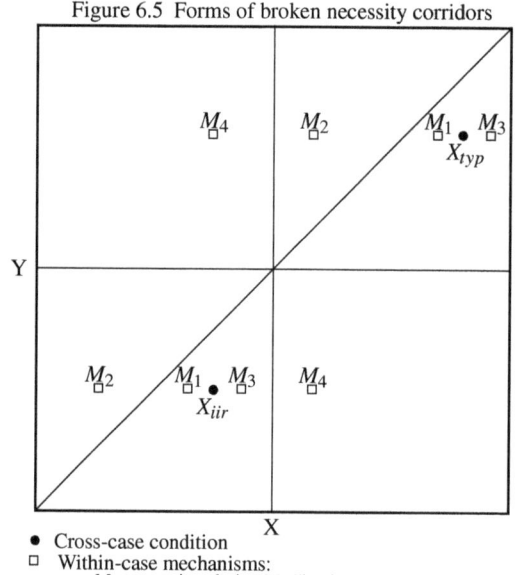

Figure 6.5 Forms of broken necessity corridors

● Cross-case condition
□ Within-case mechanisms:
 M_1 necessity chain; M_2 "broken floor" (nec-suf chain); M_3 "broken ceiling" (suf-nec chain); M_4 noncausal

If the mechanism is located inside the corridor, it provides evidence for a necessity chain. Mechanism M_1 in Figure 6.5 visualizes this scenario: condition X is necessary for mechanism M_1, which, in turn, is necessary for outcome Y ($X \Leftarrow M_1 \Leftarrow Y$). A broken ceiling happens when the case's membership in the mechanism exceeds that in the necessary condition, as represented by mechanism M_3. This situation can also be labeled as a suf-nec chain, in which X is sufficient for M_3, which, in turn, is necessary for Y ($X \Rightarrow M_3 \Leftarrow Y$). Similarly, a broken floor happens when the case's membership in the mechanism falls below that in the outcome, as represented by M_2. This can be labeled as a nec-suf chain, in which X is necessary for M_2, which, in turn, is sufficient for Y ($X \Leftarrow M_2 \Rightarrow Y$).

For all three scenarios the test corridor principle holds, which stipulates that cases should be chosen whose membership in X and Y is as similar as possible. Provided there are sound theoretical arguments, all three scenarios can be causally interpreted. This is because, in all three scenarios, membership in the mechanism is located on the expected side of the qualitative anchor: typical cases are members of the mechanism and iir cases are not members of the mechanism. Only in the fourth scenario, represented by M_4, must X be ruled out as being causal for the mechanism and the outcome. M_4 is located on the wrong side of the qualitative anchor: typical cases are not, and iir cases are, members of the mechanism.

Deviant Consistency Cases

With necessity statements, deviant consistency cases are puzzling because, like typical cases, they are members of the outcome $\sim BDT$, but, unlike typical cases, they are not members of the necessary condition $\sim DEP$. The goal of within-case analysis is to find out why outcome $\sim BDT$ is triggered in the deviant consistency case. The only model-related reason can be that a hitherto overlooked condition is enabling the mechanism $\sim M_C$ instead of $\sim DEP$. In other words, the goal of the within-case analysis of a deviant consistency case consists in identifying an omitted disjunct that acts as a functional equivalent to the known necessary condition $\sim DEP$ in enabling the mechanism $\sim M_C$.[7]

The identification of the best available deviant consistency case is guided by two principles. Both have already been introduced in the discussion of sufficiency claims (see Chapter 2). The *principle of maximum membership difference* states that deviant consistency cases should display the maximum difference in their membership in the necessary condition and the outcome. And based on the *truth table row principle*, which pays tribute to the fact that, for cases that are *not* members of a known condition (necessary or sufficient), the best starting point for finding the omitted condition is the truth table row to which they belong. With claims of necessity, the first step in the within-case analysis of a deviant consistency case is to identify which of the conditions from that truth table row could qualify as necessary conditions, either in isolation or in a disjunction.

The truth table row principle implies that deviant consistency cases from different truth table rows should be treated separately. It also implies that XY

---

[7] Or a mechanism functionally equivalent to $\sim M_C$ – see below and the discussion on mechanismic heterogeneity at the mechanism level in Chapter 1.

plots such as the one in Figure 6.1 are usually not helpful in identifying the best available deviant consistency case because the crucial information on what truth table row they belong to is not revealed. This is why it is advised to make use of the dedicated smmr() function.

In the current example by Bretthauer, there is just one deviant consistency case: Bhutan. It belongs to the truth table row $POV * DEP * {\sim}ECOD * {\sim}COR * {\sim}PIN * EDU * EEX$. By definition, it is not a member of the necessary condition $\sim DEP$. A within-case analysis should focus on whether any of the remaining conditions of which Bhutan is a member has triggered (a functional equivalent of) mechanism $\sim M_C$.[8] For instance, researchers might find evidence that Bhutan's membership in the set of a population with a high share of tertiary education (EDU) allows for an "ingenuity" mechanism (M_I) which, in turn, allows Bhutan to find solutions to pressures caused by, for instance, climate change (Bretthauer, 2015) ($EDU \Leftarrow M_I \Leftarrow \sim BDT$). The updated statement of necessity would then be $\sim DEP + EDU \Leftarrow \sim BDT$. This statement of necessity passes all empirical criteria for necessity claims at the cross-case level[9] and conceptually could be interpreted such that the two SUIN conditions $\sim DEP$ and EDU are functional equivalents for the higher-order concept "conflict pressure deflection" Z. This turns Bhutan from a deviant consistency into a typical case for this updated statement of necessity.[10]

The formula for the best available deviant consistency case for necessity claims is shown in Formula 6.4. It follows the principle of maximum set membership difference.

$$DCONnec = 1 - (Y - N) \quad \text{\small large difference in outcome and necessary term} \quad (6.4)$$

DCONnec: deviant consistency case; *N*: necessary term of interest; *Y*: outcome

Deviant Relevance Cases

Deviant relevance cases are not a puzzle in and of themselves. They display the presence of the necessary condition but the outcome is absent. Examples are Uzbekistan and Algeria (see Figure 6.1). They are perfectly in line with a statement of necessity. Yet, too many deviant relevance cases lower the empirical relevance of the necessity claim. This means that within-case

---

[8] If none of the conditions in the truth table qualifies as necessary, researchers need to extend their search to conditions hitherto omitted from the truth table.
[9] Consistency 0.933; RoN 0.689; coverage 0.791.
[10] Interestingly, Bretthauer (2015, p. 606) alludes to measurement issues rather than model-related reasons for deviance when she points out that Bhutan "[...] experienced significant ethnic strife in the early nineties," but not enough to pass her threshold of 25 battle deaths. Identifying flawed measurement or near misses can always be the result of SMMR, yet its main focus is on model-related inferences.

analyses of this type of case aims at increasing the relevance of the necessity claim. This is analogous to the motivation for studying deviant coverage cases for sufficiency claims: they, too, do not contradict any claim of sufficiency, but lower the empirical importance of those sufficiency statements.

The relevance score of 0.730 for the necessity claim $\sim DEP \Leftarrow \sim BDT$ is very high and, consequently, the XY plot in Figure 6.1 shows only few cases in the lower-right quadrant, the area for deviant relevance cases. This means that the need for within-case analyses to increase the empirical relevance of the necessity claim is not very high. If researchers nevertheless decide to go for it, then the model-related solution to reducing deviant relevance cases, and to increase the empirical relevance of the necessity claim, consists in identifying the missing conjunct from the known necessary condition. The claim that it is the absence of dependence on agriculture alone that is necessary for the absence of conflict is too sweeping and needs refinement.[11]

For instance, it could be that it is the joint absence of dependence on agriculture and of corruption that is more relevant as a necessary condition for the absence of conflict ($\sim DEP * \sim COR \Leftarrow \sim BDT$). Within-case analysis should provide evidence that deviant relevance cases that are *not* members of this conjunction also do not display the mechanism $\sim M_C$. Such cases then turn from deviant relevance into iir cases with regard to the updated conjunctural statement of necessity. This shift of cases increases the empirical relevance of the updated necessity statement. Because not only deviant relevance cases, but also typical cases, might be affected and be turned into deviant consistency cases, any refinement of the necessity statement based on within-case evidence must pass the consistency threshold at the cross-case level. In our current example, the updated necessity claim $\sim DEP * \sim COR \Leftarrow \sim BDT$ fails to pass this test: it has a consistency score of 0.647 as a necessary condition for the outcome. This suggests that the empirical relevance of the necessity claim $\sim DEP \Leftarrow \sim BDT$ cannot be enhanced (at least not by adding the absence of corruption $\sim COR$).

The formula for identifying the best available deviant relevance case is given in Formula 6.5. It identifies the case closest to the lower-right corner of an XY plot as the most deviant relevance case.

$$DREL = [1 - (N - Y)] \quad \text{\small large difference between necessary term and outcome}$$
$$+ (1 - N) \quad \text{\small large membership in necessary term} \tag{6.5}$$

DREL: deviant relevance case; Y: outcome; N: necessary term of interest

---

[11] With this advice, I deviate from Rohlfing and Schneider (2013) and Goertz (2017, chap. 4) who hold that the within-case analysis of deviant relevance cases is futile.

6.1.4 Comparative SMMR

Just as in SMMR on sufficiency, there are also four feasible forms of comparative SMMR designs for claims of necessity. Figure 6.6 graphically depicts them, together with the purpose they serve. The same information is contained in Table 6.3. These comparisons are governed by almost the same principles as those for SMMR on sufficiency. The formulas for identifying the best-matching pairs of cases also mostly need only minor adjustments.

The positive outcome principle, according to which at least one case must be a member of the outcome (see Chapter 2), also applies to necessity claims. It renders futile a comparison between an iir and a deviant relevance case. The *causal inference selection principle*, according to which at least one typical case must be involved, underpins the two causal inference SMMR designs: a comparison between a typical and an iir case to test the causal properties, and between two typical cases to test the regularity of the mechanism. Along similar lines, the *descriptive inference selection principle*, according to which at least one case must be deviant, motivates the two comparative descriptive inference SMMR designs: a comparison between a typical and a deviant consistency case with the goal of identifying the omitted disjunct, and between a typical and a deviant relevance case to identify the missing conjunct. Furthermore, the *truth table row principle* applies to all comparisons involving cases that are not members of the known necessary term.

Rohlfing and Schneider (2013) propose an additional comparison between an iir and a deviant consistency case, but only in combination with a simultaneous comparison of the latter case with a typical case. A comparison between three cases is indirectly implied by what I propose here. A researcher starts with a comparison between a deviant consistency and a typical case. This reveals the missing disjunct and turns the single-condition claim of necessity ($\sim DEP \Leftarrow \sim BDT$) into a disjunctive SUIN claim (e.g. $\sim DEP + EDU \Leftarrow \sim BDT$). Based on this updated, disjunctive necessity claim, the comparison between a typical and deviant consistency case addresses the "SU" (sufficient but unnecessary) part in SUIN. The "IN" (insufficient but necessary) element in SUIN is then tested in the comparison between a typical and an iir case (Rohlfing and Schneider, 2013, p. 228). In the following, I describe the two model specification designs and the two causal inference comparative SMMR designs in further detail.

Comparisons for Model Specification

There are two model-refining comparative SMMR designs, depicted by the dotted arrows in Figure 6.6. The comparison between a *typical and a deviant*

6.1 Basics, $A \Leftarrow Y$

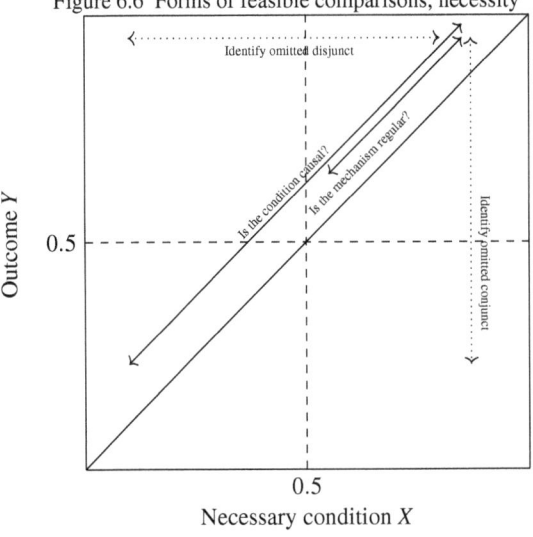

Figure 6.6 Forms of feasible comparisons, necessity

Dotted arrow: model specification; solid arrow: causal inference

Table 6.3 *Forms of comparisons and their goals in SMMR, necessity*

Comparison	Inferential goal
Causal inference	
Typical–iir	Causal properties of mechanism
Typical–typical	Generalizability of mechanism
Descriptive inference	
Typical–deviant relevance	Identify omitted conjunct
Typical–deviant consistency	Identify omitted disjunct

consistency case is governed by three principles that are only slightly modified versions of the two corresponding principles from SMMR on sufficiency. The *principle of deviance in kind* states that deviant consistency cases should qualitatively differ from typical cases in the condition, that is, the superset in necessity claims. The corresponding principle for deviant consistency case in SMMR on sufficiency required that these two cases qualitatively differ in their membership in the outcome, that is, the superset in sufficiency claims. This means that the principle of deviance in kind can be generalized to statements both of necessity and of sufficiency by requiring a qualitative difference in the superset of the set relation under investigation (Schneider and Rohlfing, 2013).

Principle of deviance in kind: Choose deviant consistency cases that are qualitatively different from typical cases in their membership in the superset.

The second principle for model-refining comparative SMMR designs on necessity is the *principle of max–min difference*. We have already encountered this principle in Chapter 2. To make it applicable to statements both of necessity and of sufficiency, this principle also requires a minor adaptation. When focusing on sufficiency statements, the principle requires the researcher to maximize the cases' difference in the outcome (superset) and to minimize the difference in the condition (subset). With necessity statements, it is the inverse: minimize the difference in the outcome (subset) and maximize the difference in the condition (superset). The principle of max–min difference can therefore be generalized to both necessary and sufficiency claims and to both forms of model specification SMMR designs as follows:

Principle of max–min difference: In model-refining comparative SMMR designs, maximize the difference of the cases' set membership in the superset and minimize the difference in the subset, or vice versa.

The third principle involved in the comparison between a typical and a deviant consistency case that needs minor adaptation is the *truth table row principle*. For sufficiency claims, it matches deviant coverage and iir cases that sit in precisely the same truth table row. By definition, for necessity claims it is not possible for a typical and a deviant consistency case to share the same truth table row: the typical case is a member of the necessary condition while the deviant consistency case is not. This is why for necessity claims the truth table row principle is fulfilled if a typical and a deviant consistency case share the same truth table row except for the necessary condition(s)[12] of interest.

Table 6.4 depicts the logic of this comparison. The values in nonbold font indicate the membership scores of cases known from the cross-case analysis and used for case selection. The values in bold font are membership scores not known prior to the within-case analysis and indicate the ideal-typical result of this analysis. By identifying the omitted disjunct *D*, the hitherto deviant consistency case turns into a typical case vis-à-vis the updated necessity

---

[12] I am using the plural here because once disjunctive and conjunctive necessity claims are allowed for, more than one condition is involved in the necessity claim and, thus, more than one condition needs to be excluded when matching cases on their truth table row membership (see Sections 6.2 and 6.3).

claim $N + D \Leftarrow Y$. As an example, I have already discussed the only deviant consistency case Bhutan and the hypothetical finding that the missing disjunct is a high share of tertiary education (EDU), which in the case of Bhutan operates as a functional equivalent to the lack of agricultural dependence ($\sim DEP$), and therefore as a necessary SUIN condition for the presence of the mechanism conflict deflection.

Table 6.4 *Matching of typical and deviant consistency cases, necessity*

Cross-case:	Known	N	$\Leftarrow$	Y
Within-case:	**Expected**		**M**	
	Typical case	1	1	1
	Dev$_{cons}$	0	1	1
	Expected	**N+D**	**M**	**Y**
	Typical case	1	1	1
	Dev$_{cons}$	1	1	1

Nonbold font: findings from QCA; bold font: target of within-case analysis

Let me briefly reflect on equifinality at either the cross-case or the within-case level. In Table 6.4, the assumption is that researchers discover in the deviant consistency case the presence of the same mechanism M as in the typical case. The puzzle to solve then is to find out which cross-case condition is needed for M in the deviant case.[13] The discovery of D produces equifinality only at the cross-case level: the two functionally equivalent conditions N and D are necessary for the same mechanism M. An equally plausible scenario is that M is not present in the deviant case. The *two* puzzles to solve in the within-case analysis then are to find both a functionally equivalent mechanism that is necessary for outcome Y in the deviant case, let us call it M_D, and the cross-case condition that is needed for the presence of M_D. In this scenario we have equifinality at both the cross-case and the within-case levels.

The formula for identifying the best-matching pair of a typical and a deviant consistency case is given in Formula 6.6. The best available pair maximizes the dissimilarity in the necessary term N and the similarity in the outcome. Furthermore, the formula is applied separately to cases from each truth table row that contains both typical and deviant consistency cases. The more truth table rows are populated by these two case types, the more potential heterogeneity there is at both the cross-case and the within-case levels.

---

[13] According to the truth table row principle, the search for this omitted condition starts, but does not have to end, with the conditions that are shared between the typical and deviant consistency cases.

$$TYPnec - DCONnec = +\left[1 - (N_{TYPnec} - N_{DCONnec})\right] \quad \text{large difference in term}$$
$$+ |Y_{TYPnec} - Y_{DCONnec}| \quad \text{similar membership in outcome}$$
(6.6)

$TYPnec$: typical case; $DCONnec$: deviant consistency case; N_{TYPnec} and $N_{DCONnec}$: membership in necessary term of typical and deviant consistency cases, respectively; Y_{TYPnec} and $Y_{DCONnec}$: membership in outcome of typical and deviant consistency cases, respectively.

The second comparative SMMR design for model refinement matches a *typical case with a deviant relevance case*. The basic logic is depicted in Table 6.5. From the cross-case analysis we know that both cases are members of the necessary term N but qualitatively differ in their membership in the outcome Y. The goal of the within-case analysis is to probe whether the typical case is a member of the mechanism M, whereas the deviant relevance case is not, and to identify a conjunct C, which, in combination with the known necessary term N, can account for the difference in the case's membership in both the outcome and the mechanism. For the omitted conjunct C to fulfill this expectation, the typical and the deviant relevance cases must qualitatively differ in their membership in C. The hitherto deviant relevance case then turns into an iir case vis-à-vis the updated necessity claim $N*C \Leftarrow Y$.

Table 6.5 *Matching of typical and deviant relevance cases, necessity*

Cross-case:	Known	N	$\Leftarrow$	Y
Within-case:	**Expected**		M_C	
	Typical	1	1	1
	Dev$_{rel}$	1	0	0
	Expected	$N*C$	M_C	Y
	Typical	1	1	1
	Dev$_{rel}$	0	0	0

Nonbold font: findings from QCA; bold font: target of within-case analysis

For example, within-case analysis might reveal that a typical case such as the Netherlands, in addition to not being dependent on agriculture ($\sim DEP$), is also not a member of the set of corrupt countries ($\sim COR$). At the same time, a deviant relevance case such as Algeria is a member of the set of corrupt countries. If there is within-case evidence for the inference that it is the joint presence of $\sim DEP$ and $\sim COR$ that is needed for the presence of the mechanism conflict deflection (M), then researchers might refine their necessity claim to $\sim DEP * \sim COR \Leftarrow \sim BDT$. As already mentioned, though, this refined necessity claim does not pass the consistency threshold at the cross-case level: too many of the typical cases shown in the XY plot in Figure 6.1 are also members of COR (e.g. Bahrain or Kuwait), and thus turn into deviant consistency cases with regard to the updated necessity claim $\sim DEP * \sim COR \Leftarrow \sim BDT$.[14]

The best available pair of a typical and a deviant relevance case is identified based on Formula 6.7. Both cases should have large and similar membership in the necessary term and they should differ a lot in their membership in the outcome.

$$
\begin{aligned}
TYPnec - DREL = &[(1 - N_{TYPnec}) + (1 - N_{DREL})] &\text{large membership in term}\\
&+ [1 - (Y_{TYPnec} - Y_{DREL})] &\text{large difference in outcome} &\quad (6.7)\\
&+ |N_{TYPnec} - N_{DREL}| &\text{similar membership in term}
\end{aligned}
$$

$TYPnec$: typical case; $DREL$: deviant relevance case; N_{TYPnec} and N_{DREL}: membership in necessary term of typical and deviant relevance cases, respectively; Y_{TYPnec} and Y_{DREL}: membership in outcome of typical and deviant relevance cases, respectively

Comparisons for Causal Inference

There are two comparative SMMR designs that aim at probing the causal properties of the necessary term. Both are governed by the *principle of max–max difference* (see Chapter 2), according to which the cases should differ as much as possible in the membership in both the outcome and the term of interest. This is visualized by the diagonal arrows depicting the two feasible causal inference comparisons in Figure 6.6.

A comparison between a *typical and an iir case* tests whether, in the absence of the necessary term, not only the outcome, but also the within-case mechanism, is absent ($\sim M$), whereas in the typical case not only the necessary term and outcome are present, but also the mechanism M (see Figure 6.6). Table 6.6 contains the logic of this comparative design.

For instance, in a comparison between the typical case Bahrain and the iir case Rwanda, the within-case analysis should test whether it is, indeed, the dependence on agriculture that triggered conflict in Rwanda and that, indeed, it is the lack of this dependence that helped Bahrain to avert such group conflict.

The formula for identifying the best-matching pair of a typical and an iir case is shown in Formula 6.8. The pair of cases should differ as much as possible

---

[14] In fact, pure logic dictates that a conjunction can pass the consistency necessity test only if and when all conjuncts in that conjunction pass this test. From this, it follows that only those conjuncts that pass the consistency threshold for necessary conditions on their own are potential candidates for solving the puzzle of deviant relevance cases.

Table 6.6 *Matching of a typical case and an iir case, necessity*

Cross-case:	Known	N	⇐	Y
Within-case:	**Expected**		**M**	
	Typical case	1	**1**	1
	iir case	0	**0**	0

Nonbold font: findings from QCA; bold font: target of within-case analysis

in their membership in both the necessary term N and the outcome Y. At the same time, they should be as close as possible to the diagonal to increase the strictness of the test and to thus adhere to the *test corridor principle*.

$$\begin{aligned}TYPnec - iir = &[1 - (N_{TYPnec} - N_{iir})] &&\text{large difference in term}\\ &+ [1 - (Y_{TYPnec} - Y_{iir})] &&\text{large difference in outcome}\\ &+ |N_{TYPnec} - Y_{TYPnec}| &&\text{small corridor for typical case}\\ &+ 2 * |N_{iir} - Y_{iir}| &&\text{small corridor for iir case}\end{aligned} \quad (6.8)$$

TYPnec: typical case; *iir*: individually irrelevant case; N_{TYPnec} and N_{iir}: membership in necessary term of typical and individually irrelevant cases, respectively; Y_{TYPnec} and Y_{iir}: membership in outcome of typical and individually irrelevant cases, respectively

The second comparison is that between *two typical cases*. As with sufficiency, the rationale is that, if mechanism M can be shown to be operative in two typical cases that differ as much as possible in their membership in N and Y, then we have good reasons to assume that the same mechanism M is also operative in all the other typical cases that fall in between the most typical and the just-so typical cases (see Figure 6.6). Table 6.7 displays the logic of this comparison and the ideal-typical membership scores in mechanism M that are revealed by this within-case comparison.

Table 6.7 *Matching of two typical cases, necessity*

Cross-case:	Known	N	⇐	Y
Within-case:	**Expected**		**M**	
	Most typical case$_1$	0.98	**0.98**	0.98
	Just-so typical case$_2$	0.51	**0.51**	0.51

Nonbold font: findings from QCA; bold font: target of within-case analysis

6.1 Basics, $A \Leftarrow Y$

As the XY plot in Figure 6.1 for the necessity claim $\sim DEP \Leftarrow \sim BDT$ shows, in the data at hand, there is no good example for a just-so typical case. Most typical cases share the same outcome membership and hold similar term membership. The assumption that the same mechanism M is operative in all typical cases sounds plausible and can only be marginally strengthened by a within-case comparison of, say Kuwait and South Korea.

The formula for identifying the best-matching pair of two typical cases is shown in Formula 6.9. Akin to the previous formula, it requires the cases to be as different as possible in their term and outcome membership and to be close to the main diagonal.

$$
\begin{aligned}
TYPnec_1 - TYPnec_2 = & [0.5 - (N_{TYPnec_1} - N_{TYPnec_2})] & \text{large difference in term} \\
& + [0.5 - (Y_{TYPnec_1} - Y_{TYPnec_2})] & \text{large difference in outcome} \\
& + 2 * (N_{TYP_1} - Y_{TYPnec_1}) & \text{small corridor for typical case 1} \\
& + 2 * (N_{TYPnec_2} - Y_{TYPnec_2}) & \text{small corridor for typical case 2}
\end{aligned}
$$
(6.9)

$TYPnec_1$: typical case 1; $TYPnec_2$: typical case 2; N_{TYPnec_1} and N_{TYPnec_2}: membership in necessary term of typical cases 1 and 2, respectively; Y_{TYPnec_1} and Y_{TYPnec_2}: membership in outcome of typical cases 1 and 2, respectively

---

Core Points 6.1: Necessity Claims

- Principles developed for SMMR on sufficiency claims remain virtually unchanged
- The main types of cases also remain unchanged, just deviance coverage cases are called deviant relevance cases
- The logic of formulas remains the same, and formulas only need adaptation to the fact that, with necessity claims, condition X is a superset of outcome Y
- In SMMR on necessity, similar single-case and comparative case study designs exist as in SMMR on sufficiency and they follow the same descriptive and causal inference goals
- In comparative SMMR designs that follow the truth table row principle, that principle needs to be applied by disregarding the case's (non)membership in the necessary condition of interest

6.1.5 Applying SMMR

Choosing cases for descriptive or causal inference on necessity claims is done with the R function smmr(). I demonstrate its use with the ongoing example by Bretthauer (2015) and her study of (non)conflict in resource-scarce countries. Code C 6.1 produces output O 6.1, which identifies $\sim DEP$ as an empirically nontrivial necessary condition of outcome $\sim BDT$.

C 6.1

```
NEC_ny <- superSubset(data = BRETT,
                     outcome = '~BDT',
                     conditions = c("POV", "DEP", "COR", "PIN", "EDU",
                     "EEX"),
                     incl.cut = 0.89,
                     ron.cut = 0.6,
                     cov.cut = 0.5,
                     depth = 1)
NEC_ny
```

O 6.1

	inclN	RoN	covN
1	~DEP	0.890	0.730	0.798

In the smmr() function, argument necessity needs to be set to TRUE if the goal is to perform SMMR on necessity claims. To perform the various descriptive and causal inference SMMR designs, values for arguments cases and match have to be set as shown in Table 6.8.

Table 6.8 *Function* smmr(), *argument* case *for SMMR on necessity*

*For single-case studies (*match = FALSE*):*	
1	Typical
2	Deviant consistency
3	Deviant relevance
*For comparative case studies (*match = TRUE*):*	
1	Typical–deviant relevance
2	Typical–deviant consistency
3	Typical–iir
4	Typical–typical

Descriptive Inference SMMR

Code C 6.2 identifies the best available deviant relevance case, as shown in output O 6.2.[15] Cases are ordered based on their value in column "Best" (using Formula 6.5). Algeria is the most deviant relevant case in the data at hand. This confirms the intuition one would get by visual inspection of XY plot in Figure 6.1 in which Algeria is closest to the position of the ideal-typical deviant relevance case in the lower-right corner.

C 6.2

```
drel <- smmr(nec.cond = "~DEP",
             results = sol_np,
             outcome = "~BDT",
             match = FALSE,
             cases = 3,
             necessity = TRUE)
drel
```

O 6.2

~DEP :

	Case	NecCond	Outcome	Best	MostDREL
1	Algeria	0.85	0.00	0.30	TRUE
6	Uzbekistan	0.83	0.30	0.64	FALSE
4	Kyrgyzstan	0.90	0.48	0.68	FALSE
3	Jamaica	0.87	0.43	0.69	FALSE
2	Egypt	0.66	0.14	0.82	FALSE
5	Lesotho	0.63	0.47	1.21	FALSE

As explained, the goal of within-case analysis of deviant relevance cases is to identify an omitted conjunct. This search is facilitated by comparing the deviant relevance case with a typical case. Code C 6.3 produces the list of best available pairs of cases, shown in output O 6.3. The ordering of pairs is based on, first, the value in column "Best" (using Formula 6.7), then whether the typical case is the most typical, and then whether the deviant relevance case is the most deviant relevance case. Based on these criteria, several pairs qualify as the best available. All of them involve deviant relevance case Algeria. While all display the same value in "Best" (after rounding), the group of pairs can be distinguished based on whether the typical cases are most typical or not. While the former are preferred, the example at hand also illustrates that such small

---

[15] Note that, for technical reasons, for SMMR designs on necessity claims, function smmr() requires the specification of argument results. This means that researchers must create a sufficiency solution object (using function minimize()) even if they are not interested in sufficiency claims and must do so prior to the analysis of necessity. That sufficiency solution object does not have to contain a substantively meaningful solution, but it must be obtained based on all conditions that the researcher deems relevant.

differences in fuzzy set membership scores should most often not be overemphasized when choosing cases for within-case analysis. In Section 7.2.6, I discuss in detail how to handle the question of coarseness of set membership scores in SMMR in more general terms.

C 6.3

```
typdrel <- smmr(nec.cond = "~DEP",
                results = sol_np,
                outcome = "~BDT",
                match = TRUE,
                cases = 1,
                max_pairs = 10,
                necessity = TRUE)
typdrel
```

O 6.3

~DEP :

	TYP	DREL	Best	MostTyp	MostDREL
3	Jordan	Algeria	0.35	TRUE	TRUE
8	South Korea	Algeria	0.35	TRUE	TRUE
9	Switzerland	Algeria	0.35	TRUE	TRUE
1	Bahrain	Algeria	0.35	FALSE	TRUE
2	Japan	Algeria	0.35	FALSE	TRUE
4	Kuwait	Algeria	0.35	FALSE	TRUE
5	Netherlands	Algeria	0.35	FALSE	TRUE
6	Qatar	Algeria	0.35	FALSE	TRUE
7	Singapore	Algeria	0.35	FALSE	TRUE
10	United Arab Emirates	Algeria	0.35	FALSE	TRUE

From the XY plot in Figure 6.1, we see that there is only one deviant consistency case (Bhutan). To identify the best available deviant consistency case, argument case needs to be set to 2 (code C 6.4). Unsurprisingly, output O 6.4 lists Bhutan as the best and only deviant consistency case. What can be seen only from this output and not from glancing at the XY plot, though, is that Bhutan's membership in its truth table row is smaller than its membership in the outcome (column "TT<=Y").

C 6.4

```
dcons <- smmr(nec.cond = "~DEP",
              results = sol_np,
              outcome = "~BDT",
              match = FALSE,
              cases = 2,
              necessity = TRUE)
dcons
```

O 6.4

~DEP :

Case	NecCond	TT_POV	TT_DEP	TT_ECOD	TT_COR	TT_PIN	TT_EDU	TT_EEX	TT_row	Outcome	TT<=Y	Best	MostDCON
1 Bhutan	0.01	1	1	0	0	0	1	1	0.72	0.95	TRUE	0.06	TRUE

As explained, the deviance of Bhutan could be rectified by identifying an omitted disjunct, or SUIN condition. This search is facilitated by contrasting a deviant consistency case with a typical case. According to the truth table row principle, adapted to the study of necessity claims, typical and deviant consistency cases are matched based on their membership in the same truth table row, excluding the necessary condition in which these two types of cases have, by definition, qualitatively different membership scores. Code C 6.5 reveals the best-matching pairs. As output O 6.5 shows, no typical case shares the same truth table row membership with Bhutan. Such forms of limited empirical diversity is common in applied set-theoretic methods.

C 6.5

```
typdcons <- smmr(nec.cond = "~DEP",
                 results = sol_np,
                 outcome = "~BDT",
                 match = TRUE,
                 cases = 2,
                 max_pairs = 10,
                 necessity = TRUE)
typdcons
```

O 6.5

~DEP :

[1] "There are no pairs in the same TT row"

Causal Inference SMMR

According to the causal inference selection principle, any SMMR design with the goal of drawing causal inference must include a typical case. If only single typical cases are selected, then code C 6.6 produces the ordered list of best available typical cases shown in output O 6.6. The ordering is based on the value in column "Best" (using Formula 6.3): the lower the value, the better.[16]

Jordan, South Korea, and Switzerland all share identical membership scores in necessary condition $\sim DEP$ and outcome $\sim BDT$ and are, thus, all listed as equally best available. Several other cases follow with almost identical membership scores and values in "Best". As mentioned, such tiny differences in degree should not be overemphasized. If there are good nonmethodological reasons (case knowledge, access to information, etc.) to choose, say,

---

[16] Once disjunctive necessity claims are allowed for, the first criterion for ordering cases will be whether or not the case is uniquely covered (see Section 6.2). In the current example with a single necessary condition, all typical cases are uniquely covered by default.

Singapore, this case can be chosen over Jordan without significant loss of methodological rigor.

C 6.6

```
typ <- smmr(nec.cond = "~DEP",
            results = sol_np,
            outcome = "~BDT",
            match = FALSE,
            cases = 1,
            necessity = TRUE)
```

O 6.6

~DEP :

	Case	NecCond	Outcome	UniqCov	Best	MostTyp
3	Jordan	0.96	0.95	TRUE	0.06	TRUE
8	South Korea	0.96	0.95	TRUE	0.06	TRUE
9	Switzerland	0.96	0.95	TRUE	0.06	TRUE
2	Japan	0.97	0.95	TRUE	0.07	FALSE
5	Netherlands	0.97	0.95	TRUE	0.07	FALSE
10	United Arab Emirates	0.97	0.95	TRUE	0.07	FALSE
1	Bahrain	0.98	0.95	TRUE	0.08	FALSE
4	Kuwait	0.98	0.95	TRUE	0.08	FALSE
6	Qatar	0.98	0.95	TRUE	0.08	FALSE
7	Singapore	0.98	0.95	TRUE	0.08	FALSE

Inference is enhanced when a typical case is matched with the appropriate iir case. Code C 6.7 produces output O 6.7 containing the list of best available pairs of typical and iir cases. In general, the ordering of pairs is based on, first, unique coverage, then globally uncovered, then low values in "Best" (using Formula 6.8), and, finally, whether the typical case is the most typical case. Because, in the current example, the necessary condition consists of the single set ~DEP, all typical cases are uniquely covered and all iir cases globally uncovered. Furthermore, since in the data at hand not only several typical cases have identical membership scores in the necessary condition and the outcome (Jordan, South Korea, Switzerland), but also several iir cases (Burundi, Nepal, Rwanda), the list of best-matching pairs shows nine combinations of these cases that are all equally good for within-case analysis.

C 6.7

```
typiir <- smmr(nec.cond = "~DEP",
               results = sol_np,
               outcome = "~BDT",
               match = TRUE,
               cases = 3,
               max_pairs = 10,
               necessity = TRUE)
typiir
```

O 6.7

~DEP :

	TYP	IIR	UniqCov	GlobUncov	Best	MostTyp
3	Jordan	Burundi	TRUE	TRUE	0.13	TRUE
8	South Korea	Burundi	TRUE	TRUE	0.13	TRUE
9	Switzerland	Burundi	TRUE	TRUE	0.13	TRUE
23	Jordan	Nepal	TRUE	TRUE	0.13	TRUE
28	South Korea	Nepal	TRUE	TRUE	0.13	TRUE
29	Switzerland	Nepal	TRUE	TRUE	0.13	TRUE
43	Jordan	Rwanda	TRUE	TRUE	0.13	TRUE
48	South Korea	Rwanda	TRUE	TRUE	0.13	TRUE
49	Switzerland	Rwanda	TRUE	TRUE	0.13	TRUE
2	Japan	Burundi	TRUE	TRUE	0.14	FALSE

Finally, the best-matching pairs of two typical cases are produced by code C 6.8 and displayed in output O 6.8. The ordering is based on the values in "Best" (using Formula 6.9), then whether both, one, or none of the typical cases qualifies as the most typical case. Here too, due to several typical cases displaying identical membership scores, there are several identical pairs of typical cases.

C 6.8

```
typtyp <- smmr( nec.cond = "~DEP",
                results = sol_np,
                outcome = "~BDT",
                match = TRUE,
                cases = 4,
                max_pairs = 10,
                necessity = TRUE)
typtyp
```

O 6.8

~DEP :

	TYP1	TYP2	UniqCov	Best	MostTyp
15	South Korea	Jordan	both	1.04	both
16	Switzerland	Jordan	both	1.04	both
49	Jordan	South Korea	both	1.04	both
50	Switzerland	South Korea	both	1.04	both
51	Jordan	Switzerland	both	1.04	both
52	South Korea	Switzerland	both	1.04	both
10	Jordan	Japan	both	1.07	typ1
12	South Korea	Japan	both	1.07	typ1
13	Switzerland	Japan	both	1.07	typ1
27	Jordan	Netherlands	both	1.07	typ1

6.2 Disjunctions, $A + B \Leftarrow Y$

Learning Goals 6.2: Disjunctive Necessity Claims

- Understand which principles and practices govern case selection in SMMR designs based on disjunctive necessity claims
- Learn that all principles and practices introduced for disjunctive sufficiency claims equally apply to disjunctive necessity claims

---

Oftentimes in applied QCA, no single condition passes the empirical and conceptual hurdles for qualifying as a necessary condition. This is not a problem per se, as applied researchers can, and most often do, proceed to the analysis of sufficiency without any claim that one or more conditions are necessary for the outcome. Sometimes, however, researchers want to further explore whether there are some "hidden" necessary conditions to be found. The strategy to find them is to open up to the possibility that it is not a single condition that is necessary, but a disjunction of two or more conditions. Disjunctions are more likely to be supersets of the outcome than single conditions because the logical OR operator (+) takes the maximum across each case's membership in the conditions that are joined into a disjunction.

Conceptually, the way toward this strategy for identifying necessary conditions has been paved by Mahoney et al. (2009) and their notion of SUIN causes. SUIN is the acronym for "a sufficient but unnecessary part of a factor that is insufficient but necessary for an outcome" (Mahoney et al., 2009, p. 126). For illustration, take Expression 6.10. Neither single condition A nor B are supersets of outcome Y, but their union $A + B$ is. To derive a meaningful claim of necessity out of this empirical superset relation, researchers need to formulate a higher-order concept Z of which A and B are functional equivalents. This newly established condition Z is the necessary but insufficient cause of Y, while both A and B are sufficient but unnecessary for Z, as shown in Expression 6.10.

$$\begin{cases} Z \Leftarrow Y \\ A + B \Rightarrow Z \end{cases} \qquad (6.10)$$

To further illustrate the logic of SUIN causes, I will present an empirical example, formulate the challenges such necessity claims create for SMMR, and offer solutions in the form of additional sub-types of cases and case selection principles. Both solutions closely resemble those formulated in Chapter 3 on the implications of equifinal sufficiency claims for SMMR.

6.2.1 Empirical Example

I continue with the study by Bretthauer (2015) on the conditions for conflict in resource-scarce countries. Unlike before, I now focus on the occurrence of conflict (BDT). Table 6.9 indicates that the parameters of fit for the disjunction of SUIN conditions $POV + COR$ are at acceptable levels. Conflict occurs in the presence of either poverty and/or political corruption. The higher-order concept that manifests itself through either POV or COR could be labeled as "weak state structure" (WSS).[17] The claim of necessity then is that weak state structures are necessary for conflicts to occur ($WSS \Leftarrow BDT$), while weak state structures manifest themselves either through high poverty or high corruption or both ($POV + COR \Rightarrow WSS$). Figure 6.7 depicts the membership scores of all cases in the outcome BDT and the logical union of the SUIN conditions $POV + COR$. We see that there are no deviant consistency cases in kind (upper-left quadrant), a few deviant consistency cases in degree (e.g. Egypt), some deviant relevance cases (e.g. Mongolia, lower-right quadrant), typical cases (e.g. Haiti, lower triangle in the upper-right quadrant), and iir cases (e.g. Qatar, lower-left quadrant).

Table 6.9 *SUIN conditions, outcome "conflict" BDT*

	inclN	RoN	covN
$WSS : POV + COR$	0.943	0.625	0.637

Conditions POV: poverty; COR: political corruption
Outcome BTD: conflict
Higher-order construct WSS: weak state structure

6.2.2 The Challenge

Similar to disjunctions in sufficiency claims (see Chapter 3), the challenge with necessity claims also consists in separating the effects of each disjunct on the mechanism(s). This problem is based on the assumption that each disjunct triggers a separate mechanism. This assumption has a lot of traction

---

[17] Bretthauer (2015, p. 596) conceptualizes weak states slightly differently as the combination of high corruption, weak institutions, and ethnic exclusion.

6.2 Disjunctions, $A + B \Leftarrow Y$

Figure 6.7 XY plot: necessary disjunction $POV + COR$, outcome BDT

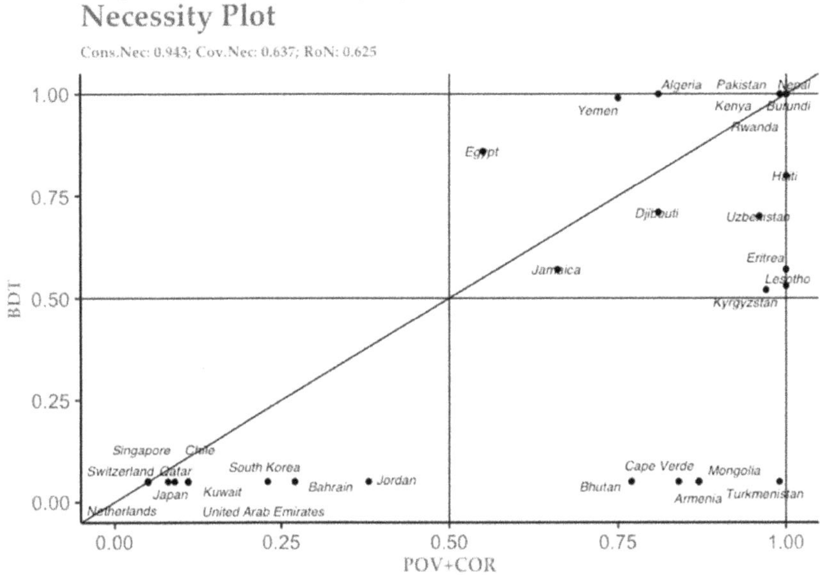

Necessity Plot

Cons.Nec: 0.943; Cov.Nec: 0.637; RoN: 0.625

[XY scatter plot with x-axis POV+COR (0.00 to 1.00) and y-axis BDT (0.00 to 1.00). Points labeled: Algeria, Pakistan, Nepal, Kenya, Burundi, Rwanda, Yemen, Egypt, Haiti, Djibouti, Uzbekistan, Eritrea, Jamaica, Lesotho, Kyrgyzstan, Singapore, Chile, Switzerland, Qatar, South Korea, Japan, Kuwait, Bahrain, Jordan, Netherlands, United Arab Emirates, Cape Verde, Mongolia, Bhutan, Armenia, Turkmenistan.]

for sufficiency claims. Yet in Chapter 3 I presented a strategy that consists of moving up the ladder of generality and subsuming two or more disjuncts under a higher-order construct. It is then this higher-order construct that is postulated as the sufficient cause for the outcome and that is expected to trigger the within-case mechanism. With this strategy the analytic challenges for SMMR created by disjunctions are resolved without reverting to new subtypes of cases and additional principles – simply because the disjunction is "conceptualized away".

With SUIN conditions it is even more plausible to assume one rather than two separate mechanisms. Why? Necessity claims based on SUIN conditions require, by definition, that a higher-order concept is defined (Schneider, 2018). To be meaningful, SUIN conditions must be understood as being functional equivalents of this higher-order concept. It therefore seems plausible to expect that these functionally equivalent conditions trigger the same mechanism.[18] One could even argue that triggering the same mechanism is the very essence of these conditions being functional equivalents.

---

[18] The difference to equifinality in sufficiency claims is also expressed by the fact that, for SUIN claims, no parameters of fit, nor XY plots, are reported for single SUIN conditions because they usually do *not* pass the criteria for being necessary. In contrast, each sufficient term in an equifinal solution formula of sufficiency counts as sufficient on its own and can be analyzed separately.

Obviously, the assumption of one mechanism triggered by all SUIN conditions can be wrong. Empirical evidence from SMMR does shed light on this question. If it turns out that each disjunct triggers separate mechanisms, then the adequate principles have to be applied, to which I turn in the next section.

Before this, Figure 6.8 depicts the two scenarios of either separate or one joint mechanism underpinning the SUIN claim of necessity. Regarding poverty, one possible mechanism is that it lowers the opportunity costs for joining rebel groups (Bretthauer, 2015, p. 597). Separate from that, corruption might trigger a grievance mechanism because, in corrupt systems, preferences of disadvantaged groups are less likely to be heard and dealt with (Bretthauer, 2015, p. 596). The mechanism for the higher-order construct weak state structures (WSS) must also be more abstract than the two SUIN condition-triggered mechanisms and could be stated as "dissatisfaction due to biased and selective state responsiveness".

Figure 6.8 Cross-case and within-case levels for disjunctive necessity claim, outcome "conflict"

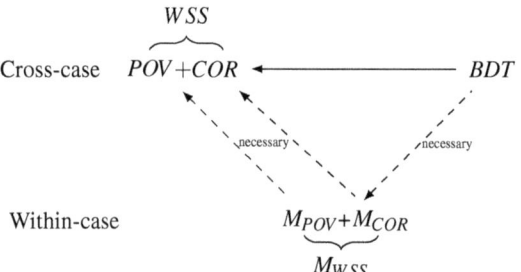

POV: poverty; COR: political corruption; WSS: weak state structure; BDT: conflict
M_{POV}: low opportunity costs for joining rebel groups
M_{COR}: increased grievance due to unresponsive political system
M_{WSS}: dissatisfaction due to biased and selective state responsiveness

6.2.3 The Solutions

The solutions to the analytic challenges for SMMR created by SUIN conditions are similar to the ones developed for equifinal sufficiency claims: the introduction of sub-types of cases, on the one hand, and of additional principles, on the other. As discussed previously, none of these sub-types of cases or principles are needed if the position of the researcher is that both SUIN conditions are functionally equivalent in a strict sense, and therefore are expected to trigger the same mechanism. In this scenario, the disjunctive SUIN claim of necessity

6.2 Disjunctions, $A + B \Leftarrow Y$

is converted into a simple claim of necessity with one condition – in the current example the claim $WSS \Leftarrow BDT$.

The sub-types of cases are depicted in Table 6.10. The new sub-types are indicated in italics. Among typical cases for the necessity claim $POV + COR \Leftarrow BDT$, we need to distinguish between those that are typical for just one of the SUIN conditions and those that are typical for more than one. The former are called uniquely covered typical cases and the latter jointly covered typical cases. For instance, Haiti has high membership in both corruption and poverty, and therefore is a jointly covered typical case. In contrast, Jamaica is classified as a member of corrupt countries, but not of poor countries. Vice versa, Eritrea is a member of the set of poor, but not of corrupt, countries. Among the iir cases, one can distinguish between those that are individually irrelevant with regard to just one of the SUIN conditions (e.g. Cape Verde for COR but not POV, for which it is a deviant relevance case) and those that are individually irrelevant for all SUIN conditions (e.g. Qatar). The latter are called globally uncovered iir cases and the former simply iir cases. Likewise, there are cases that are deviant consistent with regard to one SUIN condition, but not the other (e.g. Eritrea for COR but not POV).[19] In the current example, there are no globally deviant consistency cases, as the empty upper-left quadrant in the XY plot in Figure 6.7 shows.

Table 6.10 *Uniquely covered, jointly covered, and globally uncovered cases, necessity*

Y	Globally deviant consistency	deviant consistency or Uniquely covered typical[a]	Jointly covered typical[a]
~Y	Globally uncovered iir	Deviant relevance or iir	
	0	1	>1
		Member in how many SUIN conditions X_i	

[a] $X_i \geq Y$, new case types in italics

All three principles for confronting disjunctions that I have introduced in Chapter 3 also apply to necessity claims. The *focal disjunct principle* stipulates that each SUIN condition should be analyzed separately. Note that normally each single SUIN condition does not pass the consistency threshold as a necessary condition. It is therefore important to only choose typical cases

---

[19] This information on sub-types of cases cannot be gathered by visual representation of the XY plot in Figure 6.7, but requires either separate plots for each SUIN condition or, more efficiently, the use of the adequate arguments in the smmr() function (see Section 6.2.4).

that are consistent with the claim of necessity of the focal SUIN condition. The *uniquely covered principle*, in turn, specifies that among typical cases one should choose uniquely covered typical cases. Likewise, the *globally uncovered principle* stipulates that, among both deviant consistency and iir cases, one should select those that are not members of any SUIN condition.

Core Points 6.2: Disjunctive Necessity Claims

- All principles guiding case selection for disjunctive sufficiency claims also govern case selection for disjunctive necessity claims: focal conjunct principle, uniquely covered principle, and globally uncovered principle
- The same sub-types of case exist as for equifinal sufficiency claims: uniquely covered typical, jointly covered typical, and globally uncovered iir case. The only new sub-type is the globally deviant consistency case

---

6.2.4 Applying SMMR

Code C 6.9 produces output O 6.9, which identifies the disjunction $POV + COR$ as an empirically nontrivial necessary term for outcome BDT. As discussed above, these SUIN conditions are interpreted as functional equivalents for the higher-order concept "weak state structure" WSS.

C 6.9

```
SUIN_y <- superSubset(data = BRETT,
                     outcome = "BDT",
                     conditions = c("POV", "DEP", "COR", "PIN", "EDU",
                         "EEX"),
                     incl.cut = 0.94,
                     ron.cut = 0.6,
                     cov.cut = 0.5,
                     depth = 2)
SUIN_y
```

O 6.9

	inclN	RoN	covN
1 POV+COR	0.943	0.625	0.637

Descriptive Inference SMMR

The identification of the best available *deviant relevance case* is done by code C 6.10. Output O 6.10 automatically displays deviant relevance cases for each SUIN condition – *POV* and *COR* – and for the disjunction – the higher-order

6.2 Disjunctions, $A + B \Leftarrow Y$

concept *WSS* – that they form. As explained, the goal consists in identifying a missing conjunct from either a single SUIN condition or from the higher-order concept disjunction.

For SUIN condition *POV*, Turkmenistan is the best available deviant relevance case for this analytic task, closely followed by four other cases with identical membership in the outcome and only slightly lower membership in the condition. Turkmenistan is also the best available deviant relevance case for the second SUIN condition *COR*, followed by Armenia. These two cases therefore also lead the list as the best choices when focusing on the disjunction $POV + COR$.

C 6.10

```
drel <- smmr( nec.cond = "POV+COR",
              results = sol_p,
              outcome = "BDT",
              match = FALSE,
              cases = 3,
              necessity = TRUE)
drel
```

O 6.10

POV :

	Case	NecCond	Outcome	Best	MostDREL
5	Turkmenistan	0.99	0.05	0.07	TRUE
4	Mongolia	0.87	0.05	0.31	FALSE
3	Cape Verde	0.84	0.05	0.37	FALSE
2	Bhutan	0.77	0.05	0.51	FALSE
1	Armenia	0.55	0.05	0.95	FALSE

COR :

	Case	NecCond	Outcome	Best	MostDREL
3	Turkmenistan	0.97	0.05	0.11	TRUE
1	Armenia	0.87	0.05	0.31	FALSE
2	Mongolia	0.79	0.05	0.47	FALSE

POV+COR :

	Case	NecCond	Outcome	Best	MostDREL
5	Turkmenistan	0.99	0.05	0.07	TRUE
1	Armenia	0.87	0.05	0.31	FALSE
4	Mongolia	0.87	0.05	0.31	FALSE
3	Cape Verde	0.84	0.05	0.37	FALSE
2	Bhutan	0.77	0.05	0.51	FALSE

Instead of counterfactually arguing that a deviant relevance case such as Turkmenistan is a nonmember of a missing conjunct of which a typical case is a member, it is advisable, and empirically often possible, to match a *deviant relevance case with an appropriate typical case*. Code C 6.11 produces the list of best available pairs of typical and deviant relevance cases, shown in output O 6.11, again separated by SUIN conditions and the higher-order concept. For SUIN condition *POV*, it turns out that typical case Eritrea forms the best-matching pair with Turkmenistan, whereas for SUIN condition *COR* it is Kyrgyzstan with Turkmenistan, and for *POV* + *COR* Burundi with Turkmenistan. Note that the best pair does not always involve the most typical case. What matters more, instead, is that the typical case is uniquely covered.

C 6.11

```
typdrel <- smmr(nec.cond = "POV+COR",
                results = sol_p,
                outcome = "BDT",
                match = TRUE,
                cases = 1,
                max_pairs = 6,
                necessity = TRUE)
typdrel
```

O 6.11

POV :

	TYP	DREL	UniqCov	Best	MostTyp	MostDREL
39	Eritrea	Turkmenistan	TRUE	0.50	FALSE	TRUE
30	Eritrea	Mongolia	TRUE	0.74	FALSE	FALSE
21	Eritrea	Cape Verde	TRUE	0.80	FALSE	FALSE
12	Eritrea	Bhutan	TRUE	0.94	FALSE	FALSE
3	Eritrea	Armenia	TRUE	1.38	FALSE	FALSE
37	Burundi	Turkmenistan	FALSE	0.07	TRUE	TRUE

COR :

	TYP	DREL	UniqCov	Best	MostTyp	MostDREL
16	Kyrgyzstan	Turkmenistan	TRUE	0.59	FALSE	TRUE
4	Kyrgyzstan	Armenia	TRUE	0.79	FALSE	FALSE
10	Kyrgyzstan	Mongolia	TRUE	0.95	FALSE	FALSE
15	Jamaica	Turkmenistan	TRUE	1.16	FALSE	TRUE
3	Jamaica	Armenia	TRUE	1.16	FALSE	FALSE
9	Jamaica	Mongolia	TRUE	1.16	FALSE	FALSE

POV+COR :

	TYP	DREL	Best	MostTyp	MostDREL
45	Burundi	Turkmenistan	0.07	TRUE	TRUE
52	Nepal	Turkmenistan	0.07	TRUE	TRUE
53	Pakistan	Turkmenistan	0.07	TRUE	TRUE
54	Rwanda	Turkmenistan	0.07	TRUE	TRUE
48	Haiti	Turkmenistan	0.27	FALSE	TRUE
1	Burundi	Armenia	0.31	TRUE	FALSE

Deviant consistency cases are rare in the current example. As can be seen in the XY plot in Figure 6.7, for the necessity claim $POV + COR \Leftarrow BDT$, not even a single deviant consistency case exists. In such a situation, there is no need to perform SMMR designs with the goal of identifying omitted disjuncts from the disjunctive necessity claim. If, however, there were some deviant consistency cases for the disjunctive claim of necessity, the best starting point for identifying missing disjuncts would be the single SUIN conditions. Code

6.2 Disjunctions, $A + B \Leftarrow Y$

C 6.12 can be used to reveal deviant consistency cases for each SUIN condition and for the higher-order construct.

Output O 6.12, in fact, shows that, for condition *POV*, four such deviant consistency cases exist. Since all four of them are situated in different truth table rows, they all represent best available deviant consistency cases for their truth table row. For SUIN condition *COR*, Eritrea is the only deviant consistency case. For all five deviant consistency cases it holds, though, that they are already taken care of by the other SUIN condition. For instance, Egypt is not a member of *POV* but of *COR*. Vice versa, Eritrea is not a member of *COR* but of *POV*. Researchers therefore need to select deviant consistency cases that are not members of any SUIN condition – so-called globally deviant consistency cases (see Table 6.10) – which in this particular example do not exist.

C 6.12

```
dcons <- smmr( nec.cond = "POV+COR",
               results = sol_p,
               outcome = "BDT",
               match = FALSE,
               cases = 2,
               necessity = TRUE)
dcons
```

O 6.12

POV :

	Case	NecCond	TT_POV	TT_DEP	TT_ECOD	TT_COR	TT_PIN	TT_EDU	TT_EEX	TT_row	Outcome	GlobUncov	TT<=Y	Best	MostDCONS
2	Egypt	0.16	0	0	1	0	0	1	0.55	0.86	FALSE	TRUE	0.30	TRUE
1	Algeria	0.32	0	0	0	1	0	1	0.55	1.00	FALSE	TRUE	0.32	TRUE
4	Kyrgyzstan	0.24	0	0	1	1	1	1	0.55	0.52	FALSE	FALSE	0.72	TRUE
3	Jamaica	0.07	0	0	1	1	0	0	0.54	0.57	FALSE	TRUE	0.50	TRUE

COR :

	Case	NecCond	TT_POV	TT_DEP	TT_ECOD	TT_COR	TT_PIN	TT_EDU	TT_EEX	TT_row	Outcome	GlobUncov	TT<=Y	Best	MostDCONS
1	Eritrea	0.21	1	1	0	0	0	0	0.79	0.57	FALSE	FALSE	0.64	TRUE

POV+COR :

[1] "No cases"

6.2 Disjunctions, $A + B \Leftarrow Y$

As before, rather than relying on counterfactual reasoning (what would happen to the within-case mechanism if the deviant consistency case was a member of a specific omitted disjunct), light can be shed on this question via a comparison with a typical case. Code C 6.13 provides the list of best-matching *pairs of typical and deviant consistency cases*. Since there are no deviant consistency cases for the disjunction $POV + COR$, there are, of course, also no pairs with typical cases. In addition, output O 6.13 reveals that, for SUIN condition POV also, no typical case sits together in the same truth table row with any of the four deviant relevance cases.

Only for SUIN condition COR it happens that deviant consistency case Eritrea shares the same truth table row with typical case Haiti. Note that, as explained, "same truth table row" here means same qualitative membership in all conditions except the focal SUIN condition under investigation.[20] This is why in output O 6.13 SUIN condition COR is not listed because, by definition, Eritrea and Haiti, as typical and deviant consistency cases, respectively, hold qualitatively different membership scores in this SUIN condition.

C 6.13

```
typdcons <- smmr( nec.cond = "POV+COR",
                  results = sol_p,
                  outcome = "BDT",
                  match = TRUE,
                  cases = 2,
                  max_pairs = 10,
                  necessity = TRUE)
typdcons
```

---

[20] If the necessary condition consists of a conjunction (see Section 6.3), then typical and deviant consistency cases are matched based on their membership in all conditions except the ones involved in the conjunction. And if the focus is on a specific conjunct in a necessary conjunction (see also Section 6.3), then typical and deviant consistency cases are matched based on their membership in all conditions except that specific conjunct in the conjunction.

O 6.13

POV :

[1] "There are no pairs in the same TT row"

COR :

DCONS	TYP	TT_POV	TT_DEP	TT_ECOD	TT_PIN	TT_EDU	TT_EEX	UniqCov	GlobUncov	Best	MostTyp	MostDCON
1 Eritrea	Haiti	1	1	0	0	0	0	FALSE	FALSE	0.47	TRUE	TRUE

POV+COR :

[1] "There are no pairs in the same TT row"

Causal Inference SMMR

The only single-case causal SMMR inference design consists of the within-case analysis of a *typical case*. Code C 6.14 generates output O 6.14. As before, typical cases are listed for each SUIN condition and for the disjunction *POV + COR*, which we interpreted as "weak state structure" *WSS*. The best available typical case is uniquely covered. For SUIN condition *POV* only Eritrea fulfills this criterion. If more than one case is uniquely covered – such as Jamaica and Kyrgyzstan for SUIN condition *POV* – then lower values in column "Best" indicate which of them is better. Note that in the output for disjunctions (e.g. *POV + COR*), column UniqCov show value TRUE for cases such as Burundi or Haiti that are listed as *not* uniquely covered for one or even both SUIN conditions in isolation. This is because, when conceptually treating disjunction *POV + COR* as a single set, such cases are covered only by that single and necessary set. The ordering of best available typical cases for disjunctive necessity claims is therefore based on the value in column "Best" and whether the case is the most typical case.

C 6.14

```
typ <- smmr( nec.cond = "POV+COR",
             results = sol_p,
             outcome = "BDT",
             match = FALSE,
             cases = 1,
             necessity = TRUE)
typ
```

O 6.14

POV :

	Case	NecCond	Outcome	UniqCov	Best	MostTyp
3	Eritrea	1.00	0.57	TRUE	0.86	FALSE
1	Burundi	1.00	1.00	FALSE	0.00	TRUE
6	Nepal	1.00	1.00	FALSE	0.00	TRUE
7	Pakistan	1.00	1.00	FALSE	0.00	TRUE
8	Rwanda	1.00	1.00	FALSE	0.00	TRUE
2	Djibouti	0.79	0.71	FALSE	0.37	FALSE
4	Haiti	1.00	0.80	FALSE	0.40	FALSE
9	Uzbekistan	0.96	0.70	FALSE	0.56	FALSE
5	Lesotho	1.00	0.53	FALSE	0.94	FALSE

COR :

	Case	NecCond	Outcome	UniqCov	Best	MostTyp
3	Jamaica	0.66	0.57	TRUE	0.52	FALSE
4	Kyrgyzstan	0.97	0.52	TRUE	0.93	FALSE
2	Haiti	0.97	0.80	FALSE	0.37	TRUE
1	Djibouti	0.81	0.71	FALSE	0.39	FALSE
6	Uzbekistan	0.96	0.70	FALSE	0.56	FALSE
5	Lesotho	0.81	0.53	FALSE	0.75	FALSE

POV+COR :

	Case	NecCond	Outcome	UniqCov	Best	MostTyp
1	Burundi	1.00	1.00	TRUE	0.00	TRUE
8	Nepal	1.00	1.00	TRUE	0.00	TRUE
9	Pakistan	1.00	1.00	TRUE	0.00	TRUE
10	Rwanda	1.00	1.00	TRUE	0.00	TRUE
2	Djibouti	0.81	0.71	TRUE	0.39	FALSE
4	Haiti	1.00	0.80	TRUE	0.40	FALSE
5	Jamaica	0.66	0.57	TRUE	0.52	FALSE
11	Uzbekistan	0.96	0.70	TRUE	0.56	FALSE
3	Eritrea	1.00	0.57	TRUE	0.86	FALSE
6	Kyrgyzstan	0.97	0.52	TRUE	0.93	FALSE
7	Lesotho	1.00	0.53	TRUE	0.94	FALSE

The best-matching *pairs of typical and iir cases* is obtained with code C 6.15 and shown in output O 6.15. Again, researchers are automatically shown the best pairs for each focal disjunct and for the disjunction. The order of case pairs is based on whether the typical case is uniquely covered, then whether the iir case is globally uncovered, then the value in column "Best", and then whether the typical case is the most typical case.

For SUIN condition *POV*, several pairs involving the uniquely covered typical case Eritrea are identical. Similarly, for the disjunction *COV + POR* treated as one higher-order construct set, a series of case pairs are identical with typical cases being uniquely covered, iir cases globally uncovered, very low values in "Best", and the typical cases being the most typical cases. For SUIN condition *COR*, uniquely typical case Jamaica can be matched with various globally uncovered iir cases and only marginally different values in column "Best".

C 6.15

```
typiir <- smmr( nec.cond = "POV+COR",
                results = sol_p,
                outcome = "BDT",
                match = TRUE,
                cases = 3,
                max_pairs = 7,
                necessity = TRUE)
typiir
```

O 6.15

POV :

	TYP	IIR	UniqCov	GlobUncov	Best	MostTyp
3	Eritrea	Bahrain	TRUE	TRUE	1.39	FALSE
21	Eritrea	Japan	TRUE	TRUE	1.39	FALSE
39	Eritrea	Kuwait	TRUE	TRUE	1.39	FALSE
48	Eritrea	Netherlands	TRUE	TRUE	1.39	FALSE
57	Eritrea	Qatar	TRUE	TRUE	1.39	FALSE
66	Eritrea	Singapore	TRUE	TRUE	1.39	FALSE
75	Eritrea	South Korea	TRUE	TRUE	1.39	FALSE

COR :

	TYP	IIR	UniqCov	GlobUncov	Best	MostTyp
33	Jamaica	Qatar	TRUE	TRUE	1.11	FALSE
45	Jamaica	United Arab Emirates	TRUE	TRUE	1.13	FALSE
27	Jamaica	Kuwait	TRUE	TRUE	1.17	FALSE
39	Jamaica	South Korea	TRUE	TRUE	1.41	FALSE
3	Jamaica	Bahrain	TRUE	TRUE	1.49	FALSE
34	Kyrgyzstan	Qatar	TRUE	TRUE	1.57	FALSE
46	Kyrgyzstan	United Arab Emirates	TRUE	TRUE	1.59	FALSE

POV+COR :

	TYP	IIR	UniqCov	GlobUncov	Best	MostTyp
23	Burundi	Japan	TRUE	TRUE	0.1	TRUE
30	Nepal	Japan	TRUE	TRUE	0.1	TRUE
31	Pakistan	Japan	TRUE	TRUE	0.1	TRUE
32	Rwanda	Japan	TRUE	TRUE	0.1	TRUE
56	Burundi	Netherlands	TRUE	TRUE	0.1	TRUE
63	Nepal	Netherlands	TRUE	TRUE	0.1	TRUE
64	Pakistan	Netherlands	TRUE	TRUE	0.1	TRUE

Finally, the best-matching *pairs of two typical cases* is produced by code C 6.16 and shown in output O 6.16. The ordering of cases is based on whether both, just one, or none of the typical cases is uniquely covered, and then on the value in column "Best". For SUIN condition *POV*, we see that in none of the pairs of typical cases are both uniquely covered. For SUIN condition *COR*, at least one pair exists: Jamaica and Kyrgyzstan, even if none of the two qualifies as the most typical case for this SUIN condition. When treating *POV + COR* as one single higher-order construct set, again, all typical cases are uniquely covered by design and ranking is done based on values in column "Best" and then whether one or both cases qualify as most typical.

C 6.16

```
typtyp <- smmr( nec.cond = "POV+COR",
                results = sol_p,
                outcome = "BDT",
                match = TRUE,
                cases = 4,
                max_pairs = 10,
                necessity = TRUE)
typtyp
```

O 6.16

POV :

	TYP1	TYP2	UniqCov	Best	MostTyp
22	Eritrea	Lesotho	typ1	2.76	none
8	Burundi	Eritrea	typ2	1.43	typ1
11	Nepal	Eritrea	typ2	1.43	typ1
12	Pakistan	Eritrea	typ2	1.43	typ1
13	Rwanda	Eritrea	typ2	1.43	typ1
10	Haiti	Eritrea	typ2	2.03	none
9	Djibouti	Eritrea	typ2	2.09	none

14	Uzbekistan	Eritrea	typ2	2.29	none
4	Burundi	Djibouti	none	0.66	typ1
5	Nepal	Djibouti	none	0.66	typ1

COR :

	TYP1	TYP2	UniqCov	Best	MostTyp
6	Jamaica	Kyrgyzstan	both	2.34	none
11	Jamaica	Lesotho	typ1	1.85	none
15	Jamaica	Uzbekistan	typ1	2.13	none
3	Haiti	Jamaica	typ2	0.98	typ1
2	Djibouti	Jamaica	typ2	1.09	none
5	Haiti	Kyrgyzstan	typ2	1.96	typ1
4	Djibouti	Kyrgyzstan	typ2	2.07	none
8	Uzbekistan	Kyrgyzstan	typ2	2.25	none
7	Lesotho	Kyrgyzstan	typ2	2.61	none
1	Haiti	Djibouti	none	1.29	typ1

POV+COR :

	TYP1	TYP2	UniqCov	Best	MostTyp
21	Burundi	Jamaica	both	0.41	typ1
24	Nepal	Jamaica	both	0.41	typ1
25	Pakistan	Jamaica	both	0.41	typ1
26	Rwanda	Jamaica	both	0.41	typ1
4	Burundi	Djibouti	both	0.72	typ1
5	Nepal	Djibouti	both	0.72	typ1
6	Pakistan	Djibouti	both	0.72	typ1
7	Rwanda	Djibouti	both	0.72	typ1
1	Nepal	Burundi	both	1.00	both
2	Pakistan	Burundi	both	1.00	both

6.3 Conjunctions, $A * B \Leftarrow Y$

> **Learning Goals 6.3: Conjunctive Necessity Claims**
>
> - Understand the challenges for SMMR posed by conjunctive necessity claims
> - Learn that, in the presence of conjunctive necessity claims, only minor adaptations to two existing principles and to the rank systems are needed to adequately select (pairs of) cases for causal inference SMMR designs

Another form of complexity consists in the claim that a conjunction is necessary for the outcome. In applied QCA, such claims are very rare. One main reason for this is that it requires that each conjunct in such a conjunction must pass the necessity test on its own. As already mentioned, in applied QCA, researchers often do not find a single necessary condition, let alone two. Even when they do, it is still often the case that the conjunction of two necessary conditions fails to meet the empirical and conceptual criteria for a sound necessity claim. Usually, the conjunction fails the consistency threshold. Yet, while necessary conjunctions might be rare, they cannot and should not be ruled out. For instance, a single set might be highly consistent as a necessary condition, but fails to meet the empirical relevance criterion. One way of increasing relevance would be to decrease the size of the condition, which, in turn, can be done by creating a conjunction that involves this set. In the following, I therefore spell out the challenges of, and solutions to, conjunctive necessity claims in SMMR.

$$\begin{cases} Z \Leftarrow Y \\ A*B \Rightarrow Z \end{cases} \quad (6.11)$$

Expression 6.11 stipulates that condition Z is necessary for outcome Y and that Z, in turn, is defined by the joint presence of conditions A and B ($A*B \Rightarrow Z$). Conditions A and B are the ones that are subjected to empirical tests, whereas Z is the higher-order concept that manifests itself via the joint presence of A and B. The need for defining such a higher-order concept is similar to what I have introduced previously when discussing SUIN conditions created via the logical OR combination of two or more conditions. When aggregating conditions via the logical AND into one higher-order concept that is necessary for an outcome, each single condition can be classified as an ININ cause: a condition that is an insufficient (I) but necessary (N) element of a cause that is itself insufficient (I) but necessary (N) for an outcome.

6.3.1 Empirical Example

To better illustrate the challenges and solutions, I continue with the example by Bretthauer (2015). For outcome "conflict" (BDT), two conditions pass, or come very close to, the 0.9 consistency threshold: not-high economic development ($\sim ECOD$) and not-high tertiary education ($\sim EDU$). For illustration purposes, also the conjunction between the two can be considered as necessary for the occurrence of conflict. As the parameters of fit in Figure 6.9 show, consistency comes close to 0.9 and both RoN and Cov.Nec are high. The XY plot in Figure 6.9 visualizes the set relation.

The higher-order concept formed by the ININ causes $\sim ECOD$ and $\sim EDU$ could be labeled "flat socio-economic structure" (FSS). The causal mechanism linking FSS to outome BDT could be that the state is overburdened with reconciling the contrasting demands of different groups. Let us label this as the "overburden mechanisms" (M_O).

Figure 6.9 XY plot: necessary conjunction $\sim ECOD + \sim EDU$, outcome BDT

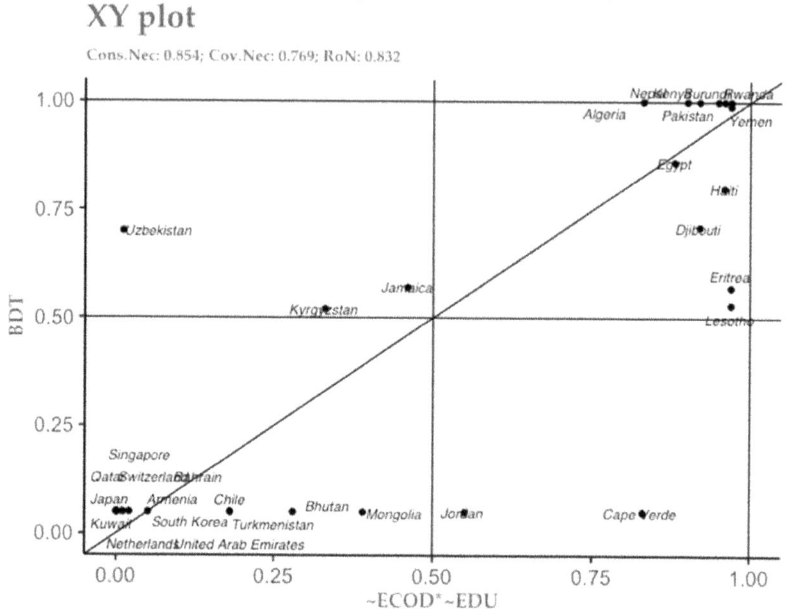

XY plot

Cons.Nec: 0.854; Cov.Nec: 0.769; RoN: 0.832

[XY plot with x-axis $\sim ECOD * \sim EDU$ (0.00 to 1.00) and y-axis BDT (0.00 to 1.00). Cases plotted include: Niger, Kenya, Burundi, Rwanda, Algeria, Pakistan, Yemen, Egypt, Haiti, Uzbekistan, Djibouti, Jamaica, Kyrgyzstan, Eritrea, Lesotho, Singapore, Qatar, Switzerland, Bahrain, Japan, Armenia, Chile, Bhutan, Mongolia, Jordan, Cape Verde, Kuwait, South Korea, Turkmenistan, Netherlands, United Arab Emirates.]

6.3.2 The Challenge

The challenges for SMMR designs posed by conjunctive claims of necessity resemble those of conjunctive sufficiency statements, detailed in Chapter 4. For a conjunction to be necessary not only for the outcome but also for the within-case mechanism, it must be shown that each conjunct is necessary for the mechanism.[21] Applied to our example, we need to investigate whether $\sim ECOD$ is needed for mechanism M_O and whether $\sim EDU$ is needed for M_O.[22] Note that, as with conjunctive sufficiency claims, the challenge exists only for causal inference SMMR designs.

6.3.3 The Solutions

The solution to the challenge of conjunctive necessity claims is the same as for conjunctive sufficiency claims: we need to disentangle the conjunction and

---

[21] We already know that each conjunct is necessary for the outcome at the cross-case level because otherwise the conjunction could not pass the necessity test.

[22] I am skipping here the possibility of mechanismic complexity in which each ININ condition triggers separate mechanisms.

perform tests on each conjunct.[23] The test consists in finding out whether in the presence of the complementary conjuncts the absence of the focal conjunct leads to the absence of the mechanism. Applied to our example: Is the overburden mechanism M_O absent in cases that are not members of the focal conjunct of not having high tertiary education ($\sim EDU$) but are members of the complementary conjunct of not being economically developed ($\sim ECOD$)?

To achieve the disentangling of conjuncts, some of the principles introduced in Chapter 4 on conjunctive sufficiency claims need adaptation. The *focal conjunct principle* remains unaltered and stipulates that, in causal inference SMMR designs, within-case analyses need to be performed on each conjunct separately. The focal conjunct principle is needed because the claim about each conjunct is that it is insufficient but necessary for the outcome (and the mechanism), that is, the focal conjunct principle helps test the "I" and "N" in the ININ claim.

Modified Principles

As explained in the excursus in Section 4.4, the attribution principle needs to be slightly modified. This adaptation is triggered by the fact that necessary conditions are supersets of the outcome. The difference to the attribution principle for sufficiency claims is that now the focal conjunct needs to provide the *maximum* rather than the minimum.

Attribution principle, necessity: The typical and iir cases should have their maxima in the focal conjunct.

In Section 4.4, I have discussed the handling of INUS conditions that are necessary for the outcome. The discussion revealed that this creates a trade-off between two principles: the attribution principle for necessity and the iir FC unique nonmembership principle. To mitigate this trade-off, I introduced the weaker version of the latter principle: the iir FC nonmembership principle. The same trade-off and its mitigation exists when handling ININ conditions. If the iir case holds nonmembership in the focal conjunct FC, then the FC cannot provide the maximum. Vice versa, if the focal conjunct provides the maximum in an iir case, it cannot be the only conjunct in which the iir case has nonmembership. Both scenarios are impossible in iir cases and are possible only in deviant relevance cases. I therefore introduced a softer variant of the principle in Chapter 4 when discussing necessary INUS conditions. The same

---

[23] Needless to say, akin to disjunctive claims, the challenges of conjunctions are also resolved if the conjunction is "conceptualized away" by creating a higher-order concept that subsumes the conjunction under one single set, here "flat state structure" (FSS).

principle holds for ININ conditions. It requires that iir cases are chosen that are not members of the focal conjunct.

Principle of iir FC nonmembership for necessity: In a comparison with a typical case, an iir case should be a nonmember of the focal conjunct.

Figure 6.10 displays all possible constellations between the focal and the complementary conjuncts in both the typical and the iir cases and the ranks of each possible pair of typical and iir cases. In a typical case, the attribution principle for necessity is either met or not met, that is, the focal conjunct either provides the maximum (typical case 1 in Figure 6.10) or it does not (typical case 2). In the second scenario, the corridor can be clean or contaminated, whereas in the first scenario it is contaminated by default.[24]

In iir cases, more constellations are possible. In general, fulfilling the iir FC (unique) nonmembership principle(s) is more important than fulfilling the attribution principle. The best scenario is when the focal conjunct is the only conjunct below 0.5 and thus the iir FC unique nonmembership principle is fulfilled (iir_1 in Figure 6.10). In this scenario the corridor is clean by default. The worst constellation is when the iir case is a member of the focal conjunct (iir_4). In between, two scenarios exist; in both, the iir FC unique nonmembership principle is violated, but at least the weaker FC nonmembership principle holds. The difference between the two scenarios is whether the attribution principle for necessity is fulfilled (iir_2) or not (iir_3). For both scenarios the corridor can be clean or contaminated. Clean corridors are preferred.

Matching the different possible constellations of focal and complementary conjuncts in typical and iir cases produces eight possible comparisons that can be ranked in terms of how helpful they are in causal inference on ININ causes in a necessary conjunction. The best-ranked pair is between a typical case that fulfills the attribution principle and an iir case that fulfills the iir FC unique nonmembership principle. The worst-ranked comparison is one in which none of the principles is fulfilled by both the typical and the iir cases.

Remember, a corridor is clean if no complementary conjunct falls between the focal conjunct and the outcome. Contaminated corridors in either the typical and/or iir case can happen in all ranks. Corridors are contaminated by default in the typical case for all uneven-numbered ranks. This is an expression of the fact that, for necessity claims, the attribution principle is incompatible with a clean corridor in a typical case. For iir cases, these two principles

---

[24] The only exception is when the typical case holds identical membership in the focal and complementary conjuncts.

6.3 Conjunctions, $A * B \Leftarrow Y$

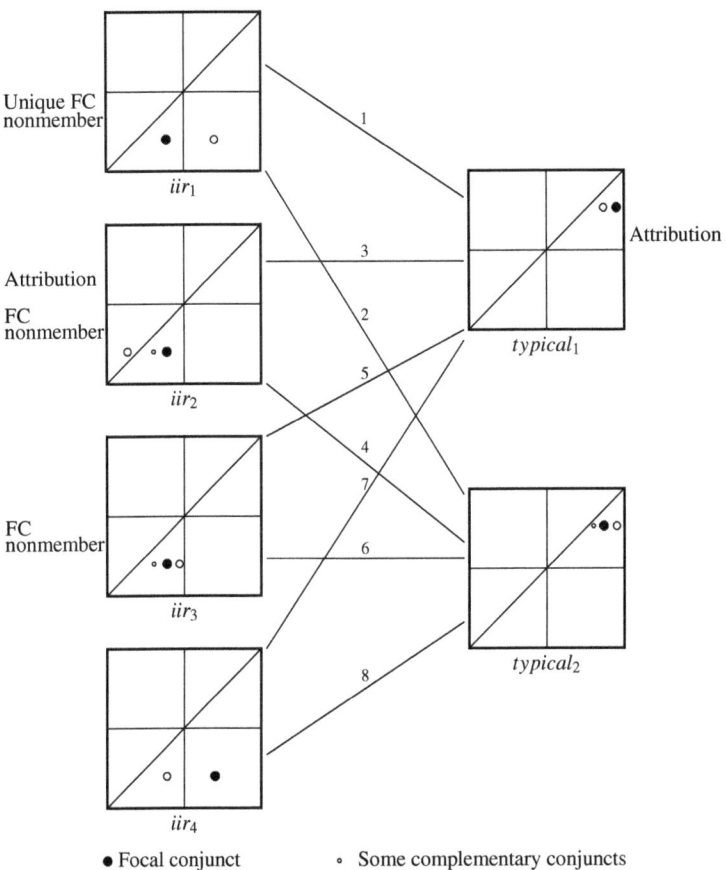

Figure 6.10 Rank order of typical and iir case pairs for focal conjuncts in necessary conjunctions

● Focal conjunct   ○ Some complementary conjuncts
○ Conjunction of complementary conjuncts

can go together. In rank 3, for instance, the focal conjunct in the iir case does provide the maximum (attribution principle fulfilled), and whether or not the complementary conjuncts exceed the case's membership in the outcome depends on the data at hand. If some complementary conjuncts do, then the corridor is contaminated, if none does, then the corridor is clean. Researchers should try to choose case pairs in the same rank for which the corridor is clean.

Additional Formulas

As explained, conjunctions affect only the causal inference SMMR designs. The formulas for identifying the best (pair of) cases introduced in Section 6.1

need to be adapted if the attention is on the focal conjunct rather than the entire necessary term. These adapted formulas are identical to those developed for identifying the best (pairs of) cases in conjunctive claims of sufficiency (see Section 4.3.3).

Formula 6.12 identifies the best available typical case for each focal conjunct in a conjunctive claim of necessity. It gives a premium to cases whose membership in the focal conjunct and the outcome are similar, thus adhering to the test corridor principle. In addition, cases with higher membership in the conjunction score higher.

$$
\begin{aligned}
TYP = & (2 * |Y - FC|) && \text{small corridor focal conjunct} \\
& + (1 - N) && \text{large membership in necessary term}
\end{aligned}
\quad (6.12)
$$

Formula 6.13 identifies the best-matching pairs of typical and iir cases. Since more aspects need to be taken into account, the formula is slightly more complex. The typical and iir cases should be as different as possible in their membership in the outcome and the focal conjunct, but as similar as possible with regard to their membership in the complementary conjuncts. Furthermore, the test corridors should be small for both cases.

$$
\begin{aligned}
TYP - IIR = & [1 - (FC_{TYP} - FC_{IIR})] && \text{large difference in focal conjunct} \\
& + [1 - (Y_{TYP} - Y_{IIR})] && \text{large difference in outcome} \\
& + |CC_{TYP} - CC_{IIR}| && \text{small difference in complementary conjuncts} \\
& + 2 * |Y_{TYP} - FC_{TYP}| && \text{small corridor for typical case} \\
& + |Y_{IIR} - FC_{IIR}| && \text{small corridor for iir case}
\end{aligned}
\quad (6.13)
$$

Finally, the formula for identifying the best-matching pair of two typical cases is shown in Formula 6.14. Also here, the two cases should be as different as possible in their membership in the outcome and the focal conjunct, and as similar as possible in their membership in the complementary conjuncts. In addition, the smaller the test corridor in both cases, the better.

$$
\begin{aligned}
TYP_1 - TYP_2 = & [0.5 - (FC_{TYP_1} - FC_{TYP_2})] && \text{large difference in focal conjunct} \\
& + [0.5 - (Y_{TYP_1} - Y_{TYP_2})] && \text{large difference in outcome} \\
& + |(CC_{TYP_1} - CC_{TYP_2})| && \text{small difference in complementary conjuncts} \\
& + 2 * |Y_{TYP_1} - FC_{TYP_1}| && \text{small corridor for typical case 1} \\
& + 2 * |Y_{TYP_2} - FC_{TYP_2}| && \text{small corridor for typical case 2}
\end{aligned}
\quad (6.14)
$$

6.3 Conjunctions, $A * B \Leftarrow Y$

Core Points 6.3: Conjunctive Necessity Claims

- Only causal inference SMMR designs are affected by the presence of necessary conjunctions
- Only two principles need to be adapted to conjunctive necessity claims: the attribution principle for necessity and the principle of iir FC nonmembership
- The rank orders follow the same logic as for conjunctive sufficiency claims: the more principles are fulfilled, the higher the rank
- Likewise, formulas follow the same logic and are adapted to the presence of necessary focal and complementary conjuncts

---

6.3.4 Applying SMMR

Code C 6.17 produces output O 6.17, which identifies the disjunction $\sim ECOD * \sim EDU$ as a consistent enough and empirically nontrivial necessary term for outcome BDT. For a graphical representation in the form of an XY plot, see Figure 6.9.

C 6.17

```
NEC_conj <- pof(data = BRETT, ~ECOD * ~EDU <- BDT)
NEC_conj
```

O 6.17

		inclN	RoN	covN
1	~ECOD*~EDU	0.854	0.832	0.769

As explained, conjunctions trigger consequences only for causal inference SMMR designs. Descriptive, model-refining SMMR designs remain unaffected because, in them, conjunctions are treated as one single set without focusing on specific conjuncts in the conjunction. This is why in this section I demonstrate only how causal inference SMMR designs are applied in R package `SetMethods`. The code is identical to what has already been introduced so far. Only the output needs some further explanation. For all three causal inference designs, the output automatically displays cases or case pairs for both focal conjuncts and for the conjunction as a whole, respectively.[25]

Code C 6.18 produces the list of best available typical cases shown in output O 6.18. When focusing on a specific conjunct, the order of cases is based on

---

[25] In SMMR designs for sufficiency claims, in contrast, two different values in argument `cases` need to be specified for focal conjuncts and for conjunctions.

low values in "Rank", then whether the corridor is clean, then whether the typical case is uniquely covered, then its value in "Best" (based on Formula 6.12), and then whether it is the most typical case. For focal conjunct $\sim ECOD$, it reveals Egypt as the best available typical case for within-case analysis. For $\sim EDU$, it is Djibouti. When treating the conjunction as one set, the ordering of cases is based on its value in "Best"[26] and whether it is the most typical case. Egypt turns out to be the best available typical case for the necessary conjuntion $\sim ECOD * \sim EDU$.

C 6.18

```
typ <- smmr(nec.cond = "~ECOD*~EDU",
            results = sol_p,
            outcome = "BDT",
            match = FALSE,
            cases = 1,
            necessity = TRUE)
typ
```

O 6.18

~ECOD :

	Case	NecCond	Outcome	Rank	CleanCorr	UniqCov	Best	MostTyp
2	Egypt	0.92	0.86	1	FALSE	FALSE	0.20	TRUE
4	Haiti	0.97	0.80	1	FALSE	FALSE	0.37	FALSE
3	Eritrea	0.98	0.57	1	FALSE	FALSE	0.84	FALSE
1	Djibouti	0.92	0.71	2	TRUE	FALSE	0.50	FALSE
5	Lesotho	0.97	0.53	2	TRUE	FALSE	0.91	FALSE

~EDU :

	Case	NecCond	Outcome	Rank	CleanCorr	UniqCov	Best	MostTyp
1	Djibouti	0.97	0.71	1	FALSE	FALSE	0.55	FALSE
2	Egypt	0.88	0.86	2	TRUE	FALSE	0.16	TRUE
4	Haiti	0.96	0.80	2	TRUE	FALSE	0.36	FALSE
3	Eritrea	0.97	0.57	2	TRUE	FALSE	0.83	FALSE
5	Lesotho	0.97	0.53	2	TRUE	FALSE	0.91	FALSE

~ECOD*~EDU :

	Case	NecCond	Outcome	UniqCov	Best	MostTyp
2	Egypt	0.88	0.86	TRUE	0.16	TRUE
4	Haiti	0.96	0.80	TRUE	0.36	FALSE
1	Djibouti	0.92	0.71	TRUE	0.50	FALSE
3	Eritrea	0.97	0.57	TRUE	0.83	FALSE
5	Lesotho	0.97	0.53	TRUE	0.91	FALSE

Code C 6.19 produces the best-matching pairs of typical and iir cases shown in output O 6.19, separated by each focal conjunct and the entire conjunction. For focal conjuncts, cases are ordered taking into account the following sequence of criteria: "PairRank" (as always, lower scores are better

---

[26] By default, all cases are uniquely covered if there is only one (conjunctive) necessary condition.

than higher); clean corridor; "Best" (based on Formula 6.13); whether the typical is the most typical case (based on Formula 6.3); whether it is uniquely covered; and then whether the iir case is globally uncovered. For focal conjunct $\sim ECOD$, this reveals the pair of Egypt and Chile as the best available pair for within-case analysis. Several other pairs matching iir case Chile to different typical cases are almost equally good. All of them are from rank 3 or lower, though, and all pairs involve cases with contaminated corridors. For focal conjunct $\sim EDU$, it is the typical case Djibouti that can be matched with various iir cases. All case pairs are from rank 1 and show relatively low values in "Best". At the same time, all case pairs from rank 1 involve the typical case of Djibouti with a contaminated corridor. For selecting a case pair with clean corridors in both cases, one would need to select pairs from rank 2, such as Egypt–Armenia, or Haiti–Armenia. Remember (e.g. see Figure 6.10) that rank 2 means that the attribution principle is violated in the typical case.

When analyzing the entire necessary conjunction, the order of case pairs is based, as outlined before, on the following criteria: is the typical case uniquely covered; then is the iir case globally uncovered, then low values in "Best" (using Formula 6.13), followed by whether the typical case is the most typical case. This identifies three pairs of cases matching Egypt with Armenia, Turkmenistan, or Bhutan as the best-matching pairs of cases.

C 6.19

```
typiir <- smmr( nec.cond = "~ECOD*~EDU",
                results = sol_p,
                outcome = "BDT",
                match = TRUE,
                cases = 3,
                max_pairs = 10,
                necessity = TRUE)
typiir
```

O 6.19

~ECOD :

	TYP	IIR	PairRank	CleanCorr	Best	MostTyp	UniqCov	GlobUncov
2	Egypt	Chile	3	none	1.68	TRUE	FALSE	TRUE
4	Haiti	Chile	3	none	1.99	FALSE	FALSE	TRUE
3	Eritrea	Chile	3	none	2.70	FALSE	FALSE	TRUE
1	Djibouti	Chile	4	typ	2.22	FALSE	FALSE	TRUE
5	Lesotho	Chile	4	none	2.81	FALSE	FALSE	TRUE

~EDU :

	TYP	IIR	PairRank	CleanCorr	Best	MostTyp	UniqCov	GlobUncov
1	Djibouti	Armenia	1	iir	0.97	FALSE	FALSE	FALSE
31	Djibouti	Turkmenistan	1	iir	1.23	FALSE	FALSE	FALSE
6	Djibouti	Bhutan	1	iir	1.43	FALSE	FALSE	FALSE
16	Djibouti	Mongolia	1	iir	1.67	FALSE	FALSE	FALSE
2	Egypt	Armenia	2	both	0.43	TRUE	FALSE	FALSE
4	Haiti	Armenia	2	both	0.68	FALSE	FALSE	FALSE
32	Egypt	Turkmenistan	2	both	0.69	TRUE	FALSE	FALSE
7	Egypt	Bhutan	2	both	0.89	TRUE	FALSE	FALSE
34	Haiti	Turkmenistan	2	both	0.94	FALSE	FALSE	FALSE
17	Egypt	Mongolia	2	both	1.13	TRUE	FALSE	FALSE

~ECOD*~EDU :

	TYP	IIR	UniqCov	GlobUncov	Best	MostTyp
2	Egypt	Armenia	TRUE	TRUE	0.40	TRUE
12	Egypt	Chile	TRUE	TRUE	0.66	TRUE
22	Egypt	Turkmenistan	TRUE	TRUE	0.66	TRUE
4	Haiti	Armenia	TRUE	TRUE	0.66	FALSE
7	Egypt	Bhutan	TRUE	TRUE	0.86	TRUE
1	Djibouti	Armenia	TRUE	TRUE	0.89	FALSE
14	Haiti	Chile	TRUE	TRUE	0.92	FALSE
24	Haiti	Turkmenistan	TRUE	TRUE	0.92	FALSE
17	Egypt	Mongolia	TRUE	TRUE	1.08	TRUE
9	Haiti	Bhutan	TRUE	TRUE	1.12	FALSE

Finally, the best-matching pair of two typical cases is obtained by code C 6.20 and shown in output O 6.20. The best pair is one with rank 1, in which both cases display a clean corridor, have a low value in "Best" (based on Formula 6.14), qualify as the most typical (using Formula 6.3) and are uniquely covered. For focal conjunct $\sim\!ECOD$, all case pairs from rank 1 fail two important other criteria: the corridor is contaminated in both cases and none of the cases is uniquely covered. As explained, in rank 1, corridors are contaminated by default. This is why one would need to choose a pair from rank 2 (e.g. Egypt–Djibouti) to obtain a clean corridor for at least one typical case (here Djibouti).

For focal conjunct $\sim\!EDU$, the best available case pairs are from rank 2 or even lower. No case pair contains uniquely covered cases. And to obtain a clean corridor for both cases, pairs from rank 4 would need to be chosen.

When analyzing the entire conjunction as a whole, the order of cases is based on low values in "Best" (using Formula 6.9), and then whether both, one, or none of them qualifies as most typical.[27] Egypt matched with either Djibouti or Lesotho comes closest to the ideal pair of typical cases.

C 6.20

```
typtyp <- smmr(nec.cond = "~ECOD*~EDU",
               results = sol_p,
               outcome = "BDT",
               match = TRUE,
               cases = 4,
               max_pairs = 7,
               necessity = TRUE)
typtyp
```

O 6.20

~ECOD :

	TYP1	TYP2	PairRank	CleanCorr	Best	MostTyp	UniqCov
6	Egypt	Haiti	1	none	1.53	typ1	none
4	Egypt	Eritrea	1	none	1.80	typ1	none
5	Haiti	Eritrea	1	none	1.95	none	none
1	Egypt	Djibouti	2	typ2	1.48	typ1	none
2	Haiti	Djibouti	2	typ2	1.63	none	none
8	Egypt	Lesotho	2	typ2	1.81	typ1	none
10	Haiti	Lesotho	2	typ2	1.96	none	none

~EDU :

	TYP1	TYP2	PairRank	CleanCorr	Best	MostTyp	UniqCov
3	Djibouti	Eritrea	2	typ2	2.24	none	none
7	Djibouti	Lesotho	2	typ2	2.27	none	none
1	Egypt	Djibouti	3	typ1	1.50	typ1	none
2	Haiti	Djibouti	3	typ1	1.81	none	none
6	Egypt	Haiti	4	both	1.43	typ1	none

[27] Again, with only one (conjunctive) condition, all cases are uniquely covered by default.

4	Egypt	Eritrea	4	both	1.70	typ1	none
8	Egypt	Lesotho	4	both	1.73	typ1	none

~ECOD*~EDU :

	TYP1	TYP2	UniqCov	Best	MostTyp
1	Egypt	Djibouti	both	1.35	typ1
6	Egypt	Haiti	both	1.38	typ1
2	Haiti	Djibouti	both	1.61	none
4	Egypt	Eritrea	both	1.64	typ1
8	Egypt	Lesotho	both	1.68	typ1
5	Haiti	Eritrea	both	1.90	none
10	Haiti	Lesotho	both	1.94	none

6.4 Conclusion and Reflections on Necessary and Sufficient Conditions, $A * B + C * D \Leftrightarrow Y$

When performing SMMR based on necessity claims, researchers do not have to reinvent the wheel. The main challenges and their solutions remain the same. Only some principles and formulas that were developed for sufficiency claims need minor adjustments in order to take into account that, with claims of necessity, condition X is a superset of outcome Y, rather than a subset.

Applied QCA is predominantly focused on the analysis of sufficiency. Yet claims of necessity can, and should, play a role. The tools presented here enable researchers to handle such claims in their SMMR design. Necessity claims can come in different forms. Either a single condition, a disjunction, or a conjunction can be considered necessary. These forms have been discussed in this chapter and they could be labelled as "stand-alone" necessity claims. Stand-alone because they are not inserted in a sufficiency claim. Sometimes, however, some conjuncts in a sufficient conjunction can be necessary for the outcome. I have discussed the details of such necessary INUS conditions in Section 4.4 and mention this here to underline the importance of understanding the logic of necessity claims even if, on the surface, QCA, and therefore most SMMR designs, are about sufficiency statements.

Yet another form in which necessity claims enter the picture is when the disjunction of conjunctions is necessary, for instance, $A*B+C*D \Leftarrow Y$. Such complex necessity statements are very rare in applied research. What is more common, though, is that a disjunction of conjunctions is both necessary and sufficient, that is, $A*B+C*D \Leftrightarrow Y$. Solution formulas such as this are the result of a sufficiency analysis if and when the coverage of the disjunction is very high. In other words, jointly, the sufficient conjunctions explain all (or most) cases that are members of the outcome. This, in turn, means that it is

6.4 Conclusion

necessary to be a member of the solution formula in order to be a member of the outcome.

What are the consequences for SMMR when the QCA yields a solution formula that is both necessary and sufficient? The consequences are minimal. All SMMR principles, types of cases, formulas, and practices remain unaffected. Note that the bidirectional arrow $\Leftrightarrow$ means that consistency of each conjunction and coverage of the disjunction are very high – otherwise the formula would not qualify as both necessary and sufficient. This, in turn, means that there are no, or only few, deviant cases. This, in turn, means that there is no, or less, need for meaningful model-refining SMMR designs. Causal inference SMMR designs should be at the center of attention.

As a matter of fact, some interpretations of a regularity theory of causation (Baumgartner, 2009) stipulate that only those solution formulas are causally interpretable that show the features of our formula here: conjunctions that are sufficient for the outcome and that form a disjunction that is necessary for the outcome: (virtually) all members of the outcome are covered and (virtually) no member of any cause contradicts the sufficiency claims. This requirement for virtually no deviation from a perfect overlap between the solution and the outcome set puts the bar very high for applied social research (Schneider, 2018). This is also one reason why SMMR stipulates different, additional requirements for causal inference, most importantly the requirement that a cross-case cause must trigger a within-case mechanism that links it to the outcome – irrespective of whether or not that cause, in combination with other causes, can exhaustively explain all instances of the outcome.

The insight that all elements of SMMR also apply to solution formulas that denote a necessary-and-sufficient relation also holds in light of the following two possible complications. First, different disjuncts in a disjunction could differ in their set relational status vis-à-vis the outcome. For instance, in the formula $A*B+C*D \Leftrightarrow Y$ it could be that $A*B$ is only necessary but not sufficient for Y, whereas $C*D$ is only sufficient but not necessary for Y. Second, also within each conjunction, single conjuncts can have a different set-relational status vis-à-vis the outcome. For instance, in conjunction $C*D$, conjunct C could be necessary for Y, whereas D is not. I discussed this issue in detail in Section 4.4. Depending on the set-relational status, which must be backed by theoretical considerations and empirical facts, the appropriate case selection protocol for either sufficiency or necessity needs to be applied to specific conjuncts and disjuncts under investigation.

7
Conclusions – SMMR in Practice

In this concluding chapter, I offer various perspectives on SMMR to shed further light both on what SMMR can and cannot deliver, and on how it can be used in applied social science research. To achieve this, I keep the summary of the book's content short and focus instead on issues of applied SMMR that researchers will most likely encounter. I explore the difference between ideal-typical and applied SMMR, point out that SMMR can also be useful for learning about nonmodel (descriptive and causal inference)-related issues, propose a sequence in which the different SMMR designs should be applied, and make suggestions on how to select among the many possible SMMR designs if and when the implementation of all of them faces practical constraints. I also briefly detail the consequences for SMMR of the choice of set type – crisp, fuzzy, multivalue, or mixes of them – and of calibration strategies. In the outlook section, I make three suggestions on how to inform SMMR with other tools in QCA that, like SMMR, produce a classification of cases into different types: theory evaluation, robustness tests, and cluster diagnostics. Finally, I dwell on the advantages of performing SMMR based on QCA results that integrate information on time, temporality, or sequencing of conditions

---

Learning Goals 7.1: SMMR in Practice

- Reflect on challenges in putting SMMR in to practice
- Understand the different ways in which to choose among the various SMMR designs
- Learn about the implications of using different types of sets in SMMR
- Develop ideas on how to combine SMMR with other, advanced tools in set-theoretic methods that share the feature of classifying cases
- Appreciate that SMMR is fully in line with, and further improves, existing, more widely accepted, methodological case selection principles

---

7.1 SMMR Principles and Established Case Selection Rules

One way of summarizing the analytic framework of SMMR is to show in one place all its principles. These principles guide the choice of the available (pairs of) cases for either descriptive or causal inference. Table 7.1 contains all 20 SMMR principles and provides information on which of them are specific to comparative SMMR and which apply also to single-case SMMR. I further indicate which principles are relevant for crisp and fuzzy sets and which ones apply only to fuzzy sets, which are used only in causal inference SMMR designs, and which principles are needed only when the QCA solution shows equifinality or conjunctural causation. Information on where in the book the SMMR principles are introduced, and their logic described, is provided in the Index. In addition, all principles are listed in Table A.1 in the Appendix.

One piece of information revealed by Table 7.1 is that no principle automatically applies to any SMMR design, regardless of the inferential goal, the type of set relation, the type of set, or the level of complexity. More than two thirds of the principle apply to both single-case and comparative SMMR designs and only six are specific to comparative SMMR. Reading the information in Table 7.1 down each column, it is revealed that a majority of principles apply to fuzzy set-based SMMR only.[1] Half of the principles apply only when the goal of the SMMR design is drawing causal inference. The two features that define the complexity of a QCA solution – equifinality and conjunctions – require nine principles. All but one of them are needed only for causal inference SMMR designs.

One further piece of information conveyed by Table 7.1 is somewhat hidden, yet important: SMMR on sufficiency and necessity follow the same principles. Only minor modifications are needed for the attribution and the iir FC unique nonmembership principles. Not only are the principles virtually identical, but also the types of cases and formulas are almost the same, with only minor adaptations.

One important point to mention about SMMR principles is this: their overall gist is to address and respond to general research design and case selection issues in social science research. In this sense, they are not specific to SMMR. Let me illustrate this point with some examples. For instance, the goal of matching a typical with an iir case such that they are identical except for their membership in the outcome and the focal conjunct mimics Mill's method of difference (Mill, 1874), the most-similar system design (Przeworski and Teune, 1970), and advice by leading comparativists (Lijphart, 1971).

---

[1] While in practice, the test corridor principle is useful only for fuzzy sets, its logic also applies to crisp sets, where the corridor is always of size 0.

Table 7.1 *Categorizing SMMR principles*

Principles	Fuzzy sets	Causal	Disjuncts	Conjuncts
Single + comparative				
Max set member	✓			
Max set member diff	✓			
Test corridor	(✓)	✓		
Causal inference sel		✓		
Descriptive inference sel				
Diff of kind and degree	✓			
Truth table row				
Focal disjunct			✓	
Uniquely covered		✓	✓	
Globally uncovered		✓	✓	
Focal conjunct		✓		✓
Clean corridor	✓	✓		✓
Attribution	✓	✓		✓
Attribution, necessity	✓	✓		✓
Only comparative				
Positive outcome				
Deviance in kind	✓			
Max–min diff	✓			
Max–max diff	✓			
iir FC unique nonmember		✓		✓
iir FC nonmember		✓		✓

In SMMR, this setup is achieved by applying several principles, such as the causal inference selection principle and the maximum set membership difference principle.

As another example that SMMR principles are formalized, set-theoretic versions of common notions of case selection strategies, consider the various principles that require maximizing differences, either between the condition and outcome memberships in a single case, or between the condition and/or outcome memberships across two cases. They all follow the general advice to select cases diversely (Rohlfing, 2012; Seawright and Gerring, 2008). Likewise, leading scholars argue that, for within-case analyses on the causal mechanism, at least one case must show the outcome of interest (e.g. Beach and Pedersen, 2016; Goertz, 2017). In SMMR, this general line of thinking is captured by the positive outcome and the causal inference selection principles.

Further SMMR principles also resonate with general methodological advice. Several SMMR principles tackle head-on the well-known inferential challenges when the outcome of interest is the result of equifinal and conjunctural causes (e.g. Rohlfing, 2012, chap. 4). For instance, the inferential problems triggered by equifinality are addressed by the focal disjunct, the uniquely covered, and the globally uncovered principles. Jointly they require that equifinality or overdetermination is "turned off" in those cases that are subjected to within-case analyses on the causal status of the term in question. This is achieved by selecting uniquely covered typical cases and globally uncovered iir cases. Similarly, the inferential problems of conjunctural causation that hamper traditional approaches, such as Mill's method of difference, are mitigated in SMMR by the focal conjunct, the attribution, and the iir FC unique nonmembership principles. Jointly, they "turn off" conjunctural causes by investigating each conjunct in a setting that allows researchers to disregard other conjuncts in the conjunction under investigation. In fully causally complex situations, the norm in applied QCA, the joint application of SMMR principles therefore increases the inferential leverage of traditional comparative designs while still being fully in line with widely shared and agreed notions of how case selection ought to occur.

All in all, the close link between existing methodological advice, on the one hand, and SMMR principle and case types, on the other, is testimony to the fact that SMMR is well inserted in the general literature on social science methodology. It does not reinvent the wheel, but rather adapts it to the vehicle of set-theoretic methods and, in so doing, further specifies and improves existing, more general methodological case selection principles.

7.2 SMMR in Research Practice

In this section, I reflect on several issues researchers unavoidably confront when applying SMMR in their research. I first address how SMMR can be seen as a bridge between the different usages of QCA identified in the literature. Then I detail the difference between ideal-typical SMMR and applied SMMR. After this, I briefly remind readers that, although SMMR is focused on model-related descriptive and causal inference, it can also help achieve other important research goals. I then outline strategies for choosing some SMMR designs over others. Finally, I reflect on the use of different types of sets – crisp, fuzzy, multivalue – and the degree of set membership coarseness more generally in SMMR.

7.2.1 SMMR and the Different Uses of QCA

To some extent, qualitative comparative analysis means different things to different people. This seems to stem from the fact that QCA can be employed in different ways and for different purposes. Thomann and Maggetti (2020) (see also Thomann and Ege, 2020) identify eight different forms of QCA. This typology is based on distinguishing three dimensions: the mode of reasoning (exploratory vs. theory-evaluating), the approach to cases (case vs. condition-oriented), and the approach to explanation (substantively interpretable vs. redundancy-free). The different QCA usages are depicted as largely mutually exclusive.

SMMR, however, can be seen as a bridge that enables researchers to integrate elements from opposite sides of these three dimensions. By definition, SMMR is case-oriented. Yet it focuses on cases to also reveal the role of conditions. Likewise, descriptive inference SMMR is more in line with exploratory approaches to QCA, whereas causal inference SMMR resonates with theory-evaluation. Finally, as explained in Sections 1.4.6 and 5.4, in SMMR the QCA solution formula can be the redundancy-free most parsimonious solution or the intermediate or conservative formula. Independent of the choice of the solution formula, the goal in causal inference SMMR remains that of explaining the outcome.

Note that the capacity of SMMR to integrate various approaches to QCA is not the same as the "hybrid approaches" identified by Thomann et al. (2022). The authors are critical of such hybrid uses and even see an inverse correlation between hybridity and adherence to good QCA practices. SMMR does not fall victim to this. It avoids the pitfall by zooming in on the post-analytic moment of QCA and then specifying – in book-length detail – which cases to choose (typical or deviant) for which purpose (descriptive or causal inference).

In short, with SMMR, one can simply achieve more than with running only a QCA. Analytic goals that seem mutually exclusive in Thomann and Maggetti (2020) and Thomann et al. (2022) can thus be reconciled and combined in and with SMMR. The conundrum of empirical predominance of hybrid approaches, on the one hand, and their substandard adherence to standards of good practice, detected by Thomann et al. (2022), on the other, can thus be mitigated, or even resolved, if QCA researchers apply in their research the principles and practices of SMMR outlined in this book.

7.2.2 Ideal-Typical vs. Applied SMMR

The list of possible within-case analyses, and sometimes even reruns of the QCA, is long and gets longer, the more complex the QCA result is. Even if the complete application of SMMR standards remains unachievable in most applied research, knowing about them is a stern reminder of just how much it takes to draw descriptive and causal inference on social phenomena based on observational data. The forms of SMMR designs introduced in this book constitute the ideal-typical scenario of what researchers should do if they have the time, resources, and access to the relevant information. Hardly ever will it be possible to put in practice the complete ideal scenario. Scarcity of time, research funds, journal space, and the limited diversity of the social world will often require hard decisions by the researcher on how to best spend the limited resources in order to get the most out of the study. Some of these limitations can sometimes be overcome by applying SMMR in a research team or a broader research project, or by providing information in online appendices of publications.

Still, nonmethodological, yet equally important, considerations, such as the substantive importance of a case, a researcher's familiarity with a case, language skills, the accessibility of research sites, etc., will often lead to the choice of cases that are not the best according to the SMMR standards presented in this book. Knowing about these standards is nevertheless an improvement. It is important for researchers to know and to be explicit about if and when they are coming short of the ideal design for descriptive and causal inference. This information should be used to calibrate the determinacy (Rohlfing, 2012) with which the inferences can be drawn. Researchers should argue why nonoptimal cases have been selected and in which sense this methodologically suboptimal choice is paid off by other important case selection rationales, to which I turn now.

7.2.3 Nonmodel-Related SMMR Goals

In this book, I have limited the discussion of SMMR to goals that relate to the model derived with QCA: we want to either refine the model or probe its causal properties. This assumed, to a large extent, that the "right" cases and conditions had been chosen and each case's membership in all sets had been calibrated "correctly". My argument is that the benefits of SMMR's dictum of going back to cases, while not explicitly discussed in this book, certainly also contributes to improving confidence in the calibration of set membership scores and the choice of scope conditions.

For instance, the primary goal of the SMMR design of matching two typical cases consists of probing the generalizability of the mechanism from one to all typical cases. At the same time, this design also sheds light on our calibration decisions. If we identify the mechanism in the just-so typical case, then our calibration decision to qualify this case as a member of both the outcome and the condition is further supported. If we do not find the mechanism in the just-so typical case, it could mean either that the mechanism cannot be generalized to all relevant typical cases or that the just-so typical case has been calibrated wrongly and should not be a just-so typical case. "Wrong" here means that the case's membership in either the condition and/or the outcome should be on the other side of the 0.5 qualitative anchor. If its membership in the outcome is wrong, it would be a deviant consistency case. If membership in the condition is wrong, it would be a deviant coverage case. And if both membership scores are wrong, it would be an iir case. By pointing researchers to within-case analyses, SMMR can help solve these empirical ambiguities of cases close to the 0.5 qualitative anchor.

Calibration decisions can also be probed in other SMMR designs. For instance, in a comparison of a typical and an iir case, imagine within-case analysis shows that the mechanism is in place regardless of whether or not the condition is present. This would be reason to dismiss this condition as causal – if we have high confidence in the membership scores of the typical and iir cases in the condition and the outcome. If either this confidence is low, or theory-driven confidence in the causal status of the condition is high, or both, then researchers should investigate in greater detail the set membership scores of the typical and iir cases in the outcome and the condition.

Explicit scope conditions are crucial for sound descriptive and causal inference. SMMR can be of help in refining them. In particular, the descriptive inference designs lend themselves to this task. When confronting deviant coverage cases, the standard analytic goal in SMMR is to identify a missing disjunct. From the study of these unexplained cases, one could also conclude, though, that some or all of them belong to a different causal universe, that is, they are not falling within the scope conditions of the study. Rather than adding as a condition to the truth table the factor(s) that make(s) deviant coverage cases different from the rest, one could specify those factors as scope conditions and therefore drop the deviant coverage cases from the analysis.

A similar logic applies to SMMR designs involving deviant consistency cases. The goal of identifying an omitted conjunct remains, but rather than adding this condition to an existing conjunction – the standard, model-related goal of SMMR – one could also conclude that this attribute makes this (and all other) deviant case(s) so different from the rest that it is warranted to add it as a scope condition to the study. Doing so results in dropping all cases that are not members of this new scope condition.

7.2.4 Sequencing and Selecting SMMR Designs

One consideration when choosing SMMR designs is the empirical fit of the QCA solution. How high is the coverage of the solution formula? And how high is the consistency of single terms? Depending on this, descriptive SMMR designs are more or less important. Figure 1.4 visualizes the logic.

7.2 SMMR in Research Practice

By and large, we can say that the lower the parameters of fit, the more reasons there are for starting with model-refining, descriptive inference SMMR designs. In more detail, if coverage of the solution formula is of concern, I suggest starting with the analysis of deviant coverage cases. As long as these analyses have not been concluded, no other within-case analysis should be performed because results from the SMMR designs focusing on deviant coverage cases are the only ones that might alter the truth table. And altering the truth table means that all other cases could change their status as typical, deviant, or iir. This means that if researchers plan to do analyses of deviant coverage cases, those should always go first. If solution coverage is not of concern, no SMMR analysis involving deviant coverage cases is needed. Note that even if solution coverage is reasonably high, it could still be of concern if either substantively or theoretically important cases are not covered by the solution.

I suggest performing analyses of deviant consistency cases, either in a single-case or a comparative case SMMR design, only if the consistency of a term is of concern. If consistency is high enough, no model-refining SMMR design is needed. If it is needed, though, then it should be implemented before any causal inference design on the term(s) in question. Also, with consistency, it is important to mention that it might be of concern if substantively or theoretically important cases contradict a set relational claim. All this implies that one should engage in causal inference SMMR designs only once the QCA solution adequately describes the underlying data as indicated by high-enough parameters of fit and nondeviance of important cases. What exactly is to be understood as high-enough and important is largely a matter of interpretation and depends on the specific research context.

Among the causal inference designs, the strongest ground for inference is provided by the comparison of a typical and an iir case. Single typical case studies are the fallback option if no adequately matching iir case exists in the data. The comparison of two typical cases should be performed after the causal status of a term has been confirmed, because this comparison aims at probing how generalizable a causal claim is.

7.2.5 Selective Focus on Some Disjuncts or Conjuncts

SMMR rests on the distinction between different disjuncts in a disjunction and conjuncts in a conjunction, and, ideally, calls for the separate analyses of each conjunct in each disjunct. The more complex a QCA solution formula, the more within-case analyses would need to be performed. The investigation of the causal status of all disjuncts and conjuncts is particularly warranted if the study is explicitly and strongly outcome-oriented (Beach and Rohlfing, 2018), that is, when the primary goal is to fully explain the outcome. Even though this seems to be the most common usage of QCA, it is also feasible to employ QCA in a more condition-centered manner (Beach and Rohlfing, 2018; Oana et al., 2021, chap. 7.3; Thomann and Maggetti, 2020).

There might be strong theoretical or substantive reasons for focusing on one specific disjunct or, even more so, on a specific conjunct in that disjunct. For instance, imagine the predominant view in a field is that the presence of condition A is terribly important for achieving outcome Y. The QCA solution, however, identifies the negated condition $\sim A$ as a conjunct in the sufficient disjunct $\sim A * B$, which itself is part of the equifinal solution $\sim A * B + C * D \Rightarrow Y$. Showing that the negation of A, if combined with condition B, is causally relevant could be a worthwhile contribution to the literature. No SMMR designs other than those focusing on conjunct $\sim A$ would be needed for this contribution.

Similarly, the contribution of a study could rest in neither explaining the outcome, nor in testing the causal properties of specific conditions, but in explaining the outcome in a specific case. Imagine that among the cases in a study there is one that is either of high substantive importance, or has consistently remained unexplained in other studies, or both. Imagine also that the researcher's QCA solution formula covers this case. In other words, it is a typical case for (at least) one of the terms in the solution. Focusing SMMR on only this term seems justified if the researcher can credibly claim that it amounts to a worthwhile contribution to the literature to finally explain why this particular case displays the outcome of interest.

7.2.6 SMMR and Different Types of Sets

Applied researchers are at liberty to choose different types of sets when performing QCA. Some use only crisp sets, others only fuzzy sets, and yet others mix both types of sets. SMMR can accommodate all these different forms of QCA. In the following, I sketch some of the implications for SMMR designs of using crisp, fuzzy, or both types of sets. I further dwell briefly on the question of how fine-grained fuzzy sets should be and what the consequences are of using fuzzy sets with different levels of coarseness. One question to address is: which type of set does the mechanism have to be in light of the choice of a set type for the QCA? I conclude with some reflections on SMMR with multivalue sets.

In general, all types of cases and principles that hold for crisp sets also hold for fuzzy sets, but the inverse is not true. Some case types and principles apply

7.2 SMMR in Research Practice

only to fuzzy sets (e.g. see Table 7.1). This extends to all SMMR formulas, which are applicable only when fuzzy sets are used. This is because fuzzy sets are the more general type of set; crisp sets can be seen as a form of fuzzy set that allows only two membership values (0 and 1).

Which types of cases apply when only crisp sets are used? The main types of cases – typical, deviant consistency, deviant coverage, deviant relevance, and iir – remain in place because they are defined based on qualitative differences and similarities in their memberships in the condition and the outcome. Even some sub-types of cases, such as the uniquely covered typical or the globally deviant coverage case, exist in crisp-set QCA-based SMMR. Only those sub-types that are based on differences in degree are limited to fuzzy-set QCA. First and foremost, these are the most typical and most deviant consistency cases.

Several of the principles apply to fuzzy sets only. Table 7.1 lists all SMMR principles and indicates which are specific to fuzzy-set QCA-based SMMR. For instance, some important principles for causal inference SMMR are available only when fuzzy sets are used, most importantly the two attribution principles, but also the test corridor and the clean corridor principles. This has implications for the ranks that are used in all causal inference SMMR designs that distinguish between focal and complementary conjuncts. As already pointed out in Section 4.3.2, with crisp sets, when matching the best available pair of typical and iir cases, pairs cannot be distinguished in eight different ranks, but only three. A similar reduction of differentiation possibilities occurs for SMMR designs focusing on single typical cases or on the matching of two typical cases.

The choice of crisp-set QCA also has implications for which set type to choose for the mechanisms. In general, the following holds: the same type of set should be chosen at the cross-case and the within-case levels. Otherwise, researchers create broken corridors *by design*. As detailed in Sections 2.4 and 6.1.3, corridors are broken when the membership in the mechanism M does not fall in between that of the condition X and the outcome Y. If researchers opt for mixing fuzzy-set within-case mechanisms with crisp-set cross-case conditions, then a typical case's membership in the mechanism is likely to be smaller than in the condition and the outcome. This means that the choice of set types unavoidably creates broken floor (sufficiency) or broken ceiling (necessity) scenarios. Similarly, if fuzzy sets are used at the cross-case level, but at the within-case level mechanisms are conceptualized as crisp sets, then researchers, by design and default, create broken ceiling (for sufficiency and necessity claims) scenarios.

Evidence for broken corridors is not a problem *per se*. However, researchers need to be aware that it is their choice of set types that predetermines broken corridors. Furthermore, broken corridors require that researchers can meaningfully interpret them as nec-suf chains or suf-nec chains (see Sections 2.4 and 6.1.3). If no such interpretation is plausible, then all SMMR designs using different set types at the within-case and the cross-case levels are bound to produce negative findings on the causal status of the cross-case conditions. Put differently, short of plausible theories for suf-nec or nec-suf chains, a mixing of set types is likely to lead to negative findings for causal inference even if the ground truth is that the conditions are causal.

What emerges from this debate is that the types of sets at the cross-case and the within-case levels should be the same. This also holds for mixed-set QCA, that is, QCA in which both crisp and fuzzy sets are used. Here what matters for SMMR is which set types (crisp or fuzzy) form part of the QCA solution formula. Ideally, by "the same", we mean not only either crisp or fuzzy sets. Among fuzzy sets, it is also preferable to calibrate with the same degree of coarseness. Fuzzy sets can come in different shapes (Ragin, 2000). So-called continuous fuzzy sets are very fine-grained and allow for any membership score between 0 and 1. Such "continuous fuzzy sets" (Goertz and Mahoney, 2012, chap. 2) look very different from more coarse fuzzy sets that allow only a specific number of discrete membership scores.[2] In SMMR, inferential problems in the form of broken corridors emerge if the level of coarseness *radically* differs between sets, both among those at the cross-case level and between the cross-case and within-case levels.

The recommendation for applied SMMR researchers is to calibrate, if possible, all sets with the same degree of coarseness. Everything else being equal, the more fine-grained the calibration, the better for SMMR. But, of course, not everything else is always equal in applied research. Researchers therefore need to carefully ponder the pros and cons of their calibration options. The mismatch of coarseness between sets at the cross- and within-case levels is one aspect to keep in mind in these considerations.

In general, one should not overemphasize small differences in set membership scores, though. Oftentimes, such minor membership differences fall into the realm of noise and are not supported by conceptually relevant differences. When selecting (pairs of) cases, applied SMMR researchers should therefore feel encouraged to back up the information provided by the output of the smmr() function with a detailed look into the membership scores of not only the best available (pairs of) cases, but also cases further down on the ranking

---

[2] If they only allow the two values 0 and 1, then we call them crisp sets.

7.2 SMMR in Research Practice

list. Maybe there are some "near misses" where, for instance, the attribution principle is violated by only a marginally higher membership of the case in the focal conjunct than in the complementary conjunct. If researchers feel confident in dismissing this minor membership difference as noise, they can, and perhaps even should, treat membership in the focal and complementary conjuncts as equal and choose this (pair of) cases for within-case analysis. Obviously, such adjustments of membership scores can count as minor only if they do not lead to a qualitative change of membership, that is, if the adjustment does not push a case to the other side of the 0.5 qualitative set membership anchor.

***

Before moving to an outlook on further developments, I briefly address the use of multivalue sets (Cronqvist and Berg-Schlosser, 2009) in SMMR. In a sense, this is already one reflection on future developments, because, in principle, SMMR based on mvQCA can be performed. It is just that, in practice, the implementation of SMMR with multivalue qualitative comparative analysis (mvQCA) in the R package `SetMethods` is a project for the future, which would gain importance if more researchers used mvQCA than is currently the case. Only very few scholars specify at least some conditions as multivalue sets in their QCAs (Rihoux et al., 2013).

For the sake of simplification, I exclude scenarios in which the outcome is a multivalue set. Strictly speaking, there is no multivalue outcome QCA. Researchers might specify an outcome with multiple qualitatively different values, but each of these outcome categories will then be analyzed in *separate* (mv)QCA. Let us also exclude the use of multivalue sets for mechanisms and focus only on the implications of the use of cross-case mvQCA for SMMR designs.

All types of cases that exist with crisp sets also exist with multivalue sets. Likewise, all principles applicable to crisp sets also apply to multivalue sets. And none of the case types and principles that are exclusive to fuzzy sets applies to multivalue sets.[3]

The consequences of multivalue sets are primarily triggered for causal inference designs. For them, it is the difference in membership in the condition of interest that matters for case selection. The typical case should be a member and the iir case a nonmember of the condition whose causal status is under

---

[3] This would be different if, in the future, so-called generalized-set QCA (Thiem, 2014) turns from a theoretical possibility into an applied practice.

scrutiny.[4] How nonmembership is handled is what distinguishes crisp and multivalue sets. One way of looking at multivalue sets is to see them as crisp sets that provide detailed information on what it means *not* to be a member of a specific set. For instance, the crisp set "social-democratic party" puts all parties that are not social-democratic together into one group. With multivalue sets, however, one can unpack this group and distinguish between, say, conservative, green, socialist, and fascist parties.

Imagine we want to probe whether being member of the set of "social-democratic party" is causal for an outcome by triggering a within-case mechanism. When matching a typical with an iir case to answer this question, the typical case must be a member of "social-democratic party". The iir case must not be a social-democratic party, which, with multivalue sets, means several different things. And all these different meanings, captured by the multiple values that constitute the multivalue set (here best labeled as "party family"), need to be analyzed separately, because the claim is that being a social-democratic party triggers the mechanism and the outcome, rather than *any* other party family type.

For applied SMMR this means that the number of within-case analyses increases with the number of values allowed by a multivalue set. The more values, the more within-case analyses are required. This holds not only for causal inference designs, but also for descriptive inference SMMR designs. When matching a deviant coverage and an iir case, there are more possible truth table rows in which both case types can be located.

All in all, researchers can use multivalue sets in SMMR. All case types and principles relevant for crisp sets apply to multivalue sets. Their use increases the number of within-case analyses proportional to the number of values specified in a multivalue set. An implementation in the smmr() function in R that identifies all required best available (pairs) of cases based on an mvQCA is a project for the future.

7.3 Outlook – Where Could and Should We Go from Here?

Apart from adapting the smmr() function to the use of multivalue sets, there are several other developments for SMMR. I focus here on four possibilities of combining SMMR with other already existing tools for QCA researchers. Theory evaluation and robustness tests share with SMMR the feature that

---

[4] We can exclude the second causal inference comparative design, the comparison of two typical cases, because it requires differences in degree to distinguish most typical from just-so typical cases. Multivalue sets do not contain information on differences in degree.

they produce, among other things, types of cases, which can inform the SMMR-based case selection. Cluster diagnostics, too, categorizes cases and thus provides information that can be capitalized on when performing SMMR. Various approaches, such as temporal QCA, two-step QCA, and causal chains, infuse QCA solutions with notions of time, which researchers can use in their SMMR designs.

7.3.1 SMMR and Theory Evaluation

Theory evaluation (Ragin, 1987; Schneider and Wagemann, 2012) asks how the QCA solution (S) overlaps with the theory-based hunches (T) held prior to the QCA analysis. The norm in applied QCA is that this overlap is only partial. Some (parts of some) conjunctions of the QCA solution overlap with theory-guided expectations, other elements do not. Each case under analysis is therefore located in one of the four possible areas $T*S + {\sim}T*S + T*{\sim}S + {\sim}T*{\sim}S$, and depending on whether a case is a member of the outcome (Y) or not (${\sim}Y$), it belongs to one of the eight possible types of cases that are created by theory evaluation. Cases predicted by theory to be members of the outcome are called "most likely" and those not predicted to be members of the outcome are "least likely" cases (Eckstein, 1975). More details on theory evaluation, how it defines types of cases and how to obtain them via R package `SetMethods` can be found in Oana et al. (2021, chap. 6.2).[5]

Each of the four main types of cases in SMMR – typical, deviant consistency, deviant coverage, and iir – comes in two forms when looking through the theory evaluation lens: they are either most likely or least likely. Knowing the status of a case can sometimes increase the inferential leverage. For instance, when choosing a deviant coverage case, the analytic goal is, as explained in this book, to discover a disjunct that is missing from the QCA solution. That hitherto unknown disjunct must be unrelated to those conditions and theories that went into the QCA. It therefore seems recommendable to choose a least likely deviant coverage case (and a least likely iir case in a comparison with a deviant coverage case).

Similarly, among deviant consistency cases, the choice of least likely cases is to be preferred, because the goal consists in identifying a conjunct that is missing from a known sufficient conjunction. When comparing a deviant consistency case with a typical case, the latter should also be least likely, to

---

[5] So far, the tool of theory evaluation has been developed for claims of sufficiency only. I therefore restrict the discussion to its combination with SMMR designs focusing on sufficient conditions.

further increase the chances of identifying the missing conjunct. In general, one can say that descriptive inference, model-refining SMMR designs can profit from choosing least likely cases.

For causal inference designs, in contrast, the choice of most likely cases seems more recommendable. For both typical and iir cases, the most likely ones are those whose membership scores are in line with what is expected by those theories whose causal status the SMMR-based analyses of typical and iir cases aim at probing.

7.3.2 SMMR and the QCA Robustness Test Protocol

One core property of QCA is that it classifies cases based on their membership in necessary and/or sufficient conditions and the outcome. SMMR capitalizes on this property of QCA and provides guidelines on which cases to choose for within-case analyses to enhance descriptive and causal inference. Similarly, one way of conceptualizing the robustness of findings generated with QCA is to ask if the classification of cases as either typical or deviant remains unaffected if the researcher implements plausible changes to the analytic setup of the QCA.

This "case-oriented" approach plays an important role in the QCA robustness test protocol by Oana and Schneider (2021). Based on conceptually plausible changes to calibration and threshold decisions when constructing the truth table (consistency and n.cut), alternative, so-called test solutions, are created. The robustness test then consists in evaluating the overlap between the initial QCA solution and the test solution. In applied QCA, the rule is that the overlap between these two solution sets is not perfect. This gives rise to three different forms of cases. A case can either be robust, shaky, or possible. A case is robust if its status as a specific type (typical or deviant) is the same in the initial and the test solution. A case is possible if it is a member of the test solution, but not the initial QCA solution. Finally, a case is shaky if it is a member of the QCA result, but not the robustness test solution.

Figure 7.1 depicts a simplified version[6] of the conceptual framework of the QCA robustness test protocol. Intersecting the QCA solution set (S), the test set (T), and the outcome set (Y) yields eight areas. For each area, I insert the case label from the robustness test protocol and the label a case would receive without knowledge of the robustness test set (type of case in square brackets). We see that after a QCA robustness test, there are three forms of typical

---
[6] It is simplified because Oana and Schneider (2021) distinguish between two forms of the test set: the maximum test set used for identifying possible cases and a minimum test set for identifying shaky cases.

7.3 Outlook – Where Could and Should We Go from Here?

Figure 7.1 SMMR and the QCA robustness test protocol

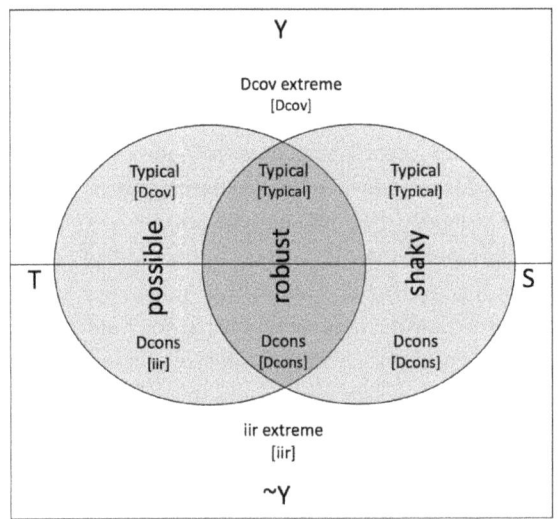

and three forms of deviant consistency cases: robust, shaky, and possible. In contrast, both deviant coverage and iir cases exist in only one form. By definition, they cannot be robust or shaky. To qualify as either robust or shaky, a case must be a member of the initial QCA solution, but deviant coverage and iir cases are, by definition, not members of the QCA solution. Thus, both case types can also not be possible cases. As soon as a deviant coverage case is part of the test solution, it is classified as a possible typical case. And an iir case covered by the test solution turns into a possible deviant consistency case.

When performing SMMR, which form of case should be chosen: robust, possible, or shaky? The answer depends on whether a descriptive or a causal inference SMMR design is implemented. For causal inference designs, I suggest the choice of robust cases. Typical cases should be qualified as such not only by the QCA solution whose causal status is under investigation. They should also be typical cases for the test solution, that is, even if different but plausible analytic setups are used for producing a QCA result. In other words, we should be reasonably sure that these cases are really typical cases and have not ended up in this category by questionable analytic choices when producing the QCA solution. The added benefit of using robustness test results when selecting typical cases is that we can avoid selecting cases that look like typical cases from the perspective of the QCA solution, but that turn out to be shaky typical cases if the QCA solution was produced with a slightly different analytic setup.

Choosing the form of iir cases in causal inference SMMR designs is straightforward because, as explained, there is just one form of iir case: the only iir cases that exist – let us label them extreme iir cases – are those that are members of neither the initial QCA solution nor the test solution. The added benefit of using robustness test results when selecting iir cases is that we can avoid selecting cases that look like iir cases from the perspective of the QCA solution, but that would turn into deviant consistency cases if the QCA solution was produced with a slightly different analytic setup.

For descriptive inference SMMR designs, a more varied scenario emerges. Designs aiming at uncovering an omitted conjunct by refining a known sufficient term have to involve a deviant consistency case. Since we want to refine a known sufficient term, choosing a possible deviant consistency case seems the best option, but a robust case is also fine. Choosing a shaky deviant consistency case, however, seems to limit the inferential value of the results obtained with this descriptive inference SMMR design. The same logic applies to a typical case when matched with a deviant consistency case: they can be either robust or possible, but should not be shaky.

Designs aiming at uncovering an omitted disjunct have to involve a deviant coverage case. From the robustness test protocol perspective, they exist in only one form. Oana and Schneider (2021) use the label of extreme deviant coverage cases, that is, cases that are not members of either the QCA solution or the test solution. I suggest their choice for descriptive inference SMMR designs that involve deviant coverage cases. They seem like the best place to start looking for new sufficient terms. The added benefit of using robustness test results when selecting deviant coverage cases is that we can avoid selecting cases that look like deviant coverage cases from the perspective of the QCA solution, but that would turn into typical cases if the QCA solution was produced with a slightly different analytic setup.

In sum, results from the robustness test protocol can provide some guidance in selecting among types of cases created by SMMR. By and large, for causal inference designs, the choice of robust cases seems warranted . For descriptive inference designs, the choice of possible cases (deviant consistency) and extreme deviant cases (deviant coverage) is preferable. The choice of shaky cases appears as the least preferred option for both causal and descriptive inference SMMR designs.

7.3.3 SMMR and Cluster Diagnostics

One frequently encountered challenge in applied QCA (and probably all of empirical social research) is that there seem to be too many factors playing

7.3 Outlook – Where Could and Should We Go from Here?

a role in explaining an outcome than what can possibly be included in the analysis. In QCA, too many conditions lead to very large truth tables with many logical remainders and often very complex solution formulas that are difficult to inject with plausible meaning. Many strategies exist to reduce the number of conditions used in the QCA. One of them is cluster diagnostics (Oana and Schneider, 2018; Oana et al., 2021, chap. 5.3).

In essence, one way of perceiving cluster diagnostics is as follows: instead of including a potentially relevant (multivalue) condition in the QCA, researchers can test whether their QCA result holds across all subgroups of cases that are formed based on each case's membership in the omitted condition. For instance, in a global study on the conditions for longevity, researchers might omit from their QCA information on which world region each case is located. Cluster diagnostics then reveals the answer to the question whether the QCA solution obtained by pooling countries from all world regions holds for each world region separately. If it does, then it does not matter for explaining longevity whether a country is located in, say Asia or Latin America. If the pooled QCA solution does not hold for all subgroups in the data, then the researcher has to make some choices. Either she can restrict the scope conditions such that the cases to which the QCA solution does not apply are excluded from further analysis. Or she can re-specify the QCA model by adding the multivalue condition "world region" to the analysis. Note that clusters can be defined based on anything that is deemed analytically relevant, including temporal clustering in panel data.

Information revealed by cluster diagnostics can be fruitfully used in SMMR. For descriptive inference SMMR designs, it could be useful to know to which subgroup deviant cases belong. This information provides a useful heuristic for identifying missing conjuncts (deviant consistency case) or disjuncts (deviant coverage and deviant relevance case). For instance, if we find that our explanation for longevity explains all cases except those located in Latin America, we have a hint of what such deviant coverage cases have in common and can start our search for a missing disjunct based on this information. Likewise, if all or most deviant consistency cases are located in, say, Asia, then this information might provide a useful cue for which conjunct is missing from the sufficient term obtained by pooling cases across all world regions. It is even useful information for SMMR if cluster diagnostics shows that there are no analytically relevant clusters in the data and, instead, the pooled QCA solution fits all subgroups equally well. This essentially means that the condition used for cluster diagnostics can be ruled out as a candidate for being a missing conjunct or missing disjunct.

For causal inference SMMR designs, information from cluster diagnostics can help decide which terms to focus on. If the goal is to draw inferences that travel as far as possible, researchers should choose for within-case analyses those sufficient and/or necessary terms that fit all subgroups. If, in contrast, researchers choose cases that are typical for terms that do not apply to all subgroups, then researchers should explicitly state this limited scope of inference. That information cannot be obtained by SMMR alone, but requires the combined use with cluster diagnostics.

7.3.4 SMMR and Time-Infused QCA Solutions

One of the weakest spots of QCA solution formulas is that, usually, they do not incorporate any analytically relevant notion of time, timing, or temporality. In their basic form, QCA solutions indicate only that the joint presence of various conditions is sufficient or necessary for the outcome. What, however, if there is a temporal order in which these conditions need to occur in order to produce the outcome? Or what if the duration for which the conditions are in place matters for their effect on the outcome? These and similar time-related aspects might matter for explaining an outcome. Formal and informal ways of integrating them into QCA exist (Pagliarin and Gerrits, 2020; Schneider and Wagemann, 2012, chap. 10.3; Verweij and Vis, 2020), but all come short of satisfactorily capturing the complexity of time-related arguments in the social sciences.

In fact, this difficulty of integrating time in truth-table based analyses is one of the main arguments why QCA should be combined with follow-up within-case analyses in the SMMR designs described in this book. The latter's capacity to capture (causal) processes and sequences counterbalances QCA's limited capacity to handle this aspect of causal complexity. Despite the limits, some notions of time can be integrated into QCA solution formulas. In the following, I briefly discuss if and how some of the strategies can improve SMMR designs. I restrict the discussion to sequences of conditions and distinguish between temporal and causal sequences. The former can be detected with temporal QCA or two-step QCA. The latter, causal chain sequences, can be detected with coincidence analysis or causal chain analysis.[7]

Temporal QCA (tQCA, Caren and Panofsky, 2005; Ragin and Strand, 2008) provides information on the sequence in which the conjuncts in a conjunction need to occur in order to be jointly sufficient for the outcome.[8] For instance, in

---

[7] For more details on these strategies and how to implement them in R, see Oana et al. (2021, chap. 5.4).
[8] tQCA for necessity claims has not yet been developed explicitly.

7.3 Outlook – Where Could and Should We Go from Here?

the sufficient conjunction $A * B * C$, let the temporal order of conjuncts be first A, then B, then C. Any other ordering would not be sufficient for the outcome Y. This information on sequence is useful when performing within-case analysis in SMMR. While no causal dependence between conditions is postulated by tQCA (but with coincidence analysis (CNA), see below), researchers could still investigate whether the first condition in the sequence (A) triggers a mechanism (M_A) that needs to be present for the second condition's mechanism (M_B) to be operative. Likewise, the second condition's mechanism might need to be present for the third condition's mechanism (M_C) to exert its impact on the outcome. And it is only this cumulative presence of $M_A * M_B * M_C$ that triggers outcome Y. Knowing about the required sequence of conditions at the cross-case level can be a helpful guidance for the within-case analysis.

A similar approach to sequencing conjuncts in a conjunction is *two-step QCA* (Schneider, 2019; Schneider and Wagemann, 2006). It proposes the separate and stepwise analysis of (temporal) remote and proximate conditions. The QCA solution formulas obtained by two-step QCA reveal the (temporal) remote context within which proximate conditions are sufficient for the outcome. As in tQCA, no causal dependence between remote and proximate conditions is postulated. In its revised version (Schneider, 2019), the remote condition analysis is an analysis of necessity and the analysis of proximate conditions an analysis of sufficiency. By design, the updated two-step QCA protocol results in sufficiency solution formulas that contain one or more necessary INUS condition(s). In Section 4.4, I discussed how to handle necessary INUS conditions in SMMR. With two-step QCA results, we have the additional knowledge that the necessary conjuncts occur prior to the sufficient conjuncts. As explained for tQCA, knowledge on this temporal sequence is informative for the within-case analysis because it structures the possibilities for causal heterogeneity at the mechanism level.

Unlike tQCA and two-step QCA, results produced with *coincidence analysis* (CNA, Baumgartner, 2009) or *causal chain analysis* (Dusa, 2019) do postulate causal dependencies between conditions. The sequence in which conditions occur is not just temporal, but causal. A is sufficient for B is sufficient for C, which then is sufficient for Y ($A \Rightarrow B \Rightarrow C \Rightarrow Y$). For within-case analyses in SMMR, this means that the focus should be on a similar sufficiency chain between the mechanisms ($M_A \Rightarrow M_B \Rightarrow M_C$).[9]

---

[9] As Baumgartner (2008) himself notes, though, for any causal chain there is what he calls a "common cause" structure, which does not imply a sequence. And with the data at hand alone, it is impossible to tell these two different models apart. This resonates with the perhaps surprising conclusion I express here that the integration of time into the cross-case QCA contributes less than expected to SMMR.

In sum, infusing QCA results with some information about the temporal or causal order among conjuncts in a conjunction can be helpful for SMMR designs. As Beach and Rohlfing (2018) argue, time-infused QCA solution formulas can enhance SMMR design-based inferences by shedding light on possible mechanismic heterogeneity and/or complexity (see also Beach and Siewert, 2019) by narrowing the possible and plausible constellations of mechanisms at the within-case level. It remains the case, though, that the best form of making QCA more time sensitive is by combining it with within-case analyses, that is, to perform SMMR.

Core Points 7.1: SMMR in Practice

- More often than not, researchers must make choices on which SMMR designs to implement and for which other designs insufficient resources are at hand
- Even if not fully implemented, the ideal SMMR protocol serves as a yardstick of what one should do to enhance descriptive and causal inference as best as possible
- SMMR's case types, principles, and formulas can be seen as translations into set-theoretic language, and the enhancement of well-known general and widely accepted case selection principles
- The coarseness of set membership scores used in the cross-case and the within-case levels should be as similar as possible
- Inferential leverage of SMMR can be enhanced by combining its use with set-theoretic robustness tests, theory evaluation, cluster diagnostics. or forms of integrating time into the cross-case QCA

***

This book has provided applied researchers with a sophisticated apparatus for best combining cross-case QCA and within-case analysis with the goal of enhancing descriptive and causal inferences. Any tool is just this: a means to achieve an end. Researchers should keep their analytic goals in mind and not get carried away by applying shiny tools just for the sake of applying them. At the same time, researchers should make use of tools rather than taking shortcuts that lead to inferior results. I hope with this book I can contribute to producing better substantive social science research.

Appendix
SMMR Principles

Table A.1 *List of SMMR principles*

Principle of differences in kind and degree:
Differences in degree should be established only among cases that are similar in kind and located on the same side of the secondary diagonal.

Truth table row principle:
For SMMR designs involving cases that are members of the outcome but not members of any term in the QCA solution formula, choose based on the membership in the truth table row to which this case belongs.

Causal inference selection principle:
A causal inference SMMR design must include a typical case.

Descriptive inference selection principle:
A descriptive inference SMMR design must include a deviant case.

Principle of maximum set membership difference:
The most deviant consistency case displays maximum difference in its set membership in the condition and the outcome.

Principle of maximum set membership:
The most typical case displays maximum set membership scores in the condition and the outcome.

Test corridor principle:
For causal inference SMMR designs, choose cases that hold membership scores in the set of interest and the outcome set that are as similar as possible.

Positive outcome principle:
At least one case must be a member of the outcome in comparative SMMR designs.

Principle of deviance in kind:
Choose deviant cases for consistency that are qualitatively different from typical cases in their membership in the superset.

Principle of max–min difference:
In model-refining comparative SMMR designs, maximize the difference of the cases' set memberships in the superset and minimize the difference in the subset, or vice versa.

Principle of max–max difference:
In causal inference comparative SMMR designs, maximize the differences of the cases' set memberships in the set of interest and the outcome.

Focal disjunct principle:
For each term, separately perform descriptive and causal inference SMMR designs.

Uniquely covered principle:
Choose typical cases that are members of just one term.

Globally uncovered principle:
Choose deviant coverage and iir cases that are not members of any term.

Focal conjunct principle:
For within-case analysis with the goal of causal inference, perform analyses for each conjunct separately.

Principle of iir focal conjunct (FC) unique nonmembership:
In a comparison with a typical case, an iir case should be a nonmember of the focal conjunct and a member of the complementary conjuncts.

Clean corridor principle:
For causal inference SMMR designs, choose cases with a clean corridor.

Attribution principle:
The typical and iir cases should have their minimum in the focal conjunct.

Attribution principle for necessity:
The typical and iir cases should have their maximum in the focal conjunct.

Principle of iir focal conjunct (FC) nonmembership, necessity:
In a comparison with a typical case, an iir case should be a nonmember of the focal conjunct.

Glossary

best available typical case Case that comes closest to the ideal typical case.

broken ceiling Situation in which a case's set membership score in the mechanism is higher than its membership score in the condition (sufficiency) or outcome (necessity).

broken corridor Situation in which a case's set membership score in the mechanism does not fall in between its membership scores in the condition and the outcome.

broken floor Situation in which a case's set membership score in the mechanism is lower than its membership score in the condition (sufficiency) or outcome (necessity).

causal mechanism see *mechanism*.

clean corridor Situation in which a case's membership score in the complementary conjuncts does not fall in between its membership scores in the focal conjunct and the outcome.

cluster diagnostics and SMMR Combination of set-theoretic cluster diagnostics and SMMR, mainly for enhancing descriptive inference and probing of scope conditions.

complementary conjunct Single or more conjuncts in a conjunction not at the center of causal inference.

complementary disjunct Single or more disjuncts in a disjunction not at the center of causal or descriptive inference.

conjunct Single set in a conjunction, that is, a group of sets combined by logical AND.

conjunction Two or more sets combined by logical AND.

corridor Range of set membership scores for a mechanism, with the case's set membership scores in the condition and the outcome constituting the floor and ceiling of the corridor.

cross-case analysis Investigation of regular patterns of association across cases between conditions and the outcome. In SMMR, patterns are defined in set relational form and investigated using QCA.

deviant consistency case Case whose membership score in the condition exceeds that in the outcome (sufficiency), or, vice versa, whose membership score in the outcome exceeds that in the condition (necessity).

deviant consistency case, in degree Case with qualitatively identical membership in the condition and the outcome but whose fuzzy set membership in the former exceeds that in the latter, such that it contradicts the statement of sufficiency.

deviant consistency case, in kind Case with qualitatively different membership in the condition and the outcome such that it contradicts the statement of sufficiency or necessity.

deviant coverage case Case with membership in the outcome without membership in any known sufficient term.

deviant relevance case Case with membership in a necessary term but not in the outcome.

difference in degree Difference between cases located on the same side of the 0.5 fuzzy-set membership score. Exists only with fuzzy sets.

difference in kind Difference between cases located on different sides of the 0.5 fuzzy-set membership score. Exists with both crisp and fuzzy sets.

disjunct Single set or conjunction in a group of sets combined by logical OR.

disjunction Two or more sets or conjunctions combined by logical OR.

enhanced XY plot Visualization for set relations between a term and the outcome and for showing types of cases. Works only with fuzzy sets. Only of limited use for case selection in SMMR, because a single XY plot cannot display all relevant (sub-) types of cases.

equifinality Attribute of a solution formula that consists of disjuncts. Denotes a situation in which different sets (single or conjunctions) are in a set relation with the outcome.

extreme deviant coverage Case that is deviant coverage based on initial solution formula and all robustness test solution formulas.

extreme iir case Case that is iir with regard to all known sufficient terms in the solution formula and all robustness test solution formulas.

focal conjunct Single conjunct in a conjunction at the center of causal inference.

focal disjunct Single disjunct in a disjunction at the center of causal or descriptive inference.

globally uncovered iir case Case that is iir with regard to all known sufficient terms in the solution formula.

ideal deviant consistency case Case with full membership in condition and full nonmembership in the outcome (sufficiency), or, vice versa, full nonmembership in the condition and full membership in the outcome (necessity).

ideal typical case Case with full membership in the condition and the outcome.

individually irrelevant (iir) case Case with nonmemberships in the condition and the outcome.

ININ A condition that is an insufficient (I) but necessary (N) element of cause that is itself insufficient (I) but necessary (N) for an outcome. For example, condition A in $Y \Leftarrow Z$, with $A * B \Rightarrow Z$.

initial solution Term used in the QCA robustness test protocol. Denotes the solution formula whose robustness is probed via test sets.

INUS A conjunct that is insufficient (I) for the outcome, yet a necessary (N) element of a conjunction that itself is unnecessary (U) but sufficient (S) for the outcome. For example, condition A in $A * B * C + C * D \Rightarrow Y$.

jointly covered typical case Case that is typical for more than one term. Antonym: uniquely covered typical case.

just-so typical case Typical case with lowest possible fuzzy-set membership in the condition and the outcome.

least likely typical case Case not expected to be a member of the outcome based on existing theories.

mechanism Located at the within-case level. Links the cross-case condition to the cross-case outcome. In SMMR, cases hold set membership in the causal mechanism. The mechanism can consist of a single set, a chain of sets, or parallel (chains of) sets.

mechanismic complexity A situation in which the mechanism at the within-case level consists of disjuncts and/or conjuncts, that is, mechanisms that present themselves in equifinal and/or conjunctural form. SMMR designs are adequate for capturing mechanismic complexity.

mechanismic heterogeneity A situation in which the level of mechanismic complexity varies across cases of the same type. SMMR designs are adequate for capturing mechanismic heterogeneity.

model ambiguity More than one solution formula of the same solution type covers the underlying data equally well.

most deviant consistency case Case in the data that comes closest to the ideal deviant consistency case.

most likely typical case Case expected to be a member of the outcome based on existing theories.

most typical case Case in the data that comes closest to the ideal typical case.

nec-suf chain Situation in which condition X is necessary for mechanism M, which, in turn, is sufficient for outcome Y ($X \Leftarrow M \Rightarrow Y$).

possible deviant consistency case Case that is deviant consistency based only on solution formulas in a robustness test, but not the initial solution formula.

possible typical case Case that is typical based only on solution formulas in a robustness test, but not the initial solution formula.

process tracing One methodological approach for within-case analysis of the causal mechanism.

robust deviant consistency case Case that remains deviant consistency after robustness tests.

robust typical case Case that remains typical after robustness tests.

robustness tests and SMMR Combination of set-theoretic robustness test-based classification of cases as either robust, shaky, or possible with SMMR types of cases for case selection for within-case analysis.

shaky deviant consistency case Case that is deviant consistency based only on the initial solution formula, but not the solution formulas in a robustness test.

shaky typical case Case that is typical based only on the initial solution formula, but not the solution formulas in a robustness test.

SMMR formula Allow for identifying the best available (pairs of) case(s) among qualitatively identical (pairs of) case(s). They are based on cases' memberships in the outcome and conditions (focal and complementary conjuncts and disjuncts, and truth table rows). Formulas work only with fuzzy sets. Lower values always indicate better choices for within-case analysis.

SMMR principles Guidelines for selecting cases for within-case analysis based on information generated at the cross-case level.

SMMR rank orders Cases (and pairs of cases) are ranked based on their memberships in the focal conjunct and the complementary conjuncts. Relevant only for single or comparative within-case analyses that aim at causal inference and only when the solution formula contains at least one conjunction.

solution type There are three QCA solutions: conservative, intermediate, and most parsimonious. They differ in their degree complexity, with the most parsimonious solution being the one without any redundant elements. Different solutions are obtained by different treatment of logical remainder rows in the process of logically minimizing the truth table. One form of handling remainders is to block all remainder rows that would lead to untenable assumptions. This yields the enhanced intermediate and enhanced most parsimonious QCA solutions. In SMMR, any type of solution can be used as the basis for selecting cases for within-case analysis.

sub-types of cases Each main type can have several sub-types, if the cross-case analysis is based on fuzzy sets, contains conjuncts and/or disjuncts, or when follow-up robustness tests or theory evaluation are performed and used for case selection.

suf-nec chain Situation in which condition X is sufficient for mechanism M, which, in turn, is necessary for outcome Y ($X \Rightarrow M \Leftarrow Y$).

sufficiency bias Expression for the empirical fact that most QCA-based research focuses on sufficiency claims rather than (also) necessity claims.

sufficiency chain Situation in which condition X is sufficient for mechanism M, which, in turn, is sufficient for outcome Y ($X \Rightarrow M \Rightarrow Y$).

SUIN A conjunct that is sufficient (S) but unnecessary (U) for the outcome, for a factor that itself is insufficient (I) but necessary (N) for the outcome. For example, condition A in $Z \Leftarrow Y$ and $A * B \Rightarrow Y$.

SUSU Sufficient but unnecessary elements of a condition, which itself is sufficient but unnecessary for the outcome. For example, condition A in $Z \Rightarrow Y$ and $A + B \Rightarrow Z$.

test set Term used in the QCA robustness test protocol. Denotes the solution formulas obtained when changing those analytic parameters that have been used for obtaining the initial solution.

theory evaluation and SMMR Combination of set-theoretic theory evaluation-based classification of cases as most likely or least likely with SMMR types of cases for case selection for within-case analysis.

truth table model The conditions that constitute the truth table. Conditions that turn out to be logically redundant during the process of logical minimization of the truth table do not appear in the solution formula.

types of cases, main The five main types of cases are defined by differences in kind in either the condition or the outcome. Membership in the five main types is mutually exclusive and jointly exhaustive.

typical case Case with memberships in the condition and the outcome that are in line with a statement of sufficiency or necessity, respectively.

uniquely covered typical case Case that is typical for just one term. Antonym: jointly covered typical case.

within-case analysis Synonym for the study of the mechanism that links the condition to the outcome at the cross-case level.

References

Adcock, Robert, and Collier, David. 2001. Measurement Validity: A Shared Standard for Qualitative and Quantitative Research. *American Political Science Review*, **95**(3), 529–546.

Ahmed, Amel, and Sil, Rudra. 2012. When Multi-Method Research Subverts Methodological Pluralism – Or, Why We Still Need Single-Method Research. *Perspectives on Politics*, **10**(4), 935–953.

Álamos-Concha, Priscilla, Pattyn, Valérie, Rihoux, Benoît, Schalembier, Benjamin, Beach, Derek, and Cambré, Bart. 2022. Conservative Solutions for Progress: On Solution Types When Combining QCA with In-Depth Process-Tracing. *Quality & Quantity*, **56**, 1965–1997.

Arel-Bundock, Vincent. 2022. The Double Bind of Qualitative Comparative Analysis. *Sociological Methods & Research*, **51**(3), 963–982.

Baumgartner, Michael. 2008. The Causal Chain Problem. *Erkenntnis*, **69**(2), 201–226.

Baumgartner, Michael. 2009. Uncovering Deterministic Causal Structures: A Boolean Approach. *Synthese*, **170**(1), 71–96.

Baumgartner, Michael, and Thiem, Alrik. 2017. Model Ambiguities in Configurational Comparative Research. *Sociological Methods & Research*, **46**(4), 954–987.

Beach, Derek. 2018. Achieving Methodological Alignment When Combining QCA and Process Tracing in Practice. *Sociological Methods & Research*, **47**(1), 64–99.

Beach, Derek, and Kaas, Jonas Gejl. 2020. The Great Divides: Incommensurability, the Impossibility of Mixed-Methodology, and What to Do about It. *International Studies Review*, **22**(2), 214–235.

Beach, Derek, and Pedersen, Rasmus Brun. 2013. *Process Tracing Methods*. Ann Arbor: University of Michigan Press.

Beach, Derek, and Pedersen, Rasmus Brun. 2016. *Causal Case Studies: Foundations and Guidelines for Comparing, Matching, and Tracing*. Ann Arbor: University of Michigan Press.

Beach, Derek, and Pedersen, Rasmus Brun. 2018. Selecting Appropriate Cases When Tracing Causal Mechanisms. *Sociological Methods & Research*, **47**(4), 837–871.

Beach, Derek, and Pedersen, Rasmus Brun. 2019. *Process-Tracing Methods: Foundations and Giudelines*. 2nd ed. Ann Arbor: University of Michigan Press.

Beach, Derek, and Rohlfing, Ingo. 2018. Integrating Cross-Case Analyses and Process Tracing in Set-Theoretic Research: Strategies and Parameters of Debate. *Sociological Methods & Research*, **47**(1), 3–36.

Beach, Derek, and Siewert, Markus. 2019. Case Selection and Nesting of Process-Tracing Case Studies. Pages 89–154 of: Beach, Derek, and Pedersen, Rasmus Brun (eds.), *Process-Tracing Methods: Foundations and Giudelines*, 2nd ed. Ann Arbor: University of Michigan Press.

Bennett, Andrew, and Checkel, Jeffrey. 2014. *Process Tracing in the Social Sciences: From Metaphor to Analytic Tool*. Cambridge: Cambridge University Press.

Bennett, Andrew, and Elman, Colin. 2006. Qualitative Research: Recent Developments in Case Study Methods. *Annual Review of Political Science*, **9**, 455–476.

Berg-Schlosser, Dirk, De Meur, Gisèle, Ragin, Charles C., and Rihoux, Benoît. 2009. Qualitative Comparative Analysis as an Approach. Pages 1–18 of: Rihoux, Benoît, and Ragin, Charles (eds.), *Configurational Comparative Methods: Qualitative Comparative Analysis (QCA) and Related Techniques*. Thousand Oaks, CA: Sage.

Blatter, Joachim, and Haverland, Markus. 2012. *Designing Case Studies: Explanatory Approaches in Small-N Research*. Basingstoke: Palgrave Macmillan.

Bretthauer, Judith M. 2015. Conditions for Peace and Conflict: Applying a Fuzzy-Set Qualitative Comparative Analysis to Cases of Resource Scarcity. *Journal of Conflict Resolution*, **59**(4), 593–616.

Bunzl, Martin. 2004. Counterfactual History: A User's Guide. *American Historical Review*, **109**(3), 845–858.

Caren, Neal, and Panofsky, Aaron. 2005. TQCA: A Technique for Adding Temporality to Qualitative Comparative Analysis. *Sociological Methods & Research*, **34**(2), 147–172.

Chatterjee, Abhishek. 2013. Ontology, Epistemology, and Multimethod Research in Political Science. *Philosophy of the Social Sciences*, **43**(1), 73–99.

Collier, D. 2014. Comment: QCA Should Set Aside the Algorithms. *Sociological Methodology*, **44**(1), 122–126.

Crasnow, Sharon, Goertz, Gary, and Haggard, Stephan. Pluralism and Partnerships:The Evidential Foundations of Multimethod Research in Political Science. Pages (not yet available) of: Box-Steffensmeier, Janet M. et al. (eds), *Oxford Handbook of Methodological Pluralism*. Oxford: Oxford University Press, in press.

Cronqvist, Lasse, and Berg-Schlosser, Dirk. 2009. Multi-Value QCA (mvQCA). Pages 69–86 of: Rihoux, Benoît, and Ragin, Charles C (eds.), *Configurational Comparative Methods. Quanlitative Comparative Analysis (QCA) and Related Techniques*. Thousand Oaks, CA: Sage.

de Block, Debora, and Vis, Barbara. 2019. Addressing the Challenges Related to Transforming Qualitative into Quantitative Data in Qualitative Comparative Analysis. *Journal of Mixed Methods Research*, **13**(4), 503–535.

Dessler, David. 1991. Beyond Correlations: Toward a Causal Theory of War. *International Studies Quarterly*, **35**(3), 337–355.

Dusa, Adrian. 2019. *QCA with R: A Comprehensive Resource*. Cham: Springer.

Eckstein, Harry. 1975. Case Study and Theory in Political Science. Pages 79–137 of: Greenstein, Fred I, and Polsby, Nelson W (eds.), *Strategies of Inquiry. Handbook of Political Science, vol. 7*. Reading, MA: Addison-Wesley.

Emmenegger, Patrick. 2011. How Good Are Your Counterfactuals? Assessing Quantitative Macro-Comparative Welfare State Research with Qualitative Criteria. *Journal of European Social Policy*, **21**(4), 365–380.

Falleti, Tulia G., and Lynch, Julia F. 2009. Context and Causal Mechanisms in Political Analysis. *Comparative Political Studies*, **42**(9), 1143–1166.

Fearon, James D. 1991. Counterfactuals and Hypothesis Testing in Political Science. *World Politics*, **43**(2), 169–195.

Fiss, Peer C. 2011. Building Better Causal Theories: A Fuzzy Set Approach to Typologies in Organization Research. *Academy of Management Journal*, **54**(2), 393–420.

George, Alexander L., and Bennett, Andrew. 2005. *Case Studies and Theory Development in the Social Sciences*. Cambridge, MA: MIT Press.

Gerring, John. 2017. *Case Study Research: Principles and Practices*. 2nd ed. Cambridge: Cambridge University Press.

Gerrits, Lasse, and Verweij, Stefan. 2018. *The Evaluation of Complex Infrastructure Projects*. Cheltenham: Edward Elgar.

Goertz, Gary. 2017. *Multimethod Research, Causal Mechanisms, and Case Studies: An Integrated Approach*. Princeton, NJ and Oxford: Princeton University Press.

Goertz, Gary, and Haggard, Stephan. Large-N Qualitative Analysis (LNQA): Causal Generalization in Case Study and Multimethod Research. *Perspectives on Politics*, **21**(3), in press.

Goertz, Gary, and Mahoney, James. 2012. *A Tale of Two Cultures: Contrasting Qualitative and Quantitative Paradigms*. Princeton, NJ: Princeton University Press.

Goertz, Gary, and Starr, Harvey. 2003. *Necessary Conditions: Theory, Methodology, and Applications*. Lanham: Rowman & Littlefield.

Hackett, Ursula. 2016. The Goldilocks Principle: Applying the Exclusive Disjunction to Fuzzy Sets. *International Journal of Social Research Methodology*, **19**(5), 551–574.

Haesebrouck, Tim, and Thomann, Eva. 2022. Introduction: Causation, Inferences, and Solution Types in Configurational Comparative Methods. *Quality & Quantity*, **56**, 1867–1888.

Haesebrouck, Tim, and Van Immerseel, Anouschka. 2020. When Does Politics Stop at the Water's Edge? A QCA of Parliamentary Consensus on Military Deployment Decisions. *European Political Science Review*, **12**(3), 371–390.

Humphreys, Macartan, and Jacobs, Alan. 2015. Mixing Methods: A Bayesian Approach. *American Political Science Review*, **109**(4), 653–673.

Kahwati, Leila C., and Kane, Heather L. 2019. *Qualitative Comparative Analysis in Mixed Methods Research and Evaluation*. Mixed Methods Research Series. Thousand Oaks, CA: Sage.

Kapiszewski, Diana. 2015. *Field Research in Political Science Practices and Principles*. Cambridge: Cambridge University Press.

Koivu, Kendra, Schneider, Carsten, and Vis, Barbara. 2019. Set-Analytic Approaches, Especially Qualitative Comparative Analysis (QCA). American Political Science Association Organized Section for Qualitative and Multi-Method Research, Qualitative Transparency Deliberations, Working Group Final Reports, Report III.4, https://papers.ssrn.com/sol3/papers.cfm?abstract_id=3333474.

Lebow, Richard Ned. 2010. *Forbidden Fruit: Counterfactuals and International Relations*. Princeton, NJ: Princeton University Press.

Lieberman, Evan S. 2005. Nested Analysis as a Mixed-Method Strategy for Comparative Research. *American Political Science Review*, **99**(3), 435–452.

Lijphart, Arend. 1971. Comparative Politics and the Comparative Method. *American Political Science Review*, **65**(3), 682–693.

Lijphart, Arend. 1975. Comparable-Cases Strategy in Comparative Research. *Comparative Political Studies*, **8**(2), 158–177.

Mackie, John L. 1965. Causes and Conditions. *American Philosophical Quarterly*, **2**(4), 245–264.

Mahoney, James. 2000. Strategies of Causal Inference in Small-N Analysis. *Sociological Methods & Research*, **28**(4), 387–424.

Mahoney, James. 2021. *The Logic of Social Science*. Princeton, NJ and Oxford: Princeton University Press.

Mahoney, James, and Acosta, Laura. 2022. A Regularity Theory of Causality for the Social Sciences. *Quality & Quantity*, **56**, 1889–1911.

Mahoney, James, Kimball, Erin, and Koivu, Kendra L. 2009. The Logic of Historical Explanation in the Social Sciences. *Comparative Political Studies*, **42**(1), 114–146.

Marx, Axel, Rihoux, Benoît, and Ragin, Charles. 2014. The Origins, Development, and Application of Qualitative Comparative Analysis: The First 25 Years. *European Political Science Review*, **6**(3), 115–142.

Mello, Patrick A. 2021. *Qualitative Comparative Analysis: An Introduction to Research Design and Application*. Washington, DC: Georgetown University Press.

Meuer, Johannes, and Rupietta, Christian. 2017a. A Review of Integrated QCA and Statistical Analyses. *Quality and Quantity*, **51**(5), 2063–2083.

Meuer, Johannes, and Rupietta, Christian. 2017b. Integrating QCA and HLM for Multilevel Research on Organizational Configurations. *Organizational Research Methods*, **20**(2), 324–342.

Mikkelsen, Kim Sass 2017. Fuzzy-Set Case Studies. *Sociological Methods & Research*, **46**(3), 422–455.

Mill, John Stuart. 1874. *A System of Logic, Ratiocinative and Inductive*. New York: Harper & Brothers.

Nielsen, Richard A. 2016. Case Selection via Matching. *Sociological Methods & Research*, **45**(3), 569–597.

Oana, Ioana-Elena, and Schneider, Carsten Q. 2018. SetMethods: an Add-on R Package for Advanced QCA. *The R Journal*, **10**(1), 507–533.

Oana, Ioana-Elena, and Schneider, Carsten Q. 2021. A Robustness Test Protocol for Applied QCA: Theory and R Software Application. *Sociological Methods & Research*. https://doi.org/10.1177/00491241211036158.

Oana, Ioana-Elena, Schneider, Carsten Q., and Thomann, Eva. 2021. *Qualitative Comparative Analysis (QCA) Using R: A Beginner's Guide*. Cambridge: Cambridge University Press.

Pagliarin, Sofia, and Gerrits, Lasse. 2020. Trajectory-Based Qualitative Comparative Analysis: Accounting for Case-Based Time Dynamics. *Methodological Innovations*, **13**(3). https://doi.org/10.1177/2059799120959170.

Pagliarin, Sofia, La Mendola, Salvatore, and Vis, Barbara. 2023. The "Qualitative" in Qualitative Comparative Analysis (QCA): Research Moves, Case-Intimacy and Face-to-Face Interviews. *Quality & Quantity*, **57**, 489–507.

Pattyn, Valérie, Álamos-Concha, Priscilla, Cambré, Bart, Rihoux, Benoît, and Schalembier, Benjamin. 2022. Policy Effectiveness through Configurational and Mechanistic Lenses: Lessons for Concept Development. *Journal of Comparative Policy Analysis: Research and Practice*, **24**(1), 33–50.

Paul, L. A., and Hall, Ned. 2013. *Causation: A User's Guide*. Oxford: Oxford University Press.

Przeworski, Adam, and Teune, Henry. 1970. *The Logic of Comparative Social Inquiry*. New York: Wiley-Interscience.

R Core Team. 2018. *R: A Language and Environment for Statistical Computing*. Vienna: R Foundation for Statistical Computing.

Ragin, Charles C. 1987. *The Comparative Method: Moving Beyond Quantitative and Qualitative Strategies*. Berkeley: University of California Press.

Ragin, Charles C. 2000. *Fuzzy-Set Social Science*. Chicago, IL: University of Chicago Press.

Ragin, Charles C. 2008. *Redesigning Social Inquiry: Fuzzy Sets and Beyond*. Chicago, IL: University of Chicago Press.

Ragin, Charles C. 2023. *Analytic Induction for Social Research*. Oakland, California: University of California Press.

Ragin, Charles C., and Becker, Howard S. 1992. *What Is a Case? Exploring the Foundations of Social Inquiry*. Cambridge: Cambridge University Press.

Ragin, Charles C., and Strand, Sarah. 2008. Using Qualitative Comparative Analysis to Study Causal Order. Comment on Caren and Panofsky (2005). *Sociological Methods & Research*, **36**(4), 431–441.

Rihoux, Benoît. 2020. *Qualitative Comparative Analysis: Discovering Core Combinations of Conditions in Political Decision Making*. Oxford: Oxford University Press.

Rihoux, Benoît, and Lobe, Bojana. 2009. The Case of Qualitative Comparative Analysis (QCA): Adding Leverage for Cross-Case Comparison. Pages 222–242 of: Byrne, David, and Ragin, Charles C. (eds.), *The Sage Handbook of Case-Based Methods*. Thousand Oaks, CA: Sage.

Rihoux, Benoît, Alamos, Priscilla, Bol, Damien, Marx, Axel, and Rezsohazy, Ilona. 2013. From Niche to Mainstream Method? A Comprehensive Mapping of QCA Applications in Journal Articles from 1984 to 2011. *Political Research Quarterly*, **66**(1), 175–184.

Rihoux, Benoît, Alamos-Concha, Priscilla, and Lobe, Bojana. 2021. Qualitative Comparative Analysis (QCA). An Integrative Approach Suited for Diverse Mixed Methods and Multimethod Research Strategies. Pages 185–197 of: Onwuegbuzie, T., and Johnson, B. (eds.), *The Routledge Reviewer's Guide to Mixed Method Analysis*. New York/London: Routledge.

Rohlfing, Ingo. 2008. What You See and What You Get: Pitfalls and Principles of Nested Analysis in Comparative Research. *Comparative Political Studies*, **41**(11), 1492–1514.

Rohlfing, Ingo. 2012. *Case Studies and Causal Inference: An Integrative Framework*. Basingstoke: Palgrave Macmillan.

Rohlfing, Ingo, and Schneider, Carsten Q. 2013. Improving Research on Necessary Conditions: Formalized Case Selection for Process Tracing after QCA. *Political Research Quarterly*, **66**(1), 220–235.

Rohlfing, Ingo, and Schneider, Carsten Q. 2018. A Unifying Framework for Causal Analysis in Set-Theoretic Multimethod Research. *Sociological Methods & Research*, **71**(1), 37–63.

Runhardt, Rosa W. 2022. Limits to Evidential Pluralism: Multi-Method Large-N Qualitative Analysis and the Primacy of Mechanistic Studies. *Synthese*, **200**(2), 171.

Russo, Federica, and Williamson, Jon. 2007. Interpreting Causality in the Health Sciences. *International Studies in the Philosophy of Science*, **21**(2), 157–170.

Rutten, Roel. 2022. Applying and Assessing Large-N QCA : Causality and Robustness From a Critical Realist Perspective. *Sociological Methods & Research*, **51**(3), 1211–1243.

Sartori, Giovanni. 1970. Concept Misformation in Comparative Politics. *American Political Science Review*, **64**(4), 1033–1053.

Schneider, Carsten Q. 2008. *The Consolidation of Democracy: Comparing Europe and Latin America*. London: Routledge.

Schneider, Carsten Q. 2018. Realists and Idealists in QCA. *Political Analysis*, **26**(2), 246–254.

Schneider, Carsten Q. 2019. Two-Step QCA Revisited: The Necessity of Context Conditions. *Quality & Quantity*, **53**(3), 1109–1126.

Schneider, Carsten Q., and Maerz, Seraphine F. 2017. Legitimation, Cooptation, and Repression and the Survival of Electoral Autocracies. *Zeitschrift für Vergleichende Politikwissenschaft*, **11**, 213–235.

Schneider, Carsten Q., and Makszin, Kristin. 2014. Forms of Welfare Capitalism and Education-Based Participatory Inequality. *Socio-Economic Review*, **12**(2), 437–462.

Schneider, Carsten Q., and Rohlfing, Ingo. 2013. Combining QCA and Process Tracing in Set-Theoretic Multi-Method Research. *Sociological Methods & Research*, **42**(4), 559–597.

Schneider, Carsten Q., and Rohlfing, Ingo. 2016. Case Studies Nested in Fuzzy-Set QCA on Sufficiency: Formalizing Case Selection and Causal Inference. *Sociological Methods & Research*, **45**(3), 526–568.

Schneider, Carsten Q., and Rohlfing, Ingo. 2019. Set-Theoretic Multimethod Research: The Role of Test Corridors and Conjunctions for Case Selection. *Swiss Political Science Review*, **25**(3), 253–275.

Schneider, Carsten Q., and Wagemann, Claudius. 2006. Reducing Complexity in Qualitative Comparative Analysis (QCA): Remote and Proximate Factors and the Consolidation of Democracy. *European Journal of Political Research*, **45**(5), 751–786.

Schneider, Carsten Q., and Wagemann, Claudius. 2010. Standards of Good Practice in Qualitative Comparative Analysis (QCA) and Fuzzy-Sets. *Comparative Sociology*, **9**(3), 397–418.

Schneider, Carsten Q., and Wagemann, Claudius. 2012. *Set-Theoretic Methods for the Social Sciences: A Guide to Qualitative Comparative Analysis*. Cambridge: Cambridge University Press.

Schneider, Martin R., Schulze-Bentrop, Conrad, and Paunescu, Mihai. 2010. Mapping the Institutional Capital of High-Tech Firms: A Fuzzy-Set Analysis of Capitalist Variety and Export Performance. *Journal of International Business Studies*, **41**(2), 246–266.

Seawright, Jason. 2016. *Multi-Method Social Science. Combining Qualitative and Quantitative Tools*. Cambridge: Cambridge University Press.

Seawright, Jason, and Gerring, John. 2008. Case Selection Techniques in Case Study Research: A Menu of Qualitative and Quantitative Options. *Political Research Quarterly*, **61**(2), 294–308.

Shan, Yafeng, and Williamson, Jon. 2023. *Evidential Pluralism in the Social Sciences*. Abingdon: Routledge.

Stevens, Alex. 2016. Configurations of Corruption: A Cross-national Qualitative Comparative Analysis of Levels of Perceived Corruption. *International Journal of Comparative Sociology*, **57**(4), 183–206.

Thiem, Alrik. 2013. Clearly Crisp, and Not Fuzzy: A Reassessment of the (Putative) Pitfalls of Multi-value QCA. *Field Methods*, **25**(2), 197–207.

Thiem, Alrik. 2014. Unifying Configurational Comparative Methodology: Generalized-Set Qualitative Comparative Analysis. *Sociological Methods & Research*, **43**(2), 313–337.

Thomann, Eva, and Ege, Jörn. 2020. *Qualitative Comparative Analysis (QCA) in Public Administration*. Oxford: Oxford University Press.

Thomann, Eva, and Maggetti, Martino. 2020. Designing Research With Qualitative Comparative Analysis (QCA): Approaches, Challenges, and Tool. *Sociological Methods & Research*, **49**(2), 356–386.

Thomann, Eva, Ege, Jörn, and Paustyan, Ekaterina. 2022. Approaches to Qualitative Comparative Analysis and Good Practices: A Systematic Review. *Swiss Political Science Review*, **28**(3), 557–580.

Tóth, Zsófia, Henneberg, Stephan C., and Naudé, Peter. 2017. Addressing the 'Qualitative' in Fuzzy Set Qualitative Comparative Analysis: The Generic Membership Evaluation Template. *Industrial Marketing Management*, **63**, 192–204.

Verweij, Stefan, and Vis, Barbara. 2021. Three Strategies to Track Configurations over Time with Qualitative Comparative Analysis. *European Political Science Review*, **13**(1), 95–111.

Vis, Barbara. 2009. Governments and Unpopular Social Policy Reform: Biting the Bullet or Steering Clear? *European Journal of Political Research*, **48**(1), 31–57.

Vis, Barbara, and Dul, Jan. 2018. Analyzing Relationships of Necessity Not Just in Kind But Also in Degree: Complementing fsQCA With NCA. *Sociological Methods & Research*, **47**(4), 872–899.

Wagemann, Claudius, and Schneider, Carsten Q. 2015. Transparency Standards in Qualitative Comparative Analysis. *Qualitative & Multi-Method Research Newsletter*, **13**(1), 38–42.

Weller, Nicholas, and Barnes, Jeb. 2016. Pathway Analysis and the Search for Causal Mechanisms. *Sociological Methods & Research*, **45**(3), 424–457.

Index

best available typical, *see* types of cases
broken ceiling, *see* corridor
broken corridor, *see* corridor
broken floor, *see* corridor

causal mechanism, *see* mechanism
clean corridor, *see* corridor
cluster diagnostics, 222, 235, 238–240
complementary conjunct, 98–108, 111–114, 128, 133, 154, 211, 212, 214, 231, 233, 244
complementary disjunct, 78, 79
configuration, *see* conjunction
contaminated corridor, *see* corridor
corridor, 42–44, 46–48, 101, 102, 110, 111, 113, 116, 153, 155, 156, 158, 214
   broken ceiling, 46, 47, 116, 117, 153, 155, 174, 231
   broken corridor, 46–48, 101, 111–117, 141, 151, 174–175, 231, 232
   broken floor, 46–48, 116, 117, 155, 158, 174, 231
   clean corridor, 101–102, 104–108, 110, 113, 115, 134, 136, 138, 151, 212, 213, 219
   contaminated corridor, 102, 104, 105, 108, 113, 115, 212, 219

deviant consistency, *see* types of cases
deviant consistency in degree, *see* types of cases
deviant consistency in kind, *see* types of cases
deviant coverage, *see* types of cases
deviant relevance, *see* types of cases

equifinality, 28, 43, 62, 64, 67, 68, 71, 73, 90, 97, 101, 141, 181, 195, 223, 225

equivalence, 29
extreme deviant, *see* types of cases
extreme iir, *see* types of cases

focal conjunct, 38, 59, 98–115, 117, 126, 128, 131, 133, 150–158, 211–214, 233, 244
focal disjunct, 38, 75–79, 85–90, 150, 198, 244

globally uncovered, *see* types of cases

ideal deviant, *see* types of cases
ideal typical, *see* types of cases
iir, *see* types of cases
implication, 28
ININ, 29, 166, 209, 211, 212
INUS, 8, 14, 29, 88, 92, 96, 111–115, 141, 147, 161, 211, 220, 241

jointly covered, *see* types of cases
just-so typical, *see* types of cases

least likely typical, *see* types of cases

mechanism, 5, 7, 9–13, 16, 29, 32, 40–48, 50, 51, 53–57, 62, 71–73, 75–77, 83, 84, 86, 87, 89, 93–102, 105, 113, 116, 117, 124–126, 131, 140, 141, 143, 144, 147–151, 153–155, 158–164, 167, 170, 171, 173–179, 181–185, 194–196, 209–211, 221, 224, 227, 228, 230, 231, 233, 234, 241, 242
   mechanismic complexity, 9, 10, 39, 40, 210, 242
   mechanismic heterogeneity, 9, 10, 48, 99, 164, 175, 241, 242

Index

mechanismic homogeneity, 9, 10, 99
nec-suf chain, 46–48, 57, 115–117, 155, 158, 171, 175, 232
process tracing, 9, 10, 29, 38
suf-nec chain, 46–48, 57, 115, 116, 153, 155, 171, 232
suffiency chain, 43, 46, 47, 57, 115, 153–155, 158, 160, 171
mechanismic complexity, *see* mechanism
mechanismic heterogeneity, *see* mechanism
mechanismic homogeneity, *see* mechanism
method of agreement, *see* Mill's methods
method of difference, *see* Mill's methods
Mill's methods, 8, 18, 79, 101, 223, 225
model ambiguity, 28
most deviant, *see* types of cases
most likely typical, *see* types of cases
most typical, *see* types of cases
most-different system design, *see* Mill's methods
most-similar system design, *see* Mill's methods

nec-suf chain, *see* mechanism

possible deviant, *see* types of cases
process tracing, *see* mechanism

QCA model, 11

robust deviant, *see* types of cases
robust typical, *see* types of cases
robustness test, 222, 234, 236–238
  test set, 236

shaky deviant, *see* types of cases
shaky typical, *see* types of cases
SMMR principles, 8, 10, 12, 14–17, 28, 66, 92, 95, 165, 166, 178, 194, 196, 221, 223–225, 230, 231, 233, 234
  attribution, 17, 100, 103–109, 113, 128, 133, 138, 140, 154, 211, 212, 224, 231, 233, 244
  attribution, necessity, 113, 115, 211, 212, 224, 231, 244
  causal inference selection, 38, 54, 57, 99, 178, 224, 244
  clean corridor, 17, 102, 103, 113, 117, 134, 136, 138, 140, 224, 231, 244
  descriptive inference selection, 38, 57, 170, 178, 224, 244
  deviance in kind, 51, 57, 179, 180, 224, 244
  differences in kind and degree, 36, 39, 57, 170, 224, 244
  focal conjunct, 16, 98–99, 140, 150, 211, 224
  focal disjunct, 16, 75, 78, 101, 150, 197, 224, 244
  globally uncovered, 16, 78, 90, 224, 244
  iir FC nonmember, 107, 115, 140, 211, 212, 224
  iir FC unique nonmember, 99–103, 108, 140, 155, 212, 223, 224
  max–min difference, 52, 54, 57, 180, 224, 244
  maximum set membership, 42, 57, 224, 244
  maximum set membership difference, 41, 57, 224, 244
  positive outcome, 49, 57, 178, 224, 244
  test corridor, 43, 44, 47, 54, 57, 65, 99, 107, 110, 113, 172, 173, 175, 184, 214, 223, 224, 231, 244
  truth table row, 37, 39, 53, 57, 120, 175, 178, 224, 244
  uniquely covered, 16, 76, 90, 198, 224, 244
SMMR ranks, 105–115, 126, 128, 131, 133, 151, 154, 160, 212, 213, 231, 232
sub-types of cases, *see* types of cases
suf-nec chain, *see* mechanism
sufficiency bias, 13, 165
sufficiency chain, *see* mechanism
SUIN, 29, 166, 176, 178, 181, 193–198, 209
SUSU, 73

temporal sequence, 125
test corridor, *see* corridor
test set, *see* robustness test
theory evaluation, 45, 222, 234–236
types of cases
  deviant consistency, 11, 12, 16, 35, 40, 41, 48–53, 59, 61, 63, 74, 77, 124, 125, 148, 149, 168, 175, 176, 178–183, 197, 198, 228, 229, 231, 234, 235, 237, 238
  in degree, 36, 37, 45, 51, 93, 106, 169, 170, 194
  ideal deviant consistency, 36, 37, 40, 41
  in kind, 36, 37, 51, 93, 124, 169, 170, 194
  most deviant consistency, 40, 41, 63, 85, 231, 244
  possible deviant consistency, 237, 238
  shaky deviant consistency, 238

deviant coverage, 11, 16, 21, 35, 37–40, 49, 50, 52, 53, 60, 63, 66, 73–78, 80, 81, 83, 93, 120–122, 145–148, 168, 177, 231, 234, 235, 237, 238, 244
    extreme deviant coverage, 238
deviant relevance, 11, 168, 176–183, 185, 194, 197–199, 211, 231
iir, 16, 35, 37, 38, 41, 43, 46, 47, 49–57, 60, 63, 64, 66, 74, 75, 78, 93, 98–105, 107, 108, 110–115, 117, 120, 122, 128, 131, 140, 150, 151, 153–155, 158, 160, 161, 168, 175, 178, 182–184, 194, 197, 198, 211–214, 228, 229, 231, 233–238, 244
    extreme iir, 238
    globally uncovered, 16, 64, 75, 78, 128, 131, 151, 197, 225
    typical, 7, 11, 14, 16, 34, 36–46, 48–57, 59, 61, 63–66, 69, 72, 74, 75, 77–79, 81, 84–89, 98–103, 105–108, 110–115, 117, 124–126, 128, 131, 140, 148–151, 153–156, 158, 160, 161, 167–173, 175–185, 194, 197, 211, 212, 214, 223, 225, 227–229, 231, 233–236, 244

best available, 39, 42, 56, 61, 62, 86, 106, 110, 124, 126, 128, 131, 133, 173, 214
ideal typical, 37, 42, 45, 56, 170
jointly covered, 62, 74, 77, 79, 86, 88, 90, 197
just-so typical, 37, 45, 56, 89, 169, 170, 184, 185, 227, 234
least likely typical, 235–236
most likely typical, 45, 235–236
most typical, 33, 37, 42, 56, 62–64, 85, 86, 88–90, 125, 131, 151, 169, 170, 184, 185, 231, 234, 244
possible typical, 237, 238
robust deviant, 237, 238
robust typical, 45, 237, 238
shaky typical, 237, 238
uniquely covered, 16, 21, 62, 74, 76–79, 86–88, 90, 126, 128, 131, 143, 151, 197, 198, 219, 225, 231, 244
typical case, *see* types of cases

uniquely covered, *see* types of cases

Milton Keynes UK
Ingram Content Group UK Ltd.
UKHW052213240324
439817UK00022B/120